Kompetenzzentrum Informelle Bildung (Hrsg.)

Grenzenlose Cyberwelt?

Kompetenzzentrum
Informelle Bildung (Hrsg.)

Grenzenlose Cyberwelt?

Zum Verhältnis von digitaler
Ungleichheit und neuen Bildungs-
zugängen für Jugendliche

VS VERLAG FÜR SOZIALWISSENSCHAFTEN

Bibliografische Information Der Deutschen Nationalbibliothek
Die Deutsche Nationalbibliothek verzeichnet diese Publikation in der
Deutschen Nationalbibliografie; detaillierte bibliografische Daten sind im Internet über
<http://dnb.d-nb.de> abrufbar.

1. Auflage Juli 2007

Alle Rechte vorbehalten
© VS Verlag für Sozialwissenschaften | GWV Fachverlage GmbH, Wiesbaden 2007

Lektorat: Stefanie Laux

Der VS Verlag für Sozialwissenschaften ist ein Unternehmen von Springer Science+Business Media.
www.vs-verlag.de

Umschlaggestaltung: KünkelLopka Medienentwicklung, Heidelberg
Satz: <Bausatz> Frank Böhm, Siegen
Druck und buchbinderische Verarbeitung: Krips b.v., Meppel
Gedruckt auf säurefreiem und chlorfrei gebleichtem Papier

ISBN 978-3-531-15319-3

Inhaltsverzeichnis

1   *Stefan Iske, Alex Klein, Nadia Kutscher, Hans-Uwe Otto*

    Vorwort... 7

Dimensions of Educational Policy / Gesellschaftliche Herausforderungen für Bildungspolitik im Kontext des Internet

2   *Lawrence Angus*

    Implications of social inequality in internet use for educational policies and programs.. 15

3   *Neil Selwyn*

    Dealing with Digital Inequality: Refocusing our Approach towards Young People, Technology and Social Exklusion............... 31

Education and Participation in the Virtual Space and its Limitations / Bildung und Teilhabe im virtuellen Raum und ihre Grenzen

4   *Caroline Haythornthwaite*

    Digital divide – social barriers on- and offline................................ 47

5   *Stefan Iske, Alex Klein, Nadia Kutscher, Hans-Uwe Otto*

    Virtuelle Ungleichheit und informelle Bildung – Internetnutzung Jugendlicher und ihre Bedeutung für Bildung und Teilhabe............. 65

6   *Winfried Marotzki*

    Vergemeinschaftungsformen im Internet und ihre Bedeutung für Bildung und Aneignung... 93

7   *Gustavo Mesch*

    Social Networks and Social Relationships of Adolescents – offline and online.. 105

Use Differences and Social Inequality in the Internet /
Nutzungsdifferenzen und Soziale Ungleichheit im Internet

8   *Eszter Hargittai*

         Characteristics of use differences and their implications for
         dealing with digital inequality... 121

9   *Heinz Bonfadelli*
         Mediennutzung von Jugendlichen mit Migrationshintergrund........... 137

10   *Horst Niesyto*
         Medienbildung mit benachteiligten Jugendlichen.............................. 153

New Perspectives for Media Education / Neue Perspektiven für
Medienbildung

11   *David Buckingham*
         Digital Culture, Media Education and the Place of Schooling........... 177

12   *Franz Josef Röll*
         Ästhetik in der zielgruppenorientierten Medienausbildung............... 199

         Autorinnen und Autoren.. 221

Vorwort

Das Internet gilt heute als zentrale Wissens- und Informationsressource. Damit ist zunehmend die Vorstellung verbunden, dass sich jeder über dieses Medium entsprechend seiner eigenen Bedürfnisse bedienen kann und soll. Immer mehr öffentliche Dienstleistungen werden über das Internet angeboten und eröffnen den NutzerInnen auf diesem Weg spezifische, insbesondere zeitliche und informationelle Vorteile für die Bewältigung des alltäglichen Lebens. Allerdings ist der Gebrauch des Internet voraussetzungsvoll. Neuere empirische Ergebnisse und theoretische Überlegungen weisen daraufhin, dass sich auch in diesem Kontext eine erweiterte gesellschaftliche Spaltung abzeichnet. Innerhalb des Internet zeigen sich entlang sozialer Ungleichheiten unterschiedliche Nutzungsweisen und spiegeln damit die Begrenzungen des „real life" auch im virtuellen Raum wider. Somit prägen auch hier nicht nur *individuelle* Präferenzen, sondern in einem besonderen Maße auch *soziale* Strukturen und Prozesse die Vergemeinschaftungsformen und Aneignungsräume im Netz. Dies zeigt sich auf zwei Ebenen: Zum einen durch Schließungsprozesse unter den NutzerInnen und zum anderen durch Angebotsstrukturen, die – häufig entgegen ihrem eigenen Anspruch – jeweils nur spezifische Zielgruppen erreichen.

In Zusammenhang mit der allgemeinen Bildungsdebatte wird darauf hingewiesen, dass die formellen Bildungsstrukturen dringend einer Ergänzung durch informelle bzw. nonformelle Angebote bedürfen. Gerade dem Internet wird hier eine besondere Rolle zugeschrieben. Das Phänomen der digitalen Ungleichheit verweist hier jedoch auf Grenzen, die durch die Wirkmächtigkeit kultureller, sozialer und materieller Ressourcen gezogen werden: Ökonomische Ressourcen kanalisieren die Zugangsmöglichkeiten, Alltagsrelevanzen prägen die jeweiligen Nutzungsintentionen, soziale Beziehungen beeinflussen die verfügbaren Unterstützungsstrukturen, Aneignungsweisen (im Sinne von Selbstbildungsprozessen im sozialen Handeln) reproduzieren ein spezifisches Bildungsverständnis. Dies führt gerade für die nachwachsende Generation zu einer frühen Stratifizierung der Chancen und damit für viele zu einer weitreichenden Bildungsbenachteiligung.

In diesem Zusammenhang stellt sich die gesellschafts- und bildungspolitisch relevante Frage nach den Teilhabechancen und dem demokratischen Potential des virtuellen Raums. Sie wird von führenden internationalen WissenschaftlerInnen in den verschiedenen Beiträgen des Buches sowohl unter empirischen als auch theoretischen Ansätzen aus der Perspektive der für diesen Kontext grundlegenden Disziplinen diskutiert, um sie für eine zukunftsorientierte Praxis nutzbar zu machen.

Der Beitrag von Lawrence Angus untersucht mit einem qualitativ-empirischen Zugang vier Familien, die an einem australischen Programm „Virtual Communities" teilnahmen, in dem Haushalte durch staatliche Unterstützung mit verbilligten Computern ausgestattet wurden. Obwohl es sich um ein kleines Sample handelt, wird an der Studie deutlich, dass sozial benachteiligte Familien nicht allein durch den Zugang zu Informations- und Kommunikationstechnologien die Benachteiligung in Hinsicht auf Teilhabe überwinden. Über die Rekonstruktion des medialen Alltags und der habituellen Strukturen der Familien markiert Lawrence Angus eine deutliche Position in der Debatte um die Frage, inwiefern die Verfügbarkeit von Informationstechnologien zum „Empowerment der Informationsbenachteiligten" (Compaine 2001, 11) beitragen kann.

Neil Selwyn fokussiert in seinem Beitrag „New technologies, young people and social inclusion" die Diskrepanzen zwischen den nicht zuletzt in sozialpolitischen Maßnahmen unterstellten Potentialen digitaler Mediennutzung für Fragen der Teilhabe und Partizipation einerseits und der empirischen Realität andererseits. Auf dieser Basis diskutiert Selwyn ein Modell digitaler Inklusion, das weniger auf die vermeintlichen Effekte und dafür stärker auf die Transformation der sozialen Ursachen digitaler Ungleichheiten zielt.

Im Artikel „Social Facilitators and Inhibitors to Internet Access and Use" diskutiert Caroline Haythornthwaite hemmende und fördernde soziale Faktoren von „online access, use, literacy and fluency" am Beispiel von technischer Infrastruktur, individuellen Nutzungsdifferenzen, Onlineinhalten und sozialen Netzwerken. Dabei gibt Haythornthwaite einen fundierten Überblick über den Stand der gegenwärtigen Forschung zur Digitalen Spaltung und verweist in differenzierter Weise auf unterschiedliche Ebenen des statistischen Zusammenhangs sozialer Faktoren. Haythornthwaite zeichnet ein komplexes Bild unterschiedlicher Nutzungsweisen und zeigt vor allem auf, dass Zugangs- und Nutzungsunterschiede bestehen bleiben werden und neben technischen vor allem auch in sozialen Ursachen begründet liegen.

Hans-Uwe Otto, Nadia Kutscher, Alexandra Klein und Stefan Iske präsentieren in ihrem Artikel die Ergebnisse einer großen empirischen Studie des Kompetenzzentrums Informelle Bildung (KIB), in der Jugendliche in der Bundesrepublik zu ihrer Internetnutzung befragt wurden. Hierbei arbeiten die AutorInnen Band-breiten an Nutzungsweisen heraus, die vielfach in der Debatte um Mediennutzung von Jugendlichen verkürzt wahrgenommen werden, und zeigen deren Implikationen für ungleiche Teilhabe und Bildungsmöglichkeiten im Kontext des Internet auf. Vor dem Hintergrund der empirischen Ergebnisse entwickelt das KIB theoretische Überlegungen für eine differenzierte Analyse von Nutzung und Aneignung im Internet sowie Ansätze für weitere Forschung und zielgruppensensible medienpädagogische Arbeit.

Winfried Marotzki setzt sich in seinem Beitrag mit der subjektkonstituierenden Seite medialer Bildung an dem Beispiel von Erinnerungsseiten im Internet auseinander. Hierbei stellt er synchrone und diachrone Orientierungsformate im Internet als Bildungsdimensionen vor, die lebensweltliche Aspekte im Medium repräsentieren und erörtert in diesem Zusammenhang, wie – so die These – das Medium kulturelle Formationen und Praktiken verändert

Gustavo S. Mesch geht in seinem Beitrag „Social Diversification: A Perspective for the Study of Social networks of Adolescents Offline and Online" auf der Basis einer großen empirischen Studie der Frage nach, inwieweit sich Freunde, die Jugendliche im Internet kennenlernen von ihren Freunden außerhalb des Internet unterscheiden. Er kommt zu dem Ergebnis, dass mit Blick auf Alter, Geschlecht und Wohnort die Jugendliche mit ihren „virtuellen Freunden" dazu beitragen, die Heterogenität ihres sozialen Netzwerks zu erweitern.

Eszter Hargittai beschäftigt sich in ihrem Beitrag „A framework for studying differences in people's digital media uses" mit den verschiedenen Fähigkeiten und Fertigkeiten, die jugendliche InternetnutzerInnen zur Teilhabe an unterschiedlichen virtueller Arrangements benötigen. Damit eröffnet sie einen analytischen Rahmen, der es ermöglicht, die unterschiedlichen Nutzungspraktiken und Nutzungskompetenzen von InternetnutzerInnen differenziert zu erforschen und mit Blick auf die damit verbundenen ungleichen Unterstützungsbedarfe weiterführend einzuordnen.

Heinz Bonfadelli und Priska Bucher stellen Ergebnisse einer quantitativen Studie zum Stellenwert von alten und neuen Medien im Leben von Schweizer Jugendlichen mit Migrationshintergrund vor. Die Mediennutzung ethnischer Minoritäten wird dabei vor dem theoretischen Hintergrund des ‚uses and gratification'-Ansatzes sowie des Ansatzes der Medienwirkungsforschung und der Cultural Studies verortet. Kritisch hinterfragt wird dabei die häufig postulierte positive Integrationsfunktion alter Medien auf dem Hintergrund neuer Medien und die Frage nach gleichen Bildungs- und Teilhabechancen sowie Zugangsmöglichkeiten zu neuen Informations- und Kommunikationsmedien. Die empirischen Ergebnisse zeigen über jugendkulturelle Gemeinsamkeiten Jugendlicher mit und ohne Migrationshintergrund hinaus auch auf Unterschiede im Medienzugang, der Mediennutzung und der präferierten Medieninhalte und verweisen damit deutlich auf die grundsätzliche Heterogenität der Gruppen der Jugendlichen mit Migrationshintergrund.

Horst Niesyto arbeitet in seinem Kapitel Aspekte sozialer Benachteiligung im Bereich der Medien heraus und formuliert vor diesem Hintergrund Anregungen für eine differenziertere medienpädagogische Praxis, die über eine tendenzielle Mittelschichtsorientierung hinaus eine explizite Reflexivität in Bezug auf sozial benachteiligte Zielgruppen und ihre Lebenswelten entwickelt. Hierbei wirft er einen kritischen Blick auf den Mythos der Selbstsozialisation mit Medien, der gerade in vielen Publikationen zur Mediennutzung Jugendlicher zu finden ist. Demgegenüber plädiert er für eine differenzierte Perspektive auf Zielgruppen und Aneignungsweisen und wendet sich gegen eine Kulturalisierung von Benachteiligung.

David Buckingham geht in seinem Beitrag mit dem Titel „Digital Culture, Media Education and the Place of Schooling" der Frage nach welche Rolle der Schule bei der Auseinandersetzung mit neuen Technologien *und* digitalen Ungleichheiten gegenwärtig zukommt und welche Rolle ihr in Anbetracht der Tatsache, dass neue Technologien nicht per se zu einer neuen und erweiterten Bildungsteilhabe der SchülerInnen führen, bei der aktiven Erweiterung der medialen Handlungsmöglichkeiten der SchülerInnen zukommen könnte.

Den Ausgangspunkt des Artikels von Franz-Josef Röll bilden Überlegungen zum ästhetischen Denken und zur ästhetischen Bildung in Hinblick auf unterschiedliche Seh- und Wahrnehmungsweisen Jugendlicher. Um Jugendliche als Zielgruppe von Bildungsinstitutionen anzusprechen, sind demzufolge unterschiedliche zielgruppenspezifische – und vor allem ästhetische – Kommunikationsangebote erforderlich, die am Beispiel des Internetauftritts der Bundeszentrale für Gesundheitliche Aufklärung sowie der Zeitschrift 'Hessische Jugend' verdeutlicht werden. Am Beispiel des Projektes „Der virtuelle Fachbereich" der Fachhochschule Darmstadt veranschaulicht Röll sein Konzept der Pädagogik als Navigation und der damit verbundenen Fokussierung offener Lernformen sowie des Lerners als Ausgangspunkt von Bildungsprozessen.

Mit den vorliegenden Artikeln wird ein erster umfassender Überblick über die Analyse des Umgangs von Jugendlichen mit den Möglichkeiten und den Selbstbegrenzungen der „Cyberworld" geliefert, wobei insbesondere die digitale Ungleichheit und die Möglichkeiten informeller Bildung in den Mittelpunkt der Diskussion gerückt werden. Hier gilt es auch in Zukunft, noch intensiver zu forschen und breiter zu diskutieren, auch unter gesellschaftpolitischen Gesichtspunkten, um die sich

anbahnende Entwicklung einer weiteren Klassifizierung von Jugendlichen und einer damit verbundenen Benachteiligung sowie ihre subjektiven und objektiven
Folgen wahrzunehmen und zu skandalisieren.

Bielefeld/Aachen, im Februar 2007

Hans-Uwe Otto, Nadia Kutscher, Alexandra Klein und Stefan Iske

Kompetenzzentrum Informelle Bildung (KIB)

Dimensions of Educational Policy / Gesellschaftliche Herausforderungen für Bildungspolitik im Kontext des Internet

Lawrence Angus

Implications for social inequality in internet use for educational policies and programs

Because access to new technologies is unequally distributed, there has been considerable debate about the growing gap, the 'digital divide', between the information-rich and information-poor (Haywood, 1998; Bolt and Crawford 2000; Compaine 2001). In an attempt to 'redress the balance between the information rich and poor' by providing 'equal access to the World Wide Web' (Virtual Communities 2002), the Australian Council of Trade Unions (ACTU), Virtual Communities (a computer/ software distributor) and Primus (an Internet provider) formed an alliance to offer relatively inexpensive computer and Internet access to union members in order to make 'technology affordable for all Australians' (Virtual Communities 2002). This paper examines the social circumstances of four families who accepted the Virtual Communities offer and acquired relatively low-cost computers for use in their homes. Although the sample is very small, the study indicates that previously disadvantaged family members are not particularly advantaged by their access to Information and Communication Technologies (ICT).

'Family' can be defined in many ways. In this paper, I am talking about four quite conventional nuclear families. The aim is to find out how ICT are used in home settings, referred to by Sefton-Green (2001, p.164) as 'the digital bedroom'. The point is to contribute to broad discussion about whether information technology can be used to 'empower the information disadvantaged' (Compaine 2001, p. 11) and thereby make a difference to 'the digital underclass' (Bell 2001, p.13).

It has long been assumed that families and family life have been affected over time by the various waves of 'new' media such as radio, television, video recorders, computers, multimedia and the internet (Van Rompaey *et al.* 2002). The extent of use of such technologies has been linked particularly with SES and education levels (Livingstone 1999), although gender is also said to influence uptake of ICT in that men are likely to make the decisions to purchase the hardware and use it (Hellman 1996). It also appears that when and if a family does decide to purchase new ICT, 'it anticipates the effects that [such purchase] is likely to have on family life and the question of what is likely to be best for the children, in order to help prepare them for future careers and workplaces' (Van Rompaey *et al.* 2002, p.190). It is also held that the 'rapid diffusion and uptake of the Internet has been phenomenal' (Holloway 2002, p.51) compared with earlier media technologies such as telephone and television.

The rate and extent of uptake of ICT are said to be related to the bursting 'new economies', which are forms of 'knowledge economy' that are related to the 'information society'. Indeed, so strong is the 'rhetoric of inevitability' (Facer *et al.* 2001. p.92) associated with the information age that Lacroix and Tremblay (1997) conclude: 'It is as if there were only two possible kinds of future societies: information societies (the most modern and avant-garde) and the others, those that did not bite the information bullet and which will be condemned to underdevelopment'. For governments, biting the information bullet has included promotion of educational policies in which educational institutions become 'core institutions of capitalism' (Garnham 2000, p.142) in order that the nation will remain, or become, internationally competitive in the global knowledge economy. According to this line of argument, the children of the digital generation must be given access to the 'information' in order to be future workers in the knowledge economy (Facer *et al.* 2001). So there are two particular concerns in countries like Australia about the 'digital divide': first, that people without access to the new technologies will be left behind in the new economy/knowledge economy/information age; and second, that workers will need ICT access and skills in the new economy in order for the nation as a whole to be internationally competitive.

There is a minority view that the futuristic vision of this burgeoning information society and knowledge economy 'bears little, if any, relation to any concretely and graspable reality' and therefore serves as an 'ideology' (Garnham 2000, p.140). Garnham (2000, p.140) claims that 'rather than serving to enhance our understanding of the world in which we live, [such terms as 'information society' are] used to elicit uncritical assent to whatever dubious proposition is being out forward beneath [their] protective umbrella'. The importance of young people being ICT literate, which is put forward in this perspective/ideology as inevitable, necessary and exciting, is therefore seen by critics like Garnham (2000) as being either simply hype or the assertion of particular capital interests. In criticising the hype, the view is sometimes put that the 'digital divide' is not worth worrying about because it will soon heal itself since the technology, which is already spreading at a furious rate, is becoming increasingly cheap, efficient and easily available (Compaine 2001). In terms of economic and political interests, the arguments are more complex. The central point is the claim that increasing the availability of and access to ICT and the Internet will not solve the problems of the digital divide because the divide is caused by reasons of differences of culture, education, literacy, opportunity and social power as much as by gaps in ownership of hardware and software. The divide, in other words, is closely related to the same socio-political divide that has long influenced the nature and quality of people's access to education, health services, wealth and power (Griffin 2000, p.30). The Internet and ICT are socially constructed. Information technology, and the educational potential of computer education, therefore, should, as Selwyn (2002, p.429) points out, be regarded as sites of power. This is broadly the perspective that informs this paper.

Methodology

The research methodology was qualitative. Case studies were conducted of four families (three who gained computer and Internet access for the first time under the ACTU/Virtual Communities scheme, and one that had had access for five years), two of which could be described as clearly 'disadvantaged'. Members of the research team visited each family a minimum of six times in their homes between mid-2000 and mid-2001. Family members were interviewed individually and together, and were observed using ICT. Additional interviews were conducted in parents' workplaces where appropriate. More than seventy interviews were conducted with family members. The schools the children attended were visited at least three times and the children were observed in various classes using computers. The research team also interviewed their teachers, the principal or assistant principal of each school, computer co-ordinators, English teachers and curriculum co-ordinators. Altogether there were over a hundred interviews. Policy documents and school charters were viewed to help us understand the 'mission statements' of the schools in providing computer technology. Two primary and two secondary schools were included in the study.

The Participating Families
Sketches of the four families as they were in 2000-2001 are presented below.

The Rodriguez family

Fernando and Luisa Rodriguez are political refugees from Chile. They came to Australia in 1988 and now live in a new housing estate in the outer-eastern Melbourne suburb of Blue Hills. Fernando is a metal worker in a factory and Luisa is a childcare worker in a crèche. They have two children, Carmen, aged 11, who attends St. Cecilia's Catholic Primary school in a suburb 15 kilometres from Blue Hills, and Lydia, aged 5, who is in the pre-kindergarten group at the childcare centre where Luisa works. Both children are bilingual. Spanish is the language spoken at home.

Fernando explains: 'Most of my English is factory English, you know?' He did not complete secondary schooling in Chile and has not attempted any study in Australia. Nonetheless, he badly wants his daughters to succeed in their education. Fernando does not use a computer at work, and says he uses the computer at home for emailing people in Chile, accessing Chilean news websites, and following Chilean soccer results. He bought the computer through the Amalgamated Metal Workers' Union for his daughters to use primarily for educational purposes. 'Computer is everything now', he says. He is not adroit with the keyboard and has to think before finding the functions he needs. As the family never sits around the computer together (unlike the Browns and the Lakes, whom we discuss below), Fernando has to call either Luisa or Carmen to show him how to do things. During an interview with Carmen, the following exchange occurred:

[Fernando comes in and looks on and smiles. He appears proud that Carmen is so competent on the computer]

Fernando: You see? [gesturing that Carmen is operating various functions]

Interviewer: Very quick. [indicating to Fernando that Carmen knows her way round the keyboard and is not fumbling keys]

[Fernando laughs and gestures that he is not at all competent on the computer. He throws up his hands.]

Luisa Rodriguez completed her secondary education in Chile. In Australia, she has taken Migrant English classes and completed Technical and Further Education (TAFE) studies in childcare. She uses a computer in the crèche she runs, including using the Internet to search for specific information (e.g. about Rubella). She says: 'Everything computer is new for me … But if I want to communicate with my daughter I have to know about this, and I'm supposed to know more than her – because I'm the mother. I still believe that mums should know more'. She and Fernando say they seek 'excellence' in education, which is why they are prepared to pay fees and send Carmen to a Catholic girls' school so far away from home.

Carmen would like to become a veterinary surgeon and both parents are keen that she pursues this goal. She is a hard worker at school and the family rule is that she is permitted to use the computer only on Friday nights and weekends. She must finish her homework on other nights. She is able to demonstrate how she accesses the Internet, using the dedicated key on the Internet keyboard. She borrows CD-ROMs from the school library and uses the computer to listen to music, or she goes onto the Internet to use email. She shows a picture she constructed using Crayola which she calls 'Lazy Days' – explaining that it's what she sees when she lies down: 'a river and background and other things'. She also borrows books from the library and is reading *Hitler's Daughter*.

The Brown family

Jenny Brown is a single mother living on benefit payments and raising her two children, Brad, aged 14, in year nine and Lizzie, aged 12, in year 7. They live in a modest council house in Greenacres, a suburb in northwestern Melbourne about twelve kilometres from the CBD. Both children attend Greenacres Secondary College. Jenny did not complete secondary school and has never had a job. Her father, who recently retired from the Vehicle Builders' Union, leased a computer package for himself and one for Jenny and her children. The computer and the TV are in the 'lounge room'. During our visits, both were always on.

Brad and Lizzie have no contact with their biological father who walked out on Jenny two weeks after Lizzie was born. Jenny's father says his motivation for leasing the computer package was to provide his grandchildren with another source of entertainment and amusement. Jenny says she is interested in its educational benefits for Brad and Lizzie: 'I mean, they're the future and they're gonna take over everywhere and so it was like, well, it will definitely help them look up things'. All three use the computer to go to chat rooms: all three say how they enjoy meeting people from a range of countries, backgrounds and different ages. When asked how they determine whether the person to whom they are speaking is being truthful, all say confidently that it is easy to tell. Lizzie illustrates:

> One guy goes: 'Oh I'm 16. How old are you?' I go: 'I'm 12', and he goes: 'Oh, I'm 12 too.' I go: 'Why did ya say you were 16 then?' So he goes: 'So people would accept me and talk to me.'

Lizzie says she can tell someone's age by the way they 'speak' in chat sites: 'He just talks like, more adulty, instead of little kid talk sort of thing.' Jenny says she can quickly tell if people are not what they 'say' they are and she and daughter Lizzie are aware of cyber predators:

Jenny: There are ones that you don't trust and you'd more or less pick that up as soon as they say hello to you, just from different things they say, so it's normally: 'All right, thank you very much, goodbye, gotta go'.... Oh yeah, we sit there often and actually watch each other and 'have a look at this one' and like, 'yep, this one, you know straight away he's going to be a right sleeze'; and yep, 'ta ta, alright, see ya later'. We just close, that's what we do.

Lizzie: A couple of times, I've seen like these people come up to me and they go: 'Oh hello.' And I go: 'Oh hi.' And they go: 'Do you wanna cyber [have cyber-sex]?' and I go: 'No, I'm only 12.' And they go: 'Oh you're old enough.' And I go: 'No! I'm not.'

Jenny: They ask all the time, all the time, male and female, it doesn't matter. I mean you have people click on ya and you know straight away they're the people, you know just straight away, 'no thank you, goodbye'.

Jenny had been almost housebound for years – just going shopping at the local supermarket is a major expedition, as both kids have to assist and carry as many bags as they can. Now, she claims, the computer has 'changed our life'. The virtual world of chat has become her social focus and she relishes the friendships and relationships that have developed from it. She says: 'I feel like I've got friends on the computer. There's friends I can talk to, have a laugh with'. after being energised by having friends 'in the computer' after years of 'feeling like a nothing', Jenny is talking for the first time about getting a job.

Lizzie Brown wants to be a clothes designer. Her teachers describe her as quite skilled with technology, but a rather quiet and shy student. Various teachers describe her as 'a nice kid', 'quiet', 'probably below average', and 'a pleasant student who needs to be helped'. Lizzie wishes teachers would 'just to stop tellin me off'. At home, she uses the computer for email, plays on Internet sites such as Virtual Dog, Barbie.com and fan sites, and uses chatrooms a lot. She is very competent in the chatroom environment and has created images of herself (avatars) that represent her physically in the virtual world.

Brad Brown 'hates school'. He says: 'I hate wakin up for it. I hate goin to it. I hate comin home and havin to work for it …just everyfin about it. I just hate everyfin about school'. Although Greenacres Secondary College is a big school, Brad is described as the sort of student 'every teacher knows'. He was 'kept down' at the end of year 7 and made to repeat. Failing year 7 is very rare, even in schools like Greenacres that have a relatively low level of academic success. But despite being perceived as 'a loser' and as a serious discipline problem by teachers, Brad is highly competent with the computer at home. He is the one relied upon by Jenny and Lizzie to troubleshoot when the computer breaks down. He says: 'When somefin happens, I know straight away basically'. He says he uses the computer for everything: 'I just go on it, muck around, talk to my friends, get car pictures, download songs – I do everyfin on it'. He also accesses sites for job searches and uses email and chatroom functions. In contrast to his home use of computer technology, Brad asserts: 'I didn't learn nuthin at school from the computer'.

The Lawford family

Helen Ryan and Brendan Lawford have recently divorced. Brendan is a communications manager for a large union and Helen is a corporate assessor for a multinational power and resources company. Both had been actively involved in union activities during university days prior to Helen being employed as a bureaucrat in public sector administration in Victoria in the late 1980s and early 1990s. With a change in political power in 1992, Helen moved easily to a higher-paid position in the private sector. Brendan hints that the strain in their marriage may have been partly due to his perception of a change in Helen's political values. Brendan still works for the union. The couple have a six-year-old daughter, Angela, who is in grade 1 at the inner-city Rosewood Primary School. Angela lives with Helen in the family home and her father has a flat nearby where Angela stays two nights a week.

Helen has an unusual background for such a corporate high flier – quite similar in fact to that of Jenny Brown. Helen's parents were among the wave of British immigrants in the 1950s who settled in a brand new satellite city just north of Adelaide, near other working class suburbs like Happy Valley and Paradise. Few of the kids who attended schools like Satellite High in the 1970s completed their secondary schooling, much less went on to higher education. Helen did both. She recalls a major defining moment in her life – what she calls her 'Big W experience', which occurred when she had been working during the summer school holidays at a large 'Big W' supermarket where she must have impressed her superiors. At fifteen, she was offered full-time, continuing work at the store – an offer most of her friends would have jumped at. The offer caused her to seriously consider where she was headed. She talked it over with her parents and recalls thinking: 'I'm fifteen and not pregnant. Perhaps I might amount to something!'

Brendan and Helen both regard the computer as an integral part of Angela's education. They bought her first computer program when she was four years old because it was 'the best little program around and it was all about mouse skills'. It is apparent that six-year-old Angela is highly computer literate and competent. At the same time, both parents emphasise the importance of books. Helen insists that Angela 'is a very, very good reader and reads at above average levels'.

The Lake family

The Lake family live in the inner-city suburb of Kilvington and the two girls, Felicity, aged 15, in year 11 and Sally, aged 13, in year 9, attend City High School. Sara and Ray Lake both have postgraduate degrees (arts, management and labour relations law for Ray; arts and law for Sara) and hold senior trade union positions. They initially bought a computer so they could work at home, and for the girls' schoolwork. The family members see the computer as a tool for work or research but stress the superiority of books and their love of the world of paper-text. For instance, during family discussions around the dining table, at which family members linger after meals, someone will often reach for the *Encyclopedia Britannica* to settle a dispute or look up information relevant to dinner-table conversation. While actively downplaying the importance of the computer and their ICT skills in general (Ray: 'I'm never sure where to put the petrol in'), all members of the family are exceptionally competent technology users.

Felicity is a member of a band that meets on weekends and finds that Hotmail is very useful for making arrangements. Sally has used computers at school from an early age and enjoys games and emailing friends. She says she's good at Internet searches and downloads images for projects but, when asked about how much she uses the Internet for research purposes, she gestures to the *Britannica* volumes on the shelf behind her to indicate that she more often refers to them. The favourite family computer activity is playing *Civilisation*. Sally describes it as 'a particularly addictive game' and adds: 'Sadly, this is what I do most of the time'. She likes to play the part of 'someone like Catherine the Great, but called Bob – easier to remember'. The family consider this game feeds their love of history and culture.

The families, cultural resources and relationships with school

In examining the attitudes of the participating families to the use of computer technology at home and school, we find it useful to consider the concepts of cultural access and deprivation, and the relationship between processes of advantaging and disadvantaging. Bourdieu (1990) considers that 'capital', the kinds of resources that can give one social and economic advantage, can be of different forms. There are tangible forms of durable capital, such as money and quantifiable assets, which he terms 'economic capital'. There are also non-material forms of capital, called 'symbolic capital'. These forms of capital enable individuals who possess them to open or close doors to material success and power. One form of symbolic capital is social capital, which Bourdieu (1990, p. 35) defines as 'a network of kinship (or other) relations capable of being mobilized or at least manifested'. For example, Jenny Brown says her life has been 'changed by the computer' as her social network, which confers upon her greater confidence and self-esteem than she has felt for many years, is now that of Internet chatrooms where she feels she is a valued member. The final type of symbolic capital, and the main one we use in this discussion, is Bourdieu's (1990) notion of 'cultural capital'.

Cultural capital includes all the attributes, including education, literacy, and social graces, with which an individual is endowed. An example of cultural capital is the desire of some of the parents (Lake, Lawford and Rodriguez) that their children attain 'excellence' in education. In the case of the Lakes and the Lawfords, this expectation would seem a normal and 'natural' consequence of Felicity's and Sally's and Angela's 'inherent' skills, networks and 'insider' knowledge of what counts as education, knowledge and culture. This is all part of their social and cultural identities. Their backgrounds and easy familiarity with the education world (although Helen had to win such familiarity the hard way) enhance their level of cultural capital way above that of the Rodriguez family, in which the parents are striving to enhance their children's cultural opportunities and identities through private education. But the Rodriguez family is in turn way ahead of the Browns in the cultural capital stakes.

Both the Rodriguez and Lawford families consider computer skills and technology as one means of opening doors to future higher education and economic sectors. Luisa and Fernando Rodriguez are not such highly skilled users of computer technology as Helen and Brendan, but they are determined that their daughters will be. For all of them, there seems to be a clearly perceived relationship between computer competence and educational success. Yet the relationship between the schools, the children and the four families is complex and variable. For example, Angela Lawford quite likes computing classes but is disappointed that 'at school you don't get to choose what you do. They actually show you what you're meant to be doing and we're meant to be working on [that]'. Angela spends most time at Barbie.com and sites to do with witches and fairies. She enjoys spelling and number games that could be regarded as school-like. The recreational computer activities of the Lake girls could also be regarded as school-like. As a family, they love playing 'Civilisation' and looking up on the Internet ingredients from interesting restaurant dishes or the botanical names of plants. The Brown children, however, derive pleasure from decidedly un-school-like computer activities. Principal among these is chat. There's also music downloading and searching for car information and images (Brad), and celebrity news, magazine and fan sites, and virtual dog (Lizzie). One of the few times Brad spoke with enthusiasm about anything (except his job, which I discuss below) was when he said:

> I love the...when I go on the Internet, well ... yeah, and like, I'll save a few pictures to my file, like car pictures, pictures of cars, and soon as I'm offline or whatever, ya know, I'll go into paint, open file, yeah, and put a car picture. And if, like, I put a car picture, I can like chop the roof off, make it smaller, make the wheels fatter, like modify it. Yeah, it's fun. (laughs)

One startling difference between the Brown family and, say, the Lawford family, is the way the families, indeed the school communities, are perceived within their respective schools. Angela Lawford is discussed fondly by her teachers, who are impressed by the level of support she receives from her extended family. Helen knows each of Angela's teachers by their first name. She has harmonious contact with the school, where she feels welcomed. Jenny Brown, however, asserts: 'the only times I've contacted the school is when [Brad's] in trouble'. She has no rapport with teachers at all. Jenny is an 'outsider' where Helen is a valued 'insider'. This raises issues about how different 'parental voices' (Vincent and Martin 2002) are 'heard' and listened to in schools.

Angela's current classroom teacher, Alan West, says: '[Angela's] like the perfect student, the ideal child'. Over at Greenacres Secondary College, however, you can't find anyone with a very high opinion of Brad or Lizzie Brown. But there's not a high regard for the community either. In response the question, 'how would you describe Greenacres Secondary College', Mr Hall says:

> Well, a lot of strugglers. A lot of families that put education well down their list of priorities. Certainly not all. There are parents who do care and who really do try and help the school, but …. I mean we get a lot of animosity no matter what we do from the parents towards the school.

Even this teacher, who Brad says knows him best, expresses little knowledge of Brad's family: 'They're basically working class stock. Apart from that I really don't know'. The school principal adds: 'for a lot of our kids, the only stable person in their lives who has a values system is their teachers'. Such social and cultural distancing of teachers from the social and cultural milieu of the Brown family, and the neighbourhood in general, was quite noticeable, even for teachers who seemed generally 'sympathetic' towards pupils (see also Barber 2002). The above quotation indicates not only a systematic discounting of the Browns' (and working class) cultural experiences, but also a teacher view that implies working class students should endeavour to conform to what McFadden and Munns (2002) call the 'teacher paradigm'. Indeed, the general attitude displayed to the working-class community of Greenacres, and to Brad Brown in particular, seems crude and dismissive and is consistent with Reay's (2001, p.335) conclusion that:

> In Bourdieurian terms, the working classes both historically and currently are discursively constituted as unknowing, uncritical, tasteless mass from which the middle class draw their distinctions … [by] representing the children of the poor only as a measure of what they lack.

Yet, perhaps ironically in this case, there is a view at Greenacres Secondary College that the school's emphasis on technology is precisely to engage working class students and better equip them for the future. According to the Deputy Principal:

> Technology comes number one. It's used as a kind of marketing technique because we give our year 7s a really intensive computer program. We make a big thing of the fact that we have four operational computer rooms.

The principal says that schools 'have a corporate responsibility to our kids' and must train students for jobs not yet in existence that will require the acquisition of knowledge and technology'. Technology, it would seem, might be the salvation of the masses. But despite computer education being a 'big thing' for marketing as well as educational purposes, teachers have very little sense of which or how many students have computers at home; indeed teachers' estimates vary from 'perhaps up to 25 per cent' to 'at least 75 per cent'.

For example, none of the teachers we spoke to knew that Brad or Lizzie had a computer at home. When informed of this fact, one teacher volunteered:

> I'm certain that most of the time [Brad's] on the computer he's searching the Net, it's for pleasure not for anything educational. You know the sites that... Brad's heavily into skateboarding for instance. As a teacher I have a computer at home for my kids. When my kids use the computer I like to oversee it and see exactly what they're doing. But who knows what Brad is doing!

Here, within a 'powerful blaming discourse' (Reay 2001, p.338) the Browns are constructed as 'others', as being of a different world to the teachers. They and their neighbours are viewed as disconnected from education in ways that the school can say it can't really do much about.

School work, home computer play and imagined futures

The Lawfords contrast with the Browns in the ease with which school and home, work and play, are integrated – particularly in terms of information technology. The Lawfords articulate the view that playing on the computer is akin to learning computer competence, and are happy about Angela's computer play. Both parents are comfortable with Angela accessing different sites such as Barbie.com. Jenny Brown also supports the view that a computer at home is important for her children, 'to help them look things up'. The reality is, however, that little schoolwork is done on the computer in the Brown house. Although Jenny conceives of computers as 'the future, and they're gonna take over everywhere', she does not insist the computer at home be used for schoolwork, unlike Luisa Rodriguez. In the Rodriguez house, the computer is for education not play.

Luisa and Fernando regard a high level of education, and integration of computer technology into that education, as vital for successful penetration of barriers to cultural and economic power. They explain: 'We want our children to be better than we are'. They are adamant that Carmen and Lydia will obtain better, higher paid jobs than they, themselves, have and are fully supportive of Carmen's dream of becoming a veterinary surgeon. Luisa, in particular, regards acquiring knowledge and credentials as vital to improving the life chances of her children. The slightly desperate quest for academic success is putting Carmen under a lot of pressure to avoid failure. It is unlikely that she will ever experience the casual assumption of academic success that pervades the Lake girls' personas. For Felicity and Sally Lake, it would appear that the 'decision' to be successful at school and proceed to university is, as Ball *et al.* (2002, p.54) put it, 'a non-decision'. It seems part of a 'normal' and expected social trajectory. For Carmen Rodriguez, it would seem that her mother has deliberately made a similar decision for her, but this 'active' decision is more problematic. The family lacks the social and cultural resources and supports that are available to the Lawfords and Lakes.

Unlike Luisa Rodriguez, Jenny Brown is not at all desperate that her children attain high levels of education and thereby increase their cultural capital and their opportunities of acquiring greater economic capital. Yet, perhaps surprisingly, the least hazy 'imagined future' of all the young people is Brad Brown's. From his first interview Brad spoke of his plan to leave school when he turned 15 (although he would be only in year 9) and get an apprenticeship. This was aiming very high in Brad's world (although not so high for the other families) and he was advised at school that such a move would be impossible for him. One teacher said: 'I actually mentioned to him, a lot of times now, you need a minimum of year 11 for an apprenticeship. Otherwise they're not even going to look at you'. Brad was adamant, however. Once he turned 15 no-one could then make him go back to school. He said he would prove to everyone, including his family, that he *could* get a job and that he would not conform to the expectation of others that he would become 'a layabout dole bludger'. In the event, Brad did leave school when he turned 15 and has achieved exactly what he said he would achieve. He explains:

> The day after [we last spoke] I organised to go up [to the crash repairer's] and we went up there and I spoke to the boss and he said, 'Yeah come in tomorrow and we'll give you a test try'. And I went, 'Oh all right'. And that [next] day they just said, 'Don't worry about the test try, we'll give you an apprenticeship now'.

In terms of where he had set his sights, Brad has achieved huge success against the odds despite bypassing the usual institutional frameworks. Apprenticeships are like gold dust among Brad's peers, even if the work can be dirty and dangerous. He's on track to becoming a skilled tradesperson and, eventually, as Brad sees it, to having his own spray painting or crash repair business. This boy, who was a 'discipline problem', a 'loser' and a 'failure' at school, has been able to use his limited capital – including a rev-head network, an uncle in the automotive trade and Jenny's ex-de facto who is a motor-bike fanatic – to make contacts in the business in which he has now scored the kind of apprenticeship he always dreamed of.

Of the people in the four families, the person who spends most time, by far, on the computer in the home is Jenny Brown. She uses it for chat with a voraciousness that suggests she may be making up for lost time spent with little social contact. This use of Internet chat has enhanced her personal symbolic capital and enabled her, a once socially isolated and housebound woman, to engage with other people and feel good about herself. But it has not so far enhanced her social power. The virtual world of chat and email has become her social capital. Her children have also become engaged in the virtual world of chat, which has a curious relationship to their off-line social world. For Jenny, in particular, and to a lesser extent Lizzie, the life 'in the computer, to some extent fills what is lacking in 'real' life. Their engagement in this partial, virtual world is highly active, creative and complex, and requires imagination and the making of multiple judgements as cyber relationships and situations are negotiated. Much time is spent discussing avatars and identities, issues of representation, relationships, realities, emotions and truth. As Webb (2001, p.562) explains: 'Virtual identities are embodied, sensuously experienced and contingently rhythmic and mobile. If you wish, we *write identity* through them'. Potentially, the capacity to 'produce' identities, representations and alternative realities in such chat activity, rather than just be consumers of computer games and Web-based information, might become a culturally empowering and enriching activity. But at present, in the Brown household, it looks like just fantasy and escapism.

Conclusion

Overall, compared with the Lawford and Lake children, and also with the Rodriguez girls, Brad and Lizzie Brown have experienced greater inequalities of access to resources and life chances, making the reproduction of disadvantage, for them, more likely. They have a computer and Internet access in their home, making them part of that rapidly expanding group of the technology 'haves', but that's where the similarities with the other children in the study more or less end. We need to ask, therefore, how useful it is to talk about technology 'haves' and 'have-nots'. Our data suggest that we require an expanded, reconceptualised understanding of 'access' and its relation to equity. Access cannot be seen merely as having an Internet connection, but as a much more complex and multileveled social goal (Burbules and Callister 2000). The question is not only about who gets how much of the technology resources, but also who gets the benefits associated with such resources and how much of them (Comber & Green, 1999).

Some time ago Lipkin wrote of new technologies:

> Them that has, gets.... If a particular race, sex or economic group occupies an inferior position in society, you only have to be able to add one and one to see that technology will compound the problem. (Lipkin, cited in Zakariya 1984, p.29)

It seems that old inequalities have not disappeared in the increasingly networked society, but neither are they the same nor have they been simply added to. Despite being among the technology 'haves' the Browns are simply not as well off as the others. And the engagement with technology and the social world of the Rodriguez family, regardless of equal access to ICT, is clearly different to that of the Law-fords and Lakes. This paper has attempted to capture and illustrate a portion of the complexity of contemporary social and educational inequalities within and across the lives of some young people and their families. On the basis of the case studies, it does not seem that equal access to ICT, without attention to other socio-political aspects of advantage and disadvantage, will do much to close the digital or social divide.

Author's note: I wish to acknowledge that the original research reported in this chapter was supported by an Australian Research Council grant and was conducted jointly with Ilana Snyder and Wendy Sutherland-Smith.

References

Ball, S. J., Davies, J., David, M. and Reay, D. (2002): 'Classification' and 'judgement': social class and the 'cognitive structures' of choice of higher education. In: *British journal of sociology of education*. 23.1. 51-72.

Barber, T. (2002): 'A special duty of care'. exploring the narration and experience of teacher caring. In: *British journal of sociology of education*. 23.3. 383-395.

Bell, D. (2001): *An introduction to cybercultures*. London: Routledge.

Bolt, D. & Crawford, R. (2000): *Digital divide: Computers and our children's future*. New York: TV Books.

Bourdieu, P. (1990): *The Logic of Practice* (R. Nice, Trans.). Stanford: Stanford University Press.

Burbules, N.C. and Callister, T. (2000): *Watch IT. The Risks and Promises of Information Technologies for Education,* Boulder, Colorado: Westview Press.

Comber, B. and Green, B. (1999): *Information Technology, Literacy and Educational Disadvantage Research and Development*. Project Report to DETE SA, Vol. 1, Adelaide: University of South Australia.

Companie, B. (2001): *The Digital divide. Facing a crisis or creating a myth?* Cambridge, Massachusetts: MIT Press.

Facer, K., Furlong, J., Furlong, R. and Sutherland, R. (2001): Constructing the child computer user: from public policy to private practices. In: *British journal of sociology of education.* 22.1. 91-108.

Garham, N. (2000): 'Information society' as theory or ideology. In: *Information, communication and society.* 3.2. 139-152.

Griffin, M. (2000): *Digital divide.* Sydney Morning Herald e-mag. 4 May, 26-30.

Haywood, T. (1995): *Info-Rich-Info-Poor. Access and exchange in the global information society.* London: Bowker Saur.

Hellman, H. (1996): A toy for the boys only? Reconsidering the gender effects of video technology. In: *European journal of communication.* 11.1. 5-32.

Holloway, D. (2002): Disparities in Internet access: a case study of western Sydney. In: *Australian journal of social issues.* 37.1. 51-69.

Lacroix, J. and Tremblay, G. (1997): From Fordism to Gatesism. In: *Current sociology.* 45.3. 115-125.

Livingstone, S. (1999): Personal computers in the home. what do they mean for children? In: *Interme-dia.* 27.2. 4-6.

McFadden, M. and Munns, G. (2002): Student engagement and the social relations of pedagogy. In: *British journal of sociology of education.* 23.2. 357-366.

Reay, D. (2001): Finding or losing yourself?: working-class relationships to education. In: *Journal of education policy.* 16.4. 333-346.

Sefton-Green, J. (2001): The 'End of School' or just 'Out of School'?: ICT, the home and digital cultures. In: C. Durrant & C. Beavis (Eds) *P(ICT)ures of English. Teachers, learners and technolo-gy* (pp.162-175). Kent Town: Wakefield Press.

Selwyn, N. (2002): Learning to love the micro: the discursive construction of 'educational' computing in the UK. In: *British journal of sociology of education.* 23.2. 427-443.

Van Rompaey, V., Roe, K. and Struys, K. (2002): Children's influence on Internet access at home. In: *Information, communication and society.* 5.2. 189-206.

Vincent, C. and Martin, J. (2002): Class, culture and agency. researching parental voice. In: *Inter-change.* 23.1. 109-128.

Virtual Communities. (2002): Available: http://www.virtualcommunities.com.au [Accessed 17 Octo-ber 2004].

Webb, S. (2001): Avatar culture. narrative, power and identity in virtual world environments. In: *Information, communication and society.* 4.4. 560-594.

Zakariya, S. (1984): In school (as elsewhere), the rich get computers, the poor get poorer. In: *Ameri-can school board journal.* March. 29-32.

Neil Selwyn

New technologies, young people and social inclusion

I   INTRODUCTION

Information and communication technologies (ICTs) have long been promoted as a particularly apposite means of allowing young people to play active roles in society, enhancing educational and employment prospects and, crucially, offering ways in which 'previously marginalised' young people "might better participate in public culture and democracy" (Schofield Clark 2003, p.98). All told, an "intrinsically equitable, decentralised and democratic world" (Graham 2002, p.35) is anticipated by many commentators, with young people technologically re-positioned at its core rather than periphery. Of course, there is a growing sense amongst more critical commentators that these inclusive promises are tempered by persistent 'digital inequalities' which replicate and reinforce the familiar 'social fault lines' of gender, age, income, race, educational background, geography and disability (Golding 2000). Indeed the Pew study of US internet use bluntly contended that 'demography is destiny when it comes to going online' – a conclusion supported by the wealth of digital divide surveys and statistical analyses produced year on year by academics, governments, charitable foundations and market researchers the world over. Broadly speaking these data show that those who are better educated, relatively well-off, urban-dwelling, white and male continue to be more likely to enjoy a higher quality and quantity of ICT access and use (Livingstone 2004, Chinn and Fairlie 2004). In this respect, the key challenge facing policymakers in the early twenty-first century remains how best to address these imperfections of the otherwise idealised information age.

In fact there has been more than a decade's worth of social policy attempts to ameliorate the technical and technological deficiencies seen to be at the heart of digital inequality. Such policy drives have been usually built around the increased resourcing of public and municipal institutions such as schools, libraries and community centres, the development of formal computer education and support programmes, and even the subsidising of IT equipment purchases by those on low incomes. Yet from the USA to Germany, such public and social policymaking has done little to remedy the persistent patterns of digital inequality just highlighted. Thus it is heartening that there has been growing recognition in recent years that a major shortcoming of much of the digital divide policymaking of the 1990s and early 2000s was its over-emphasis on addressing the technological shortcomings of people's (non)use of ICT, and subsequent neglect of the broader social and cultural dynamics which underpin ICT (non)use. Even those nations establishing what is considered to be 'universal' access to ICT have found that providing every citizen with the technological means and basic skills to use a computer is not a fast-track to overcoming digital inequality. Instead more enduring and less easily addressed issues persist, especially in terms of the social and cultural divides in how people articulate and act upon the meanings of ICTs. Addressing these and other non-technological concerns is now seen to be an acutely important element of attempting to tackle digital exclusion of young and old alike.

Thus we are now witnessing a 'second wave' of more socially- and culturally-focussed efforts to democratise the opportunities and outcomes of ICT use for young people. Crucially these more nuanced approaches towards technology and social exclusion espouse the need for a 'bottom-up' and informal approach to digital inclusion. There is, for example, a growing number of policies and initiatives seeking to support the provision of ICTs in the informal community and domestic settings most familiar and comfortable to young people – from housing estates to petrol stations, football clubs to shopping malls. Many present digital inclusion interventions take a multifaceted approach to digital inclusion and seek to address a range of contextual limitations to technology use, such as family transience, difficult domestic circumstances, inadequate resourcing and poor literacy (Williams *et al.* 2005). In a more 'virtual' sense governments and other agencies are shifting their attention towards establishing online communities of young people clustered around common interests such as education, the environment and political representation. Online media are also being used for global, nationwide and local consultation exercises with young people. All told, some valuable lessons appear to have been learnt from the digital divide policymaking of the 1990s and early 2000s.

Yet whilst this shift in thinking is much welcomed, significant doubts remain that a truly 'bottom-up' ethos is driving this new wave of policymaking and practice. In reality many of these initiatives and interventions remain rooted in idealised 'official' conceptions of how technology should be used and how young people should participate in society. This chapter therefore argues that current socially-orientated ICT interventions and initiatives may only be successful if accompanied by a fundamental shift in the thinking which underpin them. This requires a rethinking of the relevance, utility and meaning of ICT use for young people, as well as a reconsideration of the relevance of 'socially inclusive' practices in what are increasingly 'hypercomplex' societies. The chapter concludes that sustained change in present patterns of digital inequality may only occur if genuine efforts are made to empower young people to use ICTs for what are truly their own modes of participation in society, rather than the continued pursuit of official 'digital divide' agendas based around the macro-level interests of state, economy and polity. These themes are now explored in greater detail throughout the remainder of the chapter.

II WEAKNESSES IN CURRENT THINKING OVER YOUNG PEOPLE AND DIGITAL INCLUSION

Like many areas of policy and technology, the current digital inclusion agenda suffers from a continuing mismatch between the rhetoric and the reality of technology and social inclusion. Even within ostensibly critical debates over ICTs and social inclusion, there is often a subtle and sometimes unconscious privileging of the transformatory *potentials* of ICT at the expense of acknowledging the rather less spectacular *realities* of ICT use in contemporary everyday life. Thus the current 'electronic turn' within social policymaking remains more "an article of faith" than tried and tested strategy (Caulkin 2004, p.9). Of course, the need to resist the allure of techno-romanticism has been well-argued within the social science literature. Recently, for example, Paul Michael Garrett (2005) has reasoned that those commentators concerned with social policy, young people and new technology should (at the very least) allow themselves to think both positively *and* negatively about ICTs. In other words there is a pressing need to acknowledge the flawed, unsatisfactory and ordinary aspects of new technologies alongside their more celebrated extraordinary features.

This romanticism is compounded by a continuing conceptualisation of digital inclusion in 'macro' societal, economic and political terms rather than from the perspective of the individual. Despite rhetoric to the contrary, the digital inclusion agendas of countries like the UK, Germany and US retain an over-arching concern with decidedly macro-level issues such as educatability, employability, up-skilling and re-skilling workforces and generally coercing people to make more active and productive contributions to society – what Iske (2006) refers to as "the normative discourses of economy and politics". In this sense the notion of 'social inclusion' underpinning the digital inclusion model could be more accurately described as one of *economic* inclusion. Of course this is not a unique position in social policymaking and merely echoes the wider underlying driving rationales of the general policy turn in Western democracies towards 'social inclusion'. Yet, if we are to better understand the modest impact to date of digital inclusion policymaking then we need to consider the possibility that the 'socially inclusive' ends we wish young people to use ICTs for may not be that desirable or advantageous for the individuals concerned.

With these points in mind, any attempt to address young people's digital inequality will surely stand more chance of success if time is taken to reconsider a few of the received wisdoms currently underpinning ICTs and social inclusion. What if we imagine for a moment that universal use of ICTs like the internet and computers is not necessarily an inevitable or indeed necessary part of *all* young people's lives? What if we accept that there could be some very practical, pragmatic and even empowered rationales for young people to reject the forms of ICT use that are 'officially' seen as digitally desirable? What if current patterns of digital inequality derive in part from 'digital decision' rather than 'digital division'? What if we give credence to people's own capacity to reflect critically on issues of technological (non)engagement? Thus with this less presumptive perspective on ICTs and social exclusion in mid, we can now go on to outline four underpinning assumptions of the current digital inequality debate which merit further consideration, namely:

– that young people are naturally aligned to new technologies;
– that ICT use is an inevitably empowering activity for young people;
– that ICT can prompt new patterns and types of behaviour amongst young people;
– that young people who are currently deemed to be digital excluded will necessarily benefit from ICT use.

First of these areas is the widely-held notion that young people are naturally aligned to new technologies. Indeed the mythologizing of the 'cyberkid', 'techno-tot' and an entire 'net generation' forms one of the cornerstones of current debate over technology and society. Presently, this trend is being vigorously perpetuated through the promotion of an up-coming 'generation M' of young people who are constantly connected to mobile technologies (Kaiser Family Foundation 2005). Or else we are told tales of young 'digital natives' ensconced in their 'digital bedrooms' and making rich and varied use of ICT (Prensky 2003). These idealised views of young technology users are hampered by a number of shortcomings. Firstly, not all young people are inclined toward using ICTs, just as not all young people are inclined towards reading, sport, pop music or other ostensibly 'youth' activity. 'Children' and 'young people' are not homogenous categories, and it is disingenuous for academics and policymakers to treat them as such. At best, our tendency to imagine that young people are inexorably drawn towards new technologies is more rooted in expectant wish-fulfilment rather than empirical experience. In this respect the metaphoric use of a technologically-willing and able cyber-youth is a rhetorical part of the on-going discursive construction of the information age rather than an accurate reflection of young people's actual capabilities. As such is provides a shaky foundation for sustained social change.

A second flawed presumption in the current digital inclusion debate is that ICT use is an inevitably empowering and transformative activity. This trend is currently prevalent with the emerging generation of internet-mediated communication applications such as instant messaging, texting and blogging, all of which are being widely portrayed as inherently empowering practices as well as being "cheap, fast, democratic and popular" (Herring 2004, p.26). Yet in reality, young people's use of these technologies is far less prevalent than such adult enthusiasts imagine. Indeed, although internet applications may well be deeply embedded in the social fabric of the middle-class, technologically-privileged lives of academics and their children, for many young people the internet remains a decidedly 'fragile medium', which is used (if at all) in far more limited, sporadic and often conservative ways (Livingstone 2003). Thus although maintaining a high profile in the minds and imaginations of some academics and policymakers, only a minority of young people are creating and maintaining their own websites, authoring and updating their own blogs and actively contributing to virtual communities (Livingstone *et al.* 2005). And even when young people are making use of these cutting-edge applications, the realities are often less transformatory than may be imagined. Thus in the midst of the excitement over the potential of 'web 2.0' applications such as blogs, myspace, wiki-media, flickr and podcasting it is all too easy for technologically-adept adult commentators to over-estimate the intensity and quality of young people's actual engagement with technology, as well as misjudge their overall enthusiasm and appetite for using ICTs in these ways.

Of concern here is the ease with which much of the ever-expectant hype surrounding young people and technology use ignores the 'brutal' reality of contemporary ICT use (Couldry 2003), especially the crucial role of global corporate and commercial concerns in structuring young people's technology use. Whatever the potential otherwise, issues of ICT-based empowerment, inclusion and public participation are not overriding concerns in the commercial development of the technology use most of us are subjected to, where concerns are more often centred around issues of profit, audience share and 'stickiness'. Although the technological potential for social inclusion and empowerment may well exist, commentators are often slow to accept that young people's actual uses of ICTs are heavily shaped and bounded by less socially-concerned corporate, commercial constructions. A young person's passing use of Microsoft's Instant Messenger service with their schoolfriends is a world apart from emersion in a non-hierarchical and supportive virtual community. Downloading the Crazy Frog ring tone from the Jamster website is not akin to freely accessing the entire Communist Manifesto or collected works of Shakespeare. The reality of young people's commercialised and often aimless use of ICT has little in common with the public-spirited and transformatory versions of ICT currently idealised by academics and other commentators.

There is therefore a danger of imagining that ICTs can somehow prompt young people to develop profoundly *new* patterns of behaviour and types of activity. Indeed, this logic lies at the heart of much of the current digital inclusion debate. Proponents of e-learning, for instance, continue to tout being able to learn online rather than within the confines of educational institutions as encouraging those young people who have ceased to participate in education to re-engage on their own terms. Technology-mediated contact with politicians, law enforcement agencies and other state officials is similarly portrayed as widening engagement to those young people who are otherwise reluctant to engage in 'conventional' ways of contact. Yet, most empirical studies in this area find no evidence of such an extension of empowerment. In terms of voting in state and federal elections, ICTs have been found to do little to alter patterns of disenfranchisement or abstinence from voting (Mossberger *et al.* 2003). Similar conclusions have been reached by researchers examining the use of ICTs for employment seeking, lifelong learning and social connectivity (McQuaid *et al.* 2004, Gorard *et al.* 2003, Matei and Ball-Rokeach 2003). Thus, rather than prompting young people to alter their existing behaviour there is strong evidence that whilst ICT-based interventions may be *increasing* levels of learning, voting and civic engagement, they tend to have little impact on *widening* these activities beyond those who were already doing so.

Finally, there is a need to also question the assumption that the currently digitally excluded are primarily prevented from making the rational choice of using ICTs by a distinct set of barriers. Throughout the digital divide debate, people's *non*-use of ICT (and especially young people's non-use) is widely assumed to result from economic, social, cultural or technological impediments to use. These factors may sometimes be exacerbated by deficiencies on the part of the individual concerned (such as deficits in terms of skill, know-how, attitude or personality). Most efforts to overcome digital inequality are therefore focused on ameliorating these barriers to use. Yet this logic precludes the possibility that young people's non-use of ICT could be based on pragmatic, practical and perhaps even empowered choices. This choosing *not* to use could be rooted, for example, in the perception that ICT use offers little meaningful advantage to some young people and their circumstances. Thus when a non-user offers the rationale of having 'no need' to make use of ICTs (a response which researchers usually attribute to inadequate knowledge of the true potential of ICT) it *could* be that they really do mean that they have no need of ICT use and, as rational actors, have decided not to engage.

If we accept this alternate scenario for a moment, then there are a few possibilities why young people may continue to shy away from making use of ICT for what are usually seen as empowering purposes. First is the possibility that for the young people concerned ICTs like the internet or digital television are merely 'dead space', not conducive to real empowerment and certainly not "true public space[s], alive with discussion, debate and collective action" (Couldry 2003, p.96). From this perspective, a person wishing to actively become a full member of society may reasonably conclude that they are better served by pursuing offline forms of inclusive activity. From this perspective, some young people's non-use of ICT could be more a reflection of the real usefulness of technology rather than a deficit on their part. As Couldry (2003, p.92) concludes, "the vast online universe of information and entertainment cannot be assumed to be a universal good, having the same value to everyone".

This line of reasoning also questions the value and nature of the 'empowerment' that young people are being offered through ICTs. As Masschelein and Quaghebeur (2005) remind us, the 'participation' and 'inclusion' which is promised through social policy interventions is often based on official supply-side' needs and assumptions. Whilst 'participation' is often presented and perceived as the increased and active involvement of young people in activities and decisions which concern their lives, official notions of 'participation' can also be seen as actually constituting the establishment of a decidedly non-benign mode of governmentality based around government of the individual. In other words, the individual 'participant' is not actively self-determining (and self-empowering) but submitting themselves to be an oppressed element of a wider mode of government. One could argue that in this sense all that ICT-based social policy interventions can offer young people is a conservative notion of empowerment, presupposing that young people strive for a middle-class way of life and all that goes with it. Faced with this prospect, many young people may not want equal access to the civic world as it stands, but perhaps seek a changed society and social structures. In this sense offering technologically enhanced ways of engaging with an undesirable existing form of society may hold little allure. Choosing not to use ICTs in these ways *may* then be less a matter of powerless disadvantage and more an empowered tactic of resistance.

III SO WHERE NOW? TOWARDS A NEW DIGITAL INCLUSION AGENDA

So how can this critique of the current digital inclusion agenda be used in a constructive manner? Certainly if we accept that some ICT use may *not* be especially empowering, that not all young people may necessarily *want* inclusion within the formal structures of society, that not all young people are *inherently* predisposed to ICT use and that digital behaviour is most likely to follow on from offline behaviours, then we can begin to rationalise the slight impact of the digital inclusion agenda to date. More importantly we can use this critical analysis as a catalyst to more effective future efforts. In this spirit we are led to suggest four specific areas of thinking – i.e. that:

- social problems require social solutions;
- meaningful change in young people's behaviour derives from genuinely 'bottom-up' activity;
- the state and other bodies should adopt more facilitative and supportive roles in addressing digital inclusion;
- commercial interests must play a wider role in addressing digital inclusion.

Firstly, given the inter-related nature of online and offline social exclusion it would seem logical that the best way to address patterns of digital exclusion may be to attend to the underlying social issues that they reflect. Indeed, a number of different dimensions of non-digital (dis)advantage come into play in young people's relationships with the social, economic, political, cultural and technological elements of society – many of which are not even partially surmountable via digital interventions. For example, ICTs can do little to alter some people's limited resources and vulnerable circumstances. The opportunity to purchase goods and services via the internet cannot be realised without a credit card or bank account, and then also requires the requisite means with which to fund it. Similarly, the opportunity to learn online requires adequate levels of literacy, confidence and, just as importantly, a sense that the learning will be of some personal utility.

Given the over-riding inertia of social relations and structures, the most important step in engaging young people with public, civic and societal activities would be to invest the considerable time and effort in transforming activities such as learning, voting or even just having a bank account into worthwhile, relevant and even attractive activities, rather than assuming that a technological-sheen alone will somehow make them more attractive and alluring. As Earle (2005, p.2) observes, "no amount of digital interactivity with thirteen to twenty-three year olds is likely to change the fact that the current establishment is devoid of a vision for the future that can appeal to either young or old". Social problems such as disenfranchisement, unemployment, illiteracy and innumeracy generally require social solutions rather than technical fixes. It is here that social policymakers should start.

It also follows that meaningful and sustained change in young people's ICT-based behaviours will be best achieved through truly bottom-up rather than top-down means. As we have argued throughout this chapter, the impetus for young people to engage in any type of digital activity will best come from the young people themselves, rather than from external coercion or direction. Thus it makes sense to encourage young people to pursue, develop and extend the types of digital activities that they are already participating in, rather than attempting to redirect them towards what they 'should' be doing. This flies in the face of many current approaches towards encouraging young people's ICT use which still seek to remould and re-develop young people's "naturalised degree of digital and technical ability … *into transferable adult resources*" (Beastall 2006, p.109, emphasis added). As Hudson (2003) argues, despite claims to the contrary, the majority of plans for the modernisation of public services remain rooted in the logic of utilising ICTs for the top-down and one-way delivery of services. Instead it could be worth adopting the strategy of following the activities that young people are already engaged in, rather than imposing the activities that one would want them pursuing.

In this way, there is a need to concentrate on the truly informal, experimental and embryonic elements of young people's ICT use – especially where young people are developing alternative non-traditional frameworks of political and social connection and engagement. In terms of political engagement, for example, some young people's political modes are noticeably diverging from those of older generations. Whereas youth voting patterns and membership of political parties may be declining, involvement in single-issue campaigns, environmental and global politics and anti-poverty issues are increasing – sometimes with an element of ICT use involved. As we have discussed, such uses of technology may only be the preserve of a minority of young ICT users with many others just using technology for more mundane purposes. But the point here is that *whatever* is currently taking place via ICTs is best encouraged as it may well lead onto other, more empowering uses. It is likely that much of this use will be informally learnt and informally practiced; situated in 'third places' of connections amongst acquaintances which are not easily as replicated or supported as activities pursued in formal sites such as schools or community centres. But the need to follow young people's own interests and practices rather than clumsily foist an official version of 'informal' practice on to them could well be crucial to the success of future attempts to cultivate digital inclusion.

Of course, there are a number of likely 'dangers' to this rather more laissez-faire approach to digital inclusion. On the one hand young people may well remain using ICTs for inconsequential or even trite issues which have little bearing outside of their immediate domains. There is also a danger that this bottom-up 'empowerment' takes on anti-establishment dimensions, with technology used to challenge and subvert established structures and situations. Another problematic issue is the uneasy place of any official involvement or intervention within these informal practices. In theory, what are essentially fluid, organic and chaotic virtual practices will be flourishing precisely because they are free from external control, restraints or official adult intervention. Any attempt by the state and other stakeholders to create, subsidise, organise or direct such spaces should be approached with caution. As soon as informal practices and procedures are party to some form of formal intervention then they lose much of the essence of what made them successful in the first place.

Thus it is essential that the role of state and other stakeholders in the digital inclusion debate is sensitively re-imagined, with official bodies altering their approach to ICTs and young people – adopting a facilitative and supportive roles rather than as a directive and managerial presence. Thus governmental and other official bodies should adopt a more aggressive but also more realistic stance towards encouraging young people's engagement with both ICT and society. This would involve focusing less on establishing a rhetorical universal access for all young people but instead aiming to enable effective access for all those who want it – when and where appropriate. Effective enabling of the use of ICTs such as computers and the internet would seem to be better focussed on supporting a genuine 'fit' with patterns of young people's everyday lives – concentrating on increasing the relevance of ICT and shifting the universal service debate from issues of supply to issues of demand. Crucially, 'demand' should be seen in terms of the genuine demands of individual young people rather than the usual policy conceptualisation of demand in terms of employers' demands for skills or governmental demand for economic competitiveness.

This thinking runs counter to much of the current digital inclusion policymaking. Within the knowledge economy model the provision of all services – be they civic, social or educational – tends to be approached by governments as collective concerns with collective solutions. However, there is still room to develop policies which are more individually focussed and less 'one-size-fits-all'. In short, governments need to extend choice on an individual basis to everyone regarding whether they participate in society and whether they use ICT to do so. All young people should have a chance to make an empowered choice to use ICT and to vote, learn, save and work but the over-riding concern of policymakers has to be one of facilitating the individual's opportunity to *choose* rather than attempting to *coerce* mass engagement. Thus the question of who is in control of this new technology remains a crucial one and, in this respect, it is important that control is situated in the hands of the young people. Of course, in leaving control of technology use in the hands of the individual young people introduces an over-riding danger that their eventual 'choices' to either use or not use ICTs are not empowered ones. From this perspective, the state, parents and the technology community all have roles to play in supporting and enabling all young people with the means, motivation and where-with-all to make informed, effective and empowered choices. In other words, the state can best seek to ensure that young people are not faced with the disempowering situation of 'too much choice' but instead enjoy an 'autonomy of (non)use' (c.f. DiMaggio and Hargittai 2001).

Finally, it should be the case that commercial bodies shoulder more of the burden for digital inclusion. Although important, government policies and the actions of public bodies alone do not constitute digital inclusion. The centrality of IT firms and private interests to the issue of digital inclusion is obvious but it is more often than not ignored by academic observers. It is assumed that IT firms are a neutral or even benign presence in young peoples' use of ICT – quietly providing hardware and software and then slipping away. Yet the centrality of private concerns in the domestic and public uses of technology merits sustained attention, especially regarding how young peoples' use of ICTs can be shaped by business and commercial interests. Indeed, in theory there are many ways in which the IT industry could alter their practices and thereby widen young people's use of ICT. IT firms have a clear role in shaping young peoples' initial uses of computers, from the marketing through to the bundling of free software at the initial point of purchase. On a prosaic level the large IT companies could pay more attention to the content that is supplied alongside their hardware – developing genuinely useful software for all young people which can then be supplied with machines rather than endless variations on business-orientated 'Office' applications. There is also a need for young people to be given more control over the production as well as consumption of software and content. Indeed, commentators have long argued that the real digital divide should be seen in terms of control over the means of production, with the assumption that only by participating in the creation of digital content can young people really be empowered in their use of ICTs. Much of the onus for enabling young people's co-construction of more open-source and flexible content lies with software producers, who have the power if they so wish to devolve some of the power for determining the nature of content to the end-user.

Of course, firms respond to suggestions of such 'social responsibility' with understandable ambiguity and there is little short-term incentive for IT firms to engage in any of these socially-inclusive activities, trapped as they are in what Warschauer (2003) terms the 'innovator's dilemma' of having to chase the high-margin, high-profit upper ends of the market by adding value to existing products rather than attempting to reach untapped, low-margin mass markets. Yet there is no reason why increased involvement with digital inclusion activities could not be attractive to firms given their vested interest in encouraging ICT use. As Dyson (1998) observes, "one of the problems with [public funding] is that governments and philanthropists often feel good simply by giving it away; investors feel good when the money they invest actually produces something". In this respect firms operating from a digital inclusion starting-point are in a position to contribute to the establishment of wider markets for ICT which they ultimately stand to benefit from. Indeed, the IT industry is not adverse to such philanthropy but have thus far preferred to concentrate on schools and developing countries. In the US the domestic digital divide has proved a growing area for philanthropic activity by multi-national companies and foundations such as the Bill and Melinda Gates Foundation, IBM and Cisco. We would suggest that this activity could easily be extended to the provision of young peoples in other developed countries.

IV CONCLUSION

Of course, there are many flaws to these suggestions, not least that from a political point of view that they are a profoundly unappealing and 'unsexy' set of recommendations in relation to the relatively quantifiable and high-profile social policy 'solutions' currently being pursued. Crucially, many of the suggested changes in this chapter offer no guarantee of universal success. In fact one of the only predictable outcomes is that effects will be uneven and that then will inevitably be a range of "unintended and contradictory consequences" once a looser, bottom-up approach to young people's use of ICTs is in play (Murdock 1993, p.536). Another likely unintended consequence of these suggestions is that groups of young people may become 'overly' empowered and move outside the wishes and control of the state and may well be empowered in ways which are disruptive to established order with ICTs engending a more individualistic (and perhaps selfish) orientation towards 'social' participation amongst young people– again a profoundly unappealing political prospect.

Yet, these issues of uncertainty, fluidity and chaos are at the heart of contemporary technological *and* social change, and we should therefore have little compunction with them being reflected in a reordered set of priorities for young people and digital social inclusion. Previous attempts at digital inclusion have suffered from pursuing an overly precise set of outcomes in what is one of the most imprecise and unpredictable areas of social policy. Yet given the increasing complexity and uncertainty of the twenty-first century techno-culture, perhaps the best that we can hope for are interventions which are uncertain, tentative and unpredictable. Thus, as Barry Schofield (2003) concludes, a stronger self-belief in ICT should be accompanied by more *vague* set of discourses concerning the ends of technology. To be less certain about the ends and outcomes of ICT use is a more honest and possibly more accurate stance to take concerning the open possibilities of new technologies, social inclusion and young people. It is from this vaguer, less coercive but more realistic starting-point that future efforts at engineering digital inequality should commence.

REFERENCES

Beastall, E. (2006) 'Enchanting a disenchanted child: revolutionising the means of education using Information and Communication Technology and e-learning' *British Journal of Sociology of Education*, 27, 1, pp. 97-110.

Caulkin, S. (2004) 'E-binge which will cost us dear' *The Observer* (Business section), 15th August, p. 9.

Chinn, D. and Fairlie, R. (2004) '*The determinants of the global digital divide*' eScholarship Repository, University of California.

Couldry, N. (2003) 'Digital divide or discursive design?' *Ethics and Information Technology* 5, 2, pp. 89-97.

DiMaggio, P., and Hargittai, E. (2001) '*From the 'digital divide' to digital inequality*' Centre for Arts and Cultural Policy Studies, Princeton University (Working Paper #15)

Dyson, E. (1998) '*Release 2.1*' London, Penguin.

Earle, W. (2005) 'Searching for citizenship' *Spiked Online* 5 July 2005 [http://www.spiked-online.com/Printable/0000000CAC48.htm]

Garrett, P. (2005) 'Social work's 'electronic turn'' *Critical Social Policy* 25, 4, pp. 529-553.

Golding, P. (2000) 'Forthcoming features' *Sociology*, 34, 1, pp. 165-184.

Gorard, S., Selwyn, N. and Madden, L. (2003) 'Logged on to learning?' *International Journal of Lifelong Learning*, 22, 3, pp. 281-296.

Graham, S. (2002) 'Bridging urban digital divides?' *Urban Studies* 39, 1, pp. 33-56.

Herring, S. (2004) 'Slouching toward the ordinary: current trends in computer-mediated communication' *New Media & Society* 6, 1, pp. 26-36.

Hudson, J. (2003) 'E-Galitarianism?' *Critical Social Policy* 23, 2, pp. 268-290.

Iske, S. (2006) 'Effects of young people's formal educational background on structures of use and appropriation'*paper presented to Cyberworld unlimited?* Bielefeld, Germany, February,

Kaiser Family Foundation (2005) '*Generation M*'

Livingstone, S. (2003) 'Children's use of the internet: reflections on the emerging research agenda' *New Media and Society*, 5, 2, pp. 147-166.

Livingstone, S. (2004) 'The challenge of changing audiences' *European Journal of Communication*, 19, 1, pp.75-86.

Livingstone, S., Bober, M. and Helsper, E. (2005) '*Inequalities and the digital divide in children and young people's internet use*' London, London School of Economics .

Masschelein, J. and Quaghebeur, K. (2005) 'Participation for better or for worse?' *Journal of Philosophy of Education*, 39, 1, pp. 51-65.

Matei, S. and Ball-Rokeach, S. (2003) 'The internet in the communication infrastructure of urban residential communities: macro-or mesolinkage?' *Journal of Communication* 53, 4, pp. 642-657.

McQuaid, R., Lindsay, C. and Greig, M. (2004) 'Reconnecting' the unemployed' *Information, Communication & Society* 7, 3, pp. 364-388.

Mossberger, K., Tolbert, C. and Stansbury, M. (2003) '*Virtual inequality: beyond the digital divide*' Washington DC, Georgetown University Press.

Murdock, G. (1993) 'Communications and the constitution of modernity' *Media, Culture and Society*, 15, pp. 521-539.

Prensky, M. (2003) '*Digital natives*' [www.marcprensky.com]

Schofield Clark., L. (2003) 'Challenges of social good in the world of Grand Theft Auto and Barbie' *New Media & Society* 5(1): 95-116.

Shields, R. (ed) (1996) '*Cultures of the internet*' London, Sage.

Warschauer, M. (2003) '*Technology and social inclusion*' Cambridge MA, MIT Press.

Williams, J. Wallace, C. and Sligo, F. (2005) 'Free internet as an agent of community transformation' Journal of Community Informatics, 2, 1 [http://www.ci-journal.net/]

Education and Participation in the Virtual Space and its Limitations / Bildung und Teilhabe im virtuellen Raum und ihre Grenzen

Caroline Haythornthwaite

Social Facilitators and Inhibitors to Internet Access and Use

Introduction

The current rush to put resources online – academic, educational, commercial, recreational, governmental, political, personal – is accepted as providing information and opportunity for learning and self-expression for all. But is this so? Who is online, taking part in this new way of communicating and learning? Who is left out when government information dissemination, commercial enterprises, and societal participation assume a digital presence? While statistics from surveys in the early 2000's suggested that differences in *access* to the Internet across traditional categories of age, race, gender, and socioeconomic status are disappearing, more recent surveys have led to less optimism that the digital divide is – or ever can be – closed.

These data have led researchers to question the measure of access as the primary indicator of "electronic equity" (Patterson & Wilson, 2000, p. 80), and to examine in more detail what it means to be on- or off-line. Researchers point out that regional infrastructural differences in technical and content support mean that access plays out differently according to more local variables than often included in international and national indices (Barzilai-Nahon, 2006). More detailed examination of what it means to be on- or off-line reveals that differences still appear across demographics, but now expressed in time spent online, activities engaged in online (Howard & Jones, 2003; Katz & Rice, 2002; Nie & Erbring, 2000; Cole et al., 2000), bandwidth used (Horrigan, 2005), and perceived usefulness of Internet technology (CEC, 2005; Lenhart et al., 2003). Others question whether a singular notion of universal digital inclusion can be achieved. Research suggests that some sector of users, and some countries, may always lag behind the front-runners of computer and Internet use (CEC, 2005), and that lagged use is always going to leave the legacy of deprived use (Rice, 2002). Moreover, some users are remaining non-users, by choice and inclination, suggesting that current divides are not passing phenomena, but instead represent different ways of approaching and participating online (Lenhart et al., 2003; CEC, 2005).

These many patterns of digital use belie the notion of a *digital divide* (NTIA, 2000), with its connotations of all-or-nothing access to the benefits of contemporary information society, barriers to getting online, and implications of a gap that can be bridged with the delivery of technical infrastructures. Recent work refers to *digital* or *e- inclusion and exclusion* rather than a divide, and a *digital spectrum* of choices and possibilities (e.g., Lenhart et al., 2003; Livingstone & Bober, 2005; Warschauer, 2002). Yet, even a spectrum suggests access and use that fits neatly on a line from low- to high-end use, with connotations of inferior and superior participation in today's western, technologically-oriented world. What is emerging is a multi-patterned, multi-faceted, and fluid picture of use for which ideas of literacy and fluency become more appropriate than access and use. This review brings together work on the digital divide to show how several interrelated layers of social issues are encapsulated in statistical differences in access by race, gender, socio-economic status, and region. This paper highlights social facilitators and inhibitors to access, use, literacy, and fluency with the Internet and its technologies, organized around topics of infrastructure, individual differences, online content, and social networks.

Infrastructure

Infrastructure refers to both the technical requirements necessary for getting online, and the social support structures that provide public access to these devices and training in their use. It provides the electricity, wires or wireless, computing and telephone devices that are needed for basic Internet access. Private, institutional and government agencies provide technical infrastructures at work, in libraries, and in schools. They provide funds for physical devices (e.g., computers), networking capabilities (telephone lines for dial-up, broadband services), and direction in the implementation of widespread accessibility for electricity, phones, cell phones, Internet and wireless connectivity. The digital divide plays out in differences in where individuals gain access to technology, and where societal infrastructures have provided the means for access. Basic access to a computer or other device (e.g., cell phone) that provides an Internet connection is a minimum requirement, but use can be hampered when network connectivity does not keep up with the technical requirements for new applications. It is often taken-for-granted that access via broadband or other high speed connection is available and that applications can be written that require such transfer. This becomes problematic when individuals use older hardware, live outside broadband capabilities, or cannot afford newer technologies.

Geographical constraints are often cited as a reason that Internet and other kinds of access are not widely available. Disparities across geography carry with them variation in technical, political, and market support for electricity, broadband, and wireless capabilities, typically privileging urban over rural users, and developed over developing countries (Barzilai-Nahon, 2006; Nicholas, 2003; CEC, 2005; Davidson, Sooryamoorthy & Shrum, 2002; Warschauer, 2003b; Wilhelm, 2003). This is not always because individuals cannot afford new technologies. For example, while broadband would not automatically be assumed to be available in many developing countries, it often is in the U.S.. Yet, many rural parts of the U.S. do not yet have the option of broadband connection because low population densities are insufficient to justify private company investment in the infrastructure.

Rural users are further impacted by the lack of organization on their behalf. Many cities have put efforts toward Internet infrastructures, either strategically as is the case in Philadelphia, Pennsylvania (although Philadelphia has had to navigate legal challenges from internet service provider Verizon Communications), or by grassroots growth as in Seattle, Washington, and the "patchwork of smaller wireless networks, often funded by local councils" across the U.K. (Guardian Unlimited, March 3, 2005; see also, Intel, no date). "Muni nets" are being established in many cities around the world; the Guardian Unlimited (March 3, 2005) notes initiatives worldwide, including London; New York; Taipei; Calgary; Adelaide; St. Louis Missouri; and Leiden, Netherlands.

Technical use goes hand-in-hand with social use. Those with better connections can and do make greater use of the Internet. In the U.S., a 2005 survey (Horrigan, 2005) found broadband adopters to be much more intense users that those continuing to use dial-up systems. The 53% of Americans who go online from home using broadband (33% of the American adult population) are 65% more active online than dial-up users (2.8 versus 1.7 activities per day for dial-up users). Similarly, the 54% of Canadians who use broadband are more intense users, spending 55% more time online than dial-up users, and viewing twice as many web pages (comScore Media Metrix survey 2003, cited by Nua, 2003). Those not using broadband show a disinclination toward adopting this technology. While intense U.S. Internet users are adopting broadband and want broadband when they don't have it, 58% of dial-up users say they do not want broadband (February 2004 data, Horrigan, 2005). This puts into question their ability to access new online content engineered to be broadcast and received via high speed access, and assumed to be easily accessible to online users as a general category.

Network infrastructure is important for all users, but access to computer technologies is particularly important for those who do not own computers, for intermittent users (see below, in the section 'Experience and the Landscape of Use'), and for those who use the Internet by asking others to do it for them (see below in 'Social Networks'). In the U.S., non-users are not far from access: "60% of non-users know of a place in their community where Internet access is publicly available, while 76% of Internet users know of public access sites. Most of those who know of local access points say those access points are easy to reach. The most frequently identified location of public access is a library" (Lenhart et al., 2003, p. 3-4). Access in libraries provides not only the technical access, but also access to people who can help with Internet use.

Schools also play a large role in connecting children and young adults to the Internet (NSFB, 2000; Livingstone & Bober, 2005), which in turn brings that knowledge into the house (see below in 'Social Networks'). Being at school promotes use by 18-24 year olds, with 85% of those in school or college use the Internet, compared to 52% of those not in school (NTIA, 2002). In the U.S., at-school use is particularly important for low income and African-American children who are overwhelmingly more likely to use the Internet from school than home: 68% from school and 46% from home for households with incomes less than $40,000 vs. 57% from school and 86% from home for incomes over $75,000; 56% from school and 73% from home for white children vs. 71% from school and 35% at home for African-American children. (For more on the digital divide, schools and online learning, see Haythornthwaite, forthcoming). Despite the importance of schools for technology access and instruction, in their study of U.K. children, Livingstone & Bober (2005) found students had both a lack of formal instruction about the Internet and a lack of critical skills for evaluating Internet content. They point to the schools as an important location for increasing all students' knowledge about computing and the Internet and raising information literacy skills. Combining concerns about literacy with findings about access by income and race suggests an even greater need for school-based learning as a means to address digital divide issues. Although Livingstone & Bober (2005, p. 12) note that the issue is now one of "quality of use (as assessed by time use, skills and range of online activities)" rather than of technology access, household lack of means or interest can bring the site of access into play in forging quality use.

Individual differences

Early studies of computer and Internet users revealed a population that was predominantly young, white, male, of high socio-economic status, living in developed countries, and English speaking. As more people of all descriptions come online, there has been hope that the divide was closing. Major studies in the U.S., Canada, U.K., and Europe have shown that since the early 1990s, there has been considerable growth in the percentage of formerly under-represented groups online, including women, non-whites, older users, low income earners, non-college graduates, and non-native English speakers (e.g., Katz & Rice, 2002; Nua, 2001; Fallows, 2005). Yet, overall growth is not equally distributed. Across countries, regions, and demographics, gross estimates of access show near and long-term lags and differences in daily use and preferences for being online, as well as newly identified sectors of users who, by choice and inclination, only want intermittent or no access to the Internet (Lenhart et al., 2003; CEC, 2005).

Differences in Use

Beyond issues of access, differences across age, gender, race, and socio-economic indicators persist in number of years online, time spent online each day, activities engaged in online, bandwidth used, perceptions of competence or self-efficacy, and perceived usefulness of Internet technology (Anderson & Tracey, 2002; Howard & Jones, 2003; Katz & Rice, 2002; Horrigan, 2005; CEC, 2005; Livingstone & Bober, 2005; Hargittai & Shafer, 2006; LaRose, Eastin & Gregg, 2001). Howard, Rainie & Jones (2002) found that on any given day, among those with access, more of the men, whites, higher income earners, more educated and more experienced users are likely to be online. This and other studies show differences in activities and reasons for being or not being online, and use patterns related to individual life stage and life course (Anderson & Tracy, 2002).

Gender: Several studies find that men are more likely than women to use the Internet for news, product, financial, sports and hobby information, online trading, banking and gaming (Howard, Rainie & Jones, 2002; Cole et al., 2000). Data on women's access to and use of computers and the Internet find these are related to both their work use (discussed below under 'Occupation'), and their use with family members (with parents and with children). Women (and seniors) use the Internet more for health information, often seeking information on behalf of family members (NTIA, 2002); both men and women use email extensively, but women report a stronger liking for email than men (78% of women say they look forward to reading email vs. 62% of men; Rainie et al., 2000), using it for relationship building (Boneva & Kraut, 2002), and somewhat more for connecting with family (Haythornthwaite & Kazmer, 2002; Rainie et al., 2000).

Race: A 2003 report from Pew Internet and American Life project (Madden, 2003) states "there are few instances where online whites, blacks, and English-speaking Hispanics report equal participation levels" (p. 77). Non-whites trail in use of email, but use more IM and chat rooms than whites; are less active in information activities, but more active in hobby and entertainment activities (e.g., downloading music, playing games, looking for sports information). This continues trends from 2001, when a smaller proportion of Black and Hispanic Internet users emailed, searched for news, conducted searches for product/service information or made online purchases (NTIA, 2002).

Income: Different kinds of use are evident by household income (see Table 1). The higher the income, the more likely users are to engage in email/IM, searching for information, buying online, and banking and trading. Lower income households are more likely to be playing games, doing school work, searching for jobs, and chatting online, activities that suggest younger and newer online users (patterns that match those of 'newcomers' as described by Howard, Rainie & Jones, 2002; see below).

Table 1: Online Activities by Household Family Income, 2001

	Income			Income	
	<$15,000	**>75,000**		**<$15,000**	**>$75,000**
Increases with increasing income			**Decreases with increasing income**		
Email/IM	72.0	89.1	Playing games	47.0	37.5
News/weather/sports	53.5	67.0	School assignments	37.1	24.6
Product/service information	54.9	73.5	Job search	23.0	14.6
Health information	29.5	38.9	Chat rooms/ listservs	23.0	16.5
Government information	28.1	35.1	Phone calls	6.7	5.1
Product/service purchases	26.1	49.1			
Online banking	12.8	23.0	**Approximately the same across income**		
Trade stocks, bonds, funds	3.2	13.8	Radio/TV/movies	20.0	19.8
			Online education	4.0	4.0

Percentage of Internet Users Age 3 or older. Income endpoints only; trends are consistent across categories of income. (NTIA, 2002, p. 34)

Income greatly affects use by children: younger users in high income households use the internet in much higher proportions than those in low income households. Among U.S. children (10-17 years) in the highest income level, 88% use the Internet overall, and 83% use it at home. In the lowest income level, 46% use the Internet overall, and 21% at home.

Age: Fewer older users engage in each of the different kinds of online activities, although email is a major use by all age groups. The major activities of children and young adults online are schoolwork, email, playing games, listening to radio/watching movies, and using of chatrooms; and like women, those over 55 are more likely to look for health information. In general, many studies show higher use by younger users than older users. Numbers from the U.S. for 2003 (U.S. Census Bureau, 2005) show a decline in those using the Internet from any location from 70% for those 18-24 to 55% for those 55-64, dropping even further to 25% for those 65 and older.

Lags and Delays

A recent report on the expansion of Internet use in the EU by the Commission of the European Communities (CEC, 2005) provides insight into the potential for permanent lags in *e-inclusion* across countries, cultures, and demographics. The Commission found that while the gender gap seems to be closing, and more unemployed and self-employed were coming online, "Internet penetration among housepersons, especially women, older citizens, retired people and in rural areas is clearly lagging behind" (p. 8). Similarly, in 2002, a Pew Internet and American Life study found that "56% of [the 42% of Americas who are] non-Internet users do not think they will ever go online. These people are generally the poorer, older segment of the not-online population, and are more likely to be white, female, retired and living in rural areas" (Lenhart et al., 2003, p. 4). Van Dijk & Hacker (2000), drawing from U.S. and Netherlands data, also paint a pessimistic picture about closing the digital divide. They found increasing *relative differences* across demographics: households with higher incomes, a head of household with a higher education, and a lower age of head of household had greater possession of computers with the gap widening in percentage terms from 1984 to the late 1990s. In the U.S. for which data were available on race, households of white ethnicity also had greater computer possession.

Reports such as these point to persistent patterns of lag and delay in Internet use, lags that translate into impoverished use as individuals are always behind in literacy and fluency with the technologies, and access to the resources available via these lead technologies (Rice, 2002). This is well described in the CEC report (2005) which suggests the unlikely disappearance of the digital divide. The report identifies three patterns of Internet uptake, and describes how these are evident in traditional categories of the digital divide. The first pattern suggests the digital divide may be a *temporary issue*, with groups catching up to fore-runners in the medium term. At present this looks like the case for the gender divide, and for older populations, particularly as the latter increasingly include digitally aware age co-horts. However, recent figures from a September 2005 Pew survey, which show a much higher number of Americans online (72% overall; Pew Internet and American Life Project, Dec. 8, 2005), also shows gender differences again – 75% of U.S. men online, compared to 69% of women – so perhaps the gender gap is not after all a temporary divide, but instead a recurring one (see also Liff & Shepherd, 2004).

The second pattern noted by CEC suggests the digital divide is an issue of *ever evolving delays*, with groups catching up in the very long term, but lagging behind with every new innovation. The CEC report finds this likely the case for low income and less educated groups, and possibly the case for some countries newly entering the EU, and rural areas and users. This is also likely the pattern for differences across other countries. Data on the percentage of the population online for various countries show high levels (over 50% online) for countries such as Australia, Canada, Hong Kong, Japan, New Zealand, Singapore, South Korea, Sweden, Taiwan and the U.S. (over 50% online) and in the mid- to low range for Aruba (34%), Bahrain (21%), Chile (20%), Israel (17%), Argentina (10%), Kuwait (9%), Lebanon (8%), South Africa (7%), and Brazil (7%) (for 2001, from Nua, 2005). Elsewhere in the world numbers are far lower, even in some European countries where less than 1% of the population is online, as in the Ukraine (in 2001), Bosnia (in 2001) and Albania (in 2000; Nua, 2005). The lags are likely to remain, even as each country increases its own percentages; catching up is going to be hard to do.

The third pattern suggests the digital divide is a continuing issue of *delay and exclusion*, with considerable delay between social groups, and some groups never catching up. CEC suggests this is possibly the case for low income, less educated groups, and looks like it is the case for some countries, and for rural areas and users. Other reports show that this may also be the case for the disabled. Adults and children with disabilities are proportionally under-represented online. In 2002, 38% of Americans with disabilities were online compared to 58% of all Americans; 28% of these non-users reported their disability made it "difficult or impossible for them to go online" (Lenhart et al., 2003); and Livingstone & Bober (2005) found U.K. children and young adults with disabilities used the Internet less frequently than others.

Experience and the Landscape of Use

Although experience cuts across the demographics sectors discussed, it has a profound effect on use, and hence is important to recognize as a significant difference in discussions of the digital spectrum. Experienced users spend considerably more time online than other users: 6 hours a week for those with one year of experience, and over 16 hours a week for those with over 4 years online (U.S. figures: Cole et al., 2000; see also Nie & Erbring, 200; Nie, 2001). These *Netizens* (Howard et al., 2002) are online more often, involved in more online activities than others, and online more for professional reasons. They incorporate the Internet into all aspects of their lives, with greater comfort spending and managing their money online, and communicating online to support social relationships. They are both literate and fluent with technologies, making less of a separation between being online and not being online, easily 'toggling' between on- and off-line life (Fallows, 2004).

Yet, Netizens only represent 16% of the adult U.S. Internet users (as of 2000). Along with Netizens, Howard, Rainie & Jones (2002; Howard & Jones, 2003) find: *Utilitarians* (28% of adult Internet users) who approach the Internet functionally as a tool; *Experimenters* (26%) who are on their way to becoming netizens, moving beyond fun activities to information retrieval tasks; and *Newcomers* (30%) who have arrived online more recently, using it primarily for fun activities, and generally from one place (either work or home).

Lenhart et al. (2003) also reveal a few more categories of Internet users – *Intermittent* and *Non-users*. Looking in more detail at the 42% of Americans (in 2002) who said they did not use the Internet, Lenhart et al. found that of these, 69% (24% of Americans) were *Truly Disconnected*, not using the Internet nor having others near them using it. Others were intermittent users: some currently disconnected (*Net Dropouts*, 17% of non-users), some connected (*Intermittent Users*, estimated as 27-44% of current users), and some who connect through other people's use (*Net Evaders*, 20% of non-users). In this and other studies, non-users report no need for a computer or the Internet,

These categories suggest that current divides are not passing phenomena. In some cases they represent different ways of approaching and participating online (e.g., the Net Evaders). In other cases, there is a rejection of computers and the Internet, on principle, from lack of interest, or lack of awareness of potential uses. (For more on non-users reports, see Lenhart et al., 2003; CEC, 2005; Katz & Rice, 2002, 2003; van Dijk & Hacker, 2000).

Content and Representation

The discussion so far has highlighted issues relating to users – getting them online with computers and Internet connections, examining what they are doing online. But, while many rightly concern themselves with issues of access to resources, others are turning their attention to the content of the Internet. Since the numbers are clear that certain countries, cultures, and demographics are not participating fully in populating and seeding the Internet, where then is their representation online? Fewer members of a population online means not only fewer able to access and use resources, but fewer also placing resources online, and fewer others to communicate with online from these countries, cultures, and demographics.

One gross measure of representation online is the amount of content available in different languages. Estimates put the number of English speakers online between 32% (2005) and 44% (2001) (Internet World Statistics, 30.6%, March, 2006; Global Reach, 35.8%, 2004), with later figures lower than earlier ones as the number of non-English speakers increases rapidly (with particular increases in Chinese speakers, Johnson, 2005). Yet, there is general consensus that English dominates on the web with 2003 figures suggesting 45% of the web is in English, with other high representations for German (15%), French (11%), and Spanish (10%). This leaves far fewer resources presently online for speakers of other languages. (These data are from studies by FUNREDES, http://funredes.org/lc, as reported in Paolillo, Pimienta, Prado, D. et al., 2005; for a detailed discussion of measures and estimation techniques for the amount of English language sites and language diversity, see Paolillo et al., 2005).

Not only language, but also resources that speak to particular cultures, ages and communities are important for making the move online worthwhile and relevant to potential adopters and users (e.g., Katz & Rice, 2002; Warschauer, 2002, 2003a; Stanley, 2003; Ess & Sudweeks, 2005; Brock, 2005). Many grassroots and non-profit community networking initiatives strive to do just that, bringing the Internet and its resources to the local community in a way that is relevant and representative of their needs (e.g., Bishop et al., 2001; Brock, 2005; Gaver, Dunne & Pacenti, 1999; Hagar, 2005).

As well as concerns about content and representation, being online also means adopting new ways of communicating, writing, and speaking. Users will have different levels of fluency with information technology (Committee on Information Technology Literacy, 1999) and its new literacies. These include facility with the primary language – usually English – in which resources are presented, with online language and communication norms (e.g., emoticons, SMS text), and the growing and emerging variety of online communication applications, technologies and programming environments (e.g., blogs, wikis, podcasts, html, RSS, java). Going online means adopting *multiple innovations*: not just technical innovations of computers, Internet connections, and Internet service providers, but also the complex social and organizational practices that create online venues for socializing, self-expression, learning, sharing knowledge, and working together. Users differ in their comfort with exposing their thoughts and information on the web (and also with understanding the extent of that exposure) and their confidence with presenting themselves online community (Bregman & Haythornthwaite, 2003). Learning these new practices is an important step in gaining full access to the Internet and its resources.

Social networks

Social networks are implicated in a number of ways relating to getting and staying online, as well as gaining access to resources. Work and family ties provide means of learning about and accessing Internet resources. Proxy use of the Internet is a simple way to try out the technology without adopting it, and 74% of non-users have family members and close friends who go online and potentially gain access on their behalf (Lenhart et al., 2003). Making the next step to adopting the Internet, particularly for communication purposes, is going to be easier and more advantageous when there are known others such as family to communicate with, and/or members of the same culture, region, demographic or interest group. Strongly tied communicators – friends, family – are much more likely to be able to influence each other to adopt a new means of communication, as well as to call on each other for help in getting started (Haythornthwaite, 2005). The following tours the interpersonal ties that help promote Internet access and use.

Occupation

Where an occupation involves computer use at work, it significantly enhances the likelihood of computer use at home, and thus in the household for children and other household members (NTIA, 2002; Lenhart et al., 2003). NTIA reports that in 2001, 77% of households in which someone uses a computer or the Internet at work also own a computer or use the Internet from home, compared to 35% for other households; this holds across other demographic factors (income, education, race, age of adults). "Use at work not only acquaints someone with the utility of the technology, it also provides an opportunity to climb a sometimes frustrating learning curve in an environment with technical support. This acquired knowledge can then be taken home and shared with other members of a household." (NTIA, 2002, p. 62-3).

However, use by profession differs, and thus also who has the opportunity to learn at work with others, and who can then bring that knowledge home. In 2001, 20% of those is Managerial/professional specialties, and 22% in Technical/sales/administrative support used the Internet and/or email at work compared to 8% in Precision production/craft/repair, 10% in Farming/forestry/fishing, 6% in Service, and less than 4% among Operators/fabricators/laborers (percent of employed persons, age 25 and over in 2001; NTIA, 2002). Data from the U.S. Census (2005) shows that the much higher use by Managerial/professional and Technical/sales/administration categories still holds in 2003, although overall use at work is much higher (e.g., 69% for men in managerial positions, 73% in professional, 51% in office support, 18% in service; job categories differ between the two data sources, and data are reported separately for men and women in the census data).

Use by profession also differs between men and women. While women in the U.S. have had high rates of computer use since the mid-1980s, this has largely been due to use in office support positions. Data from the U.S. Census (2005) show that in 1984, 29% of working women used a computer on the job compared to 21% of working men; in 2003, 63% of working women and 51% of men (with 47% of women and 39% of men using the Internet at work). However, in 2003, 23% of these women were employed in office and administration support, but only 7% of men; with 29% of those women using computers at work, compared to 6% of the men. (The report gives use of computers at work separately from use of the Internet at work. See the full report for complete details.) Use also differs by gender at the highest percentages of work computer and Internet use. Women are the highest computer users in the category of "management, business, and financial occupations" (86% vs. 77% for men), men in professional occupations (84% vs. 75% for women). Where what is gained at work differs by occupation, it also then differs by gender, suggesting that what knowledge can be brought home differs across work occupations and between men and women (For more on how such differences may contribute to a gender digital divide, see Liff & Shepherd, 2004).

Children and Parents

Family, children in school, and friends also bring Internet skills into the household, giving the non-user access to the resources of the Internet, either by proxy as they ask others to look things up for them, or directly as they learn to use the computer that is now situated in the household. Once online, access to others via the Internet through email, online groups, discussion lists, etc. accelerates access to resources as others online – distant family, friends, or new online acquaintances – can lead the new user to new information, products, skills, and discussions. As noted above, children who are learning to use computers at school bring new computing and learning skills into the home. Livingstone & Bober (2005) report from their U.K. study of children's use of the Internet, that "Children usually consider themselves more expert than their parents, gaining in social status within the family as a result. Among daily or weekly internet users, 19% of parents describe themselves as beginners compared with only 7% of children, and only 16% of parents consider themselves advanced compared with 32% of children" (p.14). Children are also a major reason for adoption of computers in the household (National School Board Federation, 2000; Statistics Canada, 2000; Cole et al., 2000), and women's access to the Internet has been found to be markedly higher when there are children in the household (70% versus 57%; Cole et al., 2000).

Grown children also play a role in getting the family online. In studying Internet use in a farming community, Hagar (2005) found that family members not in the household often served as online searchers for non-users (e.g., sons or daughters living on their own farms), and that farm women were the main users on behalf of the family. Among online learners report bringing the Internet to their family, as well as maintaining distant friendships because of their new found skills and confidence (Haythornthwaite, Kazmer, Robins & Shoemaker, 2000; Bregman & Haythornthwaite, 2003).

Summary

While statistics from the early 2000's offered the promise that differences in access and use of the Internet across traditional socio-economic categories were disappearing, more recent studies have been showing an emerging landscape of differentiated use. These data confirm what writers have been saying for the last five years – that notions of a divide, with a singular barrier of access separating users from non-users, is inadequate for furthering discussion of inclusion in digital society. Differences in access and use between high-tech, high-speed, experienced users and newcomers, differences in attitudes between those online and confirmed non-users, and differences between Internet affluent and Internet poor regions, reveal a digital spectrum of Internet awareness, readiness and uptake. New to the discussion is acceptance that differences in access and use will persist, and are rooted as much in social as technological factors. Studies show emergent preferences in use and non-use, creating a more nuanced view of who uses the Internet for what, and with whom. Ideas of bringing everyone up to the efficiency and effectiveness of experienced users is giving way to an acceptance of different preferences and approaches to information access and engagement in digital society. Also new is the notion that individual access is not the full picture, but that technical and social infrastructures – computer networks, computer terminals, social networks, schools, and libraries – play a major role in usage patterns and the ability to become literate and fluent by facilitating access to the Internet and access to learning about the Internet. Wider-scale social networks also matter in providing content of interest to potential and actual users, and the critical mass of others creating and exchanging these resources. This review has suggested that, amid the emerging landscape of increasing spread of computers and the Internet and the new landscapes of contemporary use and voluntary non-use, there are interrelated social issues encapsulated in statistical differences in access that act as different social facilitators and inhibitors to online access, use, literacy and fluency.

References

Anderson, B., & Tracey, K. (2002). Digital Living: The impact (or otherwise) of the Internet in everyday British life. In: B. Wellman & C. Haythornthwaite (Eds.), *The Internet In Everyday Life* (pp. 139-163). Oxford, U.K.: Blackwell.

Barzilai-Nahon, K. (2006). Gaps and bits: Conceptualizing measurements for digital divide/s. *The Information Society*, 22, 269-278.

Bishop, A. P., Bazzell, I., Mehra, B., & Smith, C. (2001). Afya: Social and digital technologies that reach across the digital divide, *First Monday*, 6(4). http://www.firstmonday.org/issues/issue6_4/bishop/index.html.

Boneva, B. & Kraut, R. (2002). Email, gender and personal relationships. In: B. Wellman & C. Haythornthwaite (Eds.), *The Internet In Everyday Life* (pp. 372-403). Oxford, U.K.: Blackwell.

Bregman, A. & Haythornthwaite, C. (2003). Radicals of presentation: Visibility, relation, and co-presence in persistent conversation. *New Media and Society*, 5(1), 117-140.

Brock, A. (2005). 'A belief in humanity is a belief in colored men:' Using culture to span the digital divide, *Journal of Computer-Mediated Communication, 11(1), article 17*. Available online at: http://jcmc.indiana.edu/vol11 /issue1/brock.html.

Cole, J.I., Suman, M., Schramm, P., van Bel, D., Lunn, B., Maguire, P., Hanson, K., Singh, R., & Aquino, J-S. (2000). *The UCLA Internet report: Surveying the Digital Future*. Retrieved May 31, 2006 from: http://www.digitalcenter.org/pdf/InternetReportYearOne.pdf.

Commission of the European Communities (2005). *eInclusion Revisited: The Local Dimension of the Information Society*. Available online at: http://europa.eu.int/comm/employment_social/news/2005/feb/eincllocal_en.pdf.

Committee on Information Technology Literacy (1999). *Being Fluent With Information Technology*. Washington, DC: National Academy Press.

Davidson, T., Sooryamoorthy, R. & Shrum, W. (2002). Kerala connections: Will the Internet affect science in developing areas? In B. Wellman & C. Haythornthwaite (Eds.), *The Internet In Everyday Life* (pp. 496-519). Oxford, U.K.: Blackwell.

Ess, C. & Sudweeks, F. (2005). Culture and computer-mediated communication: Toward new understandings. *JCMC, 11(1), article 9*. Available online at: http://jcmc.indiana.edu/vol11/ issue1/ess.html.

Fallows, D. (2004). *The Internet and Daily Life*. Available online at: http://www.pewinternet.org/ pdfs/PIP_Internet_and_Daily_Life.pdf.

Fallows, D. (2005). *How Women and Men Use the Internet*. Available online at: http://www.pewinternet.org/ pdfs/PIP_Women_and_Men_online.pdf.

Gaver, W.W., Dunne, A., Pacenti, Elena (1999). Design: Cultural probes. *Interactions, 6*(1), 21-29.

Global Reach (Sept. 2004). *Global Internet Statistics (by Language)*. Retrieved May 31, 2006 from: http://global-reach.biz/globstats/index.php3, and http://www.glreach.com/globstats/refs.php3.

Guardian Unlimited (March 3, 2005) All wired up. Retrieved Dec. 22, 2005 from http:// technology.guardian.co.uk/online/story/0,,1428626,00.html.

Hagar, C. (2005). *The Farming Community in Crisis*. Unpublished doctoral dissertation, University of Illinois at Urbana Champaign.

Hargittai, E. & Shafer, S. (2006). Differences in actual and perceived online skills: The role of gender. *Social Science Quarterly, 87*(2), 432-448.

Haythornthwaite, C. & Kazmer, M. M. (2002). Bringing the Internet home: Adult distance learners and their Internet, Home and Work worlds. In: B. Wellman & C. Haythornthwaite (Eds.), *The Internet in Everyday Life* (pp. 431-463). Oxford, U.K.: Blackwell.

Haythornthwaite, C. (2005). Social networks and Internet connectivity effects. *Information, Communication and Society, 8*(2), 125-147.

Haythornthwaite, C. (forthcoming). Digital divide and e-learning. In: R. Andrews & C. Haythornthwaite (Eds.), *Handbook of E-Learning Research*. London: Sage.

Haythornthwaite, C., Kazmer, M. M., Robins, J. & Shoemaker, S. (2000). Community development among distance learners: Temporal and technological dimensions. *Journal of Computer-Mediated Communication, 6*(1). Available online at: http://www.ascusc.org/jcmc/vol6/issue1/haythornthwaite.html.

Horrigan, J. (2005). *Broadband Adoption at Home in the United States: Growing But Slowing*. Paper presented to the 33rd Annual Telecommunications Policy Research Conference. Retrieved Dec. 22, 2005 from http://www.pewinternet.org/ pdfs/PIP_Broadband.TPRC_Sept05.pdf.

Howard, P. & Jones, S. (2003). (Eds.) *Society Online: The Internet in Context*. Thousand Oaks, CA: Sage.

Howard, P., Rainie, L. & Jones, S. (2002). Days and nights on the Internet. In: B. Wellman & C. Haythornthwaite (Eds.), *The Internet In Everyday Life* (pp. 45-73). Oxford, U.K.: Blackwell.

Intel (no date). *Most Unwired City Survey*. Retrieved Dec. 22, 2005 from http://www.intel.com/ personal/wireless/unwiredcities/.

Internet World Statistics (March, 2006). *Top Ten Languages Used in the Web*. Retrieved May 31, 2006 from: http://www.internetworldstats.com/stats7.htm.

Johnson, B. (2005). English grip on internet being eroded. *Guardian Unlimited, Technology Blog, Tuesday Aug. 16, 2005*. Retrieved Dec. 22, 2005. http://blogs.guardian.co.uk/technology/archives/ 2005/08/16/english_grip_on_internet_being_eroded.html.

Katz, J. E. & Rice, R. E. (2002). *Social Consequences of Internet Use: Access. Involvement and Expression*. Cambridge, MA: MIT Press.

LaRose, R., Eastin, M. S., & Gregg, J. (2001). Reformulating the Internet paradox: Social cognitive explanations of Internet use and depression. *Journal of Online Behavior, 1*(2). Available online at: http://www.behavior.net/JOB/v1n2/paradox.html.

Lenhart, A., Horrigan, J., Rainie, L., Allen, K., Boyce, A., Madden, M. & O'Grady, E. (2003). *The Ever-Shifting Internet Population: A New Look at Internet Access and the Digital Divide*. Retrieved Dec. 23, 2005 from: http://www.pewinternet.org/pdfs/PIP_Shifting_Net_Pop_Report.pdf.

Liff, S. & Shepherd, A. (July, 2004). An evolving gender digital divide? *Oxford Internet Institute, Internet Issue Brief No. 2*. Retrieved November 19, 2006 from: www.oii.ox.ac.uk/resources/publications/IB2all.pdf.

Livingstone, S. & Bober, M. (2005). *U.K. Children Go Online: Final Report of Key Project Findings*. Economic and Social Research Council: U.K. Retrieved January 16, 2006 from: http://news.bbc.co.uk/1/shared/bsp/hi/pdfs/28_04_05_childrenonline.pdf.

Madden, M. (Dec. 22, 2003). *America's Online Pursuits. The Changing Picture of Who's Online And What They Do*. Pew Internet and American Life Project. Retrieved May 28, 2006 from: http://www.pewinternet.org/pdfs/PIP_Online_Pursuits_Final.PDF.

Nicholas, K. (2003). Geo-policy barriers and rural internet access: The regulatory role in constructing the digital divide. *The Information Society 19* (4), 287-295.

Nie N. H. (2001). Sociability. Interpersonal relations, and the Internet: Reconciling conflicting findings. *American Behavioral Scientist*, 45(3), 420-435.

Nie, N. H. & Erbring, L. (Feb. 17, 2000). *Internet and society: A preliminary report*. Stanford Institute for the Quantitative Study of Society (SIQSS), Stanford University, and InterSurvey Inc. Available online at: http://www.stanford.edu/group/siqss/.

NSBF (National School Board Federation) (March 28, 2000). *Safe & Smart: Research and Guidelines for Children's Use of the Internet*. Retrieved January 14, 2006 fromt: http://www.nsbf.org/safesmart/full-report.htm.

NTIA (2002). *A Nation Online: How Americans Are Expanding Their Use of the Internet*. U.S. Department of Commerce.

NTIA (National Telecommunications and Information Administration) (2000). *Falling through the Net: Toward Digital Inclusion*. U.S. Department of Commerce. Available online at: http://www.ntia.doc.gov/ntiahome/digitaldivide/.

Nua (2001). *U.S. No Longer Dominates the Net*. Available online at: http://www.nua.ie/surveys/index.cgi?f=VS&art_id=905356771&rel=true.

Nua (2003). *Forrester Research: One in Five European Seniors Online*. Retrieved Jan. 19, 2006 from http://www.nua.com/surveys/index.cgi?f=VS&art_id=905358750&rel=true.

Nua (2005). *How Many Online*. Available online at: http://www.nua.com/surveys/how_many_online/europe.html.

Paolillo, J., Pimienta, D., Prado, D. et al. (2005). *Measuring Linguistic Diversity on the Internet*. Montreal, Canada: UNESCO. Retrieved May 26, 2006 from: http://unesdoc.unesco.org/images/0014/001421/142186e.pdf.

Patterson, R. & Wilson, E. J. III (2000). New IT and social inequity: Resetting the research and policy agenda. *The Information Society*, 16, 77-86.

Pew Internet and American Life Project (Dec. 8, 2005). *Data Update*. Retrieved Dec. 22, 2005 from: http://www.pewinternet.org/pipcomments.asp?m=12&y=2005.

Rainie, L., Fox, S., Horrigan, J., Lenhart, A. & Spooner, T. (May 10, 2000). *Tracking Online Life: How Women Use the Internet to Cultivate Relationships with Family and Friends*. Retrieved Dec. 22, 2005 from: http://www.pewinternet.org/pdfs/Report1.pdf.

Rice, R. E. (2002). Primary issues in Internet use: Access, civic and community involvement, and social interaction and expression. In L. Lievrouw & S. Livingstone (Eds.), *Handbook of New Media* (pp. 105-129). London: Sage.

Stanley, L. D. (2003). Beyond access: Psychosocial barriers to computer literacy. *The Information Society, 19*(5), 407-416.

Statistics Canada (2000). Plugging in: Household Internet use. *The Daily*. Monday, December 4, 2000. Available online at: http://www.statcan.ca/Daily/English/001204/d001204a.htm.

U.S. Census Bureau (October, 2005). *Computer and Internet Use in the United States: 2003*. U.S. Department of Commerce, Economics and Statistics Administration. Available online at: http://www.census.gov/prod/2005pubs/p23-208.pdf.

van Dijk, J. & Hacker, K. (2003). The digital divide as a complex and dynamic phenomenon. *The Information Society, 19*(4), 315–326.

Warschauer, M. (2002). Reconceptionalizing the digital divide. *First Monday, 7*(7), 1–15. http:// firstmonday.org/issues/issue7_7/warschauer/index.html.

Warschauer, M. (2003a). *Technology and Social Inclusion.* Cambridge, MA: MIT Press.

Warschauer, M. (2003b). Dissecting the digital divide: A case study in Egypt. *The Information Society, 19*(4), 297-304.

Wilhelm, A.G. (2003). Leveraging sunken investments in communications infrastructure: A policy perspective from the United States. *The Information Society, 19*(4), 279-286.

Stefan Iske/Alexandra Klein/Nadia Kutscher/Hans-Uwe Otto

Virtuelle Ungleichheit und informelle Bildung. Eine empirische Analyse der Internetnutzung Jugendlicher und ihre Bedeutung für Bildung und gesellschaftliche Teilhabe

1 Die Expansion des Internet und die Diversifizierung der Nutzungsweisen

Das Internet ist in den letzten 10 Jahren zu einem der bedeutendsten Informations- und Kommunikationsmedien aufgestiegen. Die Länderkennung „.de" für Deutschland tragen im November 2006 mehr als 10 Millionen Internetseiten. Nutzten 1997 hierzulande gerade 6,4% der ab 14jährigen das Internet, sind es 2006 schon 59,5% (van Eimeren/Frees 2006). Im letzten Jahr kamen allein in der Bundesrepublik 1,2 Millionen NutzerInnen hinzu. Waren von den InternetnutzerInnen 1997 noch knapp 60% auf einen außerhäuslichen Internetzugang (Büro, Schule, Universität) verwiesen, sind es 2005 unter 15% (van Eimeren/Frees 2005). Obgleich es noch immer deutliche – durch Alter, Geschlecht, Bildung, Erwerbsstatus und Einkommen vermittelte – Ungleichheiten im formalen Zugang zum Internet gibt, wird das Internet zunehmend auch von denjenigen genutzt, die gemeinhin als ‚internetferne' Bevölkerungsgruppen gelten (vgl. dazu Eimeren/Frees 2005, van Eimeren/Frees 2006, (N)Onliner Atlas 2006). Nicht nur der Glaube an die soziale, kulturelle und ökonomische Relevanz des Internet sondern auch die faktische Nutzung scheint das Internet als gesellschaftliches ‚Muss' etabliert zu haben.

Allen voran werden Jugendliche als eine tendenziell bildungs- und geschlechtsübergreifende ‚technical savvy generation' (Livingstone et al. 2004) thematisiert. Nach den Daten der JIM-Studie von 2006 nutzen 94% der GymnasiastInnen, aber auch knapp 83% der HauptschülerInnen das Internet. Neben der viel zitierten kommunikativen Nutzungspräferenz Jugendlicher, stellt auch die Informationssuche zu persönlichen Themen, wie etwa Schule und Ausbildung oder Freundschaft, Liebe und Partnerschaft eine zentrale Nutzungsorientierung dar (Feierabend/Rathgeb 2005). Dass die Unterscheidung zwischen dem Internet als Kommunikationsmedium (Email, Chat, Foren etc.) und dem Internet als Informationsmedium (Recherche in und Rezeption von bestehenden Angeboten, Webseiten, Beiträgen v.a. zur

Information) nur eine analytische Behelfskonstruktion sein kann, verdeutlicht insbesondere der Bereich der netzbasierten Unterstützungssuche von Jugendlichen. Diese Nutzungsform hat mittlerweile einen beachtlichen Umfang erreicht: Unter britischen Jugendlichen sucht – bei lediglich marginalen klassenspezifischen Unterschieden – jede/r vierte jugendliche InternetnutzerIn explizit im Internet nach Rat und Hilfe (vgl. Livingstone et al. 2004). Nach der jüngsten Studie von Lenhart et al. (2005: 42) bejahen 22% der amerikanischen Jugendlichen die Frage „if they ever look for information online about a health topic that's hard to talk about, like drug use, sexual health, or depression". Gerade bei der Suche nach Rat und Hilfe verschwimmt das Verhältnis zwischen Kommunikations- und Informationsmedium: Virtuelle Unterstützungssuche kann sich sowohl schreibend als auch lesend vollziehen. Dass beide Nutzungsweisen zusammen kommen ist insbesondere dann der Fall, wenn innerhalb eines Onlineangebots sowohl Kommunikation als auch Information strukturell ermöglicht werden, so dass prinzipiell kein Angebotswechsel zur Realisierung der einen oder der anderen Nutzungsform vollzogen werden muss, sondern dies im Sinne konvergenter Nutzung erfolgen kann.

Diese grundlegenden Basisdaten zum Internetzugang Jugendlicher verdeutlichen, dass das Medium Internet zu einem ‚Gegenstand' alltäglichen Gebrauchs geworden ist. Die vor wenigen Jahren noch eher spekulative Diagnose einer fundamentalen Durchdringung der Alltagssphäre scheint somit, gemessen an der Diffusionsrate und den Nutzungsinteressen, zumindest für jugendliche NutzerInnen zuzutreffen.

Verlässt man die Ebene des formalen Zugangs zum Internet, weisen sämtliche empirischen Studien darauf hin, dass sich auch die Art und Weise, wie unterschiedliche Menschen das Internet nutzen, erheblich unterscheidet. Mit Blick auf das Internet ist dies nicht überraschend, gilt es doch aufgrund seiner Medienmerkmale als ein so genanntes „Pull-Medium". Pull-Medien zeichnen sich dadurch aus, dass sich die Angebote erst durch die Auswahlentscheidungen der Nutzerinnen als Angebotsarrangement realisieren. Schließlich handelt es sich bei dem Internet um eine komplexe technische Infrastruktur, die vielfältige Navigationswege und Nutzungsoptionen eröffnen kann. Auf der Basis der spezifisch gestalteten vorhandenen Angebote, ihrer Interessen und ihrer Fähigkeiten und Fertigkeiten stellen sich die NutzerInnen also faktisch „ihr Angebot" aus einer Vielzahl von bestehenden und sich veränderten Angeboten permanent selbst zusammen. Hierbei ist jedoch weder davon auszugehen, dass es sich bei den Nutzungsselektionen um bewusst kalkulierte und rein rational getroffene Entscheidungen handelt, noch dass es sich um substanzielle Fähigkeiten handelt, die unabhängig von den jeweiligen Angeboten und ihrer medialen, inhaltlichen und personalen Verfasstheit betrachtet werden können (vgl. für letzteres: Klein 2004, 2006). Vielmehr bilden die NutzerInnen – mehr oder weniger bewusst – vor dem Hintergrund ihrer jeweiligen Fähigkeiten und Fertigkeiten und Nutzungsinteressen habitualisierte Nutzungspraktiken heraus, die sich „als stabile Niveauunterschiede des Umgangs mit dem neuen Medium zu verfestigen" scheinen (Oehmichen/Schröter 2006:442).

Die auf der Basis repräsentativer Daten für die Bundesrepublik empirisch gewonnenen Typologien der Internetnutzung fokussieren auf die Gesamtheit der InternetnutzerInnen[1]. Hier ist insbesondere die Typologie auf der Basis der ARD/ZDF-Online-Daten zu nennen, wie sie von Oehmichen und Schröter entwickelt wurde. Allerdings bezieht sich diese auf InternetnutzerInnen ab 14 Jahren, ohne eine gesonderte Auswertung zur Internetnutzung Jugendlicher vorzunehmen. Dieses Desiderat hinsichtlich einer differenzierten Betrachtung jugendlicher Nutzungspraktiken korrespondiert mit der eingangs thematisierten Annahme einer vermeintlichen „technical savvy youth". Dass diese diskursive Figur empirisch nicht haltbar ist, stellen jedoch mittlerweile auch Oehmichen und Schröter fest: Auch „unter den 14- bis 19-Jährigen oder den 20- bis 29- Jährigen gibt es einen relativ hohen Anteil von Usern, die die Möglichkeiten des Internets keineswegs umfassend ausschöpfen" (ebd. 447). Vielmehr, so ihre Einschätzung, gibt es „eben nicht nur die Differenz von jung und alt, sondern, und das scheint wichtiger zu sein, zwischen gebildet und ungebildet. Der knowledge gap – zwischen den ‚digital natives' und den ‚digital immigrants' – durchzieht alle Generationen. Derjenige junge Mensch, der weiß, wie man E-Mails verschickt, wie man Musik herunterlädt und der auch noch die Site mit den besten Radio Comedies kennt, muss durchaus nicht in der Lage sein, das Internet zur Informationsbeschaffung sinnvoll zu nutzen oder sich die neuesten Features von Web 2.0 zu erschließen" (ebd. 447). In all diesen Ausführungen erscheint eine, wie auch immer definierte, Medienkompetenz als „magic bullet", die es den jugendlichen NutzerInnen ermöglichen soll, die technischen Möglichkeiten des Netzes zu realisieren. Überraschenderweise findet sich in diesen großen Studien weder eine Definition dessen, was konkret unter Medienkompetenz verstanden werden soll, noch eine Kontextualisierung der Nutzungspraktiken der Jugendlichen – weder mit ihrer „Medienkompetenz", ihren Bewertungen oder einer differenzierten Betrachtung bestimmter Angebote im Internet noch mit ihrem milieuspezifischen Habitus und den daraus erwachsenden Präferenzen. Eine solche Kontextualisierung von Nutzungspraktiken, -perspektiven und -bewertun-

---

1 Interessanterweise verzichtet die größte deutsche Untersuchung zur Mediennutzung Jugendlicher, die jährlich durchgeführte JIM-Studie, auf eine empirische Typologisierung, obwohl sie deskriptiv Nutzungsunterschiede zwischen Jugendlichen unterschiedlicher sozialer Gruppen verdeutlicht.

gen einerseits und die Analyse der jeweiligen Angebote andererseits ist allerdings unverzichtbar, um zu einer umfassenden Einordnung der Potentiale und Restriktionen alltäglicher Mediennutzung unterschiedlicher NutzerInnen in verschiedenen medialen Arrangements zu gelangen. Daher will dieser Beitrag einen erweiterten Blick darauf lenken, was Medienkompetenz in Zusammenhang mit dem Internet sein kann – nicht nur als Bildungsverantwortung der NutzerInnen, sondern auch als strukturelle Verantwortung der AnbieterInnen in der zielgruppensensiblen Gestaltung der Internetangebote.

In Anlehnung an die mittlerweile klassischen Überlegungen von Dieter Baacke (1980) lässt sich (Medien-) Kompetenz von (Medien-) Performanz dahingehend unterscheiden, dass letztere als die kontextual gebundene Aktualisierung von ersterer verstanden werden kann, als „überdauernde[...] Verhaltenspattern, die jedoch nicht durch die Kompetenz allein strukturiert werden, sondern auf der Grundlage eines Regelsystems der Kompetenz durch situative, persönliche, soziale und kulturelle Variablen geschaffen sind" (Baacke 1980:102). Dementsprechend ist die Performanz der jeweiligen NutzerInnen nicht ohne die jeweiligen Angebote im Internet, ihre mediale, inhaltliche und soziale Verfasstheit einerseits und die verfüg- und verwertbaren Fähigkeiten und Fertigkeiten der NutzerInnen andererseits zu denken.

2   Das Internet als Möglichkeitsraum für Bildungsprozesse

Auch hinsichtlich seines Bildungspotentials wird das Internet als Medium stark diskutiert. In diesem Zusammenhang polarisiert es hinsichtlich der Gefahren und Chancen, die ihm zugeschrieben werden – ob man die Diskussionen um die Computerspiel-Verbotsforderungen nach Amokläufen wie in Erfurt oder Emsdetten betrachtet oder die These im Nachgang zu PISA-Auswertungen, dass internetversierte Jugendliche bessere Schulleistungen zeigen[2]. In Zusammenhang mit diesen Debatten wird häufig die Frage thematisiert, inwiefern das Internet ein Raum ist, der den NutzerInnen neue, erweiterte Möglichkeiten der Aneignung von Bildung, Wissen und Handlungskompetenzen eröffnet (vgl. Tully 2003). Die Protagonisten

---

2   vgl. OECD 2006 – diese These kann schon alleine dadurch in Frage gestellt werden, wenn man die soziodemographischen Herkunftsmerkmale betrachtet, die auf tendenziell „bildungsaffine" Herkunftsmilieus hindeuten und somit die Ursache für bessere Schulleistungen eher darin und weniger in der Tatsache der Internetnutzung zu suchen ist. Darüber hinaus werden jeweils in den öffentlichen Debatten um sog. „Killerspiele" zumindest von seiten der OnlinespielerInnen die Kompetenzdimensionen im Kontext von Computerspielen thematisiert: strategisches Denken und Handeln, Teamkooperation (,soziale Kompetenzen') etc.

dieser Sichtweise betrachten hierbei häufig gerade Jugendliche als die Internetgeneration schlechthin (s.o., „internet savvy generation"), die mit dem Medium aufwachse und daher per se mit dem Medium vertraut und im Umgang in allen Lebenslagen kompetent sei. Dieser Perspektive leistete auch das Ende der 90er Jahre veröffentlichte Buch „Net Kids" von Don Tapscott (1998) Vorschub. Darin werden Jugendliche als eine Generation bezeichnet, die generell durch das Aufwachsen mit den neuen Medien neue Formen gesellschaftlicher Beteiligung und des Verständnisses von Demokratie entwickle (vgl. kritisch zu Tapscotts und anderen Entwürfen: Stegbauer 2001, Selwyn 2003, Buckingham 2005). Doch diese Thesen, die im Übrigen mit der Verbreitung des „Web 2.0" wieder eine Renaissance erfahren, sind – wie im Folgenden gezeigt wird – vor dem Hintergrund ungleicher Nutzungsweisen grundlegend zu hinterfragen.

Soll das Internet als Raum analysiert werden, der die Möglichkeiten und Fähigkeiten der NutzerInnen erweitern und Bildungszugänge eröffnen kann, so sind zunächst die Bedingungen, unter denen Internetnutzung in der Regel stattfindet, näher zu betrachten. Die dominante Nutzungssituation ist überwiegend im informellen Kontext angesiedelt. Das bedeutet, dass die NutzerInnen das Internet zur Realisierung subjektiver Motive gebrauchen. Wie verschiedene Studien gezeigt haben (vgl. Otto et al. 2004, Iske et al. 2005, Livingstone et al. 2004) hängen diese zunächst scheinbar rein subjektiven Präferenzen deutlich mit dem soziokulturellen Hintergrund zusammen. Diese Präferenzen führen in einem ersten Schritt dazu, dass bestimmte Internetangebote als attraktiv beurteilt und genutzt werden, wenn sie diesen Interessen entgegenkommen, während andere weniger bzw. gar nicht genutzt werden. Gleichzeitig spielen in diesem Zusammenhang die jeweils den NutzerInnen verfügbaren Offline-Ressourcen eine entscheidende Rolle: Peerstrukturen, familiäre Herkunft, schulische Bildungskontexte beeinflussen das für die Internetnutzung verfügbare soziale, kulturelle und ökonomische Kapital. Insofern sind die jeweiligen Voraussetzungen, mit denen Jugendliche das Internet und die dort lokalisierten Angebote nutzen, je nach der Verfügbarkeit dieser Ressourcen unterschiedlich verteilt.

Dies wird besonders deutlich unter der Perspektive der Vesterschen Bildungsmilieus (vgl. Vester et al. 2001): Michael Vester hat in seinen Milieustudien Sozialisationsräume rekonstruiert, die sich u.a. „danach unterscheiden, welche Alltagspraktiken wertgeschätzt werden und (milieuspezifische) Anerkennung erfahren oder welche Erziehungsvorstellungen vorherrschend sind. In Auseinandersetzung mit diesen sozialisatorischen Hintergründen entwickeln Heranwachsende auf der Grundlage unterschiedlicher milieuspezifischer Anerkennungsmuster differente Relevanzstrukturen, die zu abgrenzbaren Präferenzordnungen führen.[3] Milieus liefern insofern einen besonderen Wissensvorrat, der die lebensweltlichen Handlungsorientierungen und relevanten Handlungsbefähigungen maßgeblich bestimmt. Diesem impliziten und expliziten Wissensvorrat liegt ein sozialisatorischer Erfahrungsschatz zu Grunde." (Bittlingmayer/Hurrelmann 2005: 5f.). Das bedeutet, dass die Unterschiede in der Nutzung im informellen Kontext auf milieuspezifischen Präferenzen beruhen, die nicht ausschließlich durch eine defizitäre Ressourcenausstattung begründet werden können. Vielmehr sind unter einer lebensalltagsbezogenen Perspektive bestimmte Nutzungsweisen innerhalb eines spezifischen sozialen Kontexts als relevanter zu rekonstruieren als andere. Dies kann mit Pierre Bourdieus Habituskonzept analysiert werden (vgl. Bourdieu 1987). Vor diesem Hintergrund sind Nutzungsweisen, die sich an einem eher „bildungsbürgerlichen" Habitus orientieren (z.b. gezielte, themenorientierte Suche im Netz, textbezogene Interessen, redaktionelle Tätigkeiten von Jugendlichen) ebenso zu erklären wie Nutzungsweisen, die eine eher ‚hedonistisch'-pragmatische oder instrumentell ausgeprägte Orientierung (z.b. Spiele spielen, Zeitvertreib, chatten) aufweisen. Allerdings wird in den Auseinandersetzungen um das Bildungspotential des Internet deutlich, das bestimmte Nutzungsweisen als ‚erstrebenswerter' (z.b. gezielte Informationssuche) gelten als andere (z.b. Chatten) bzw. auch in unterschiedlichen Kontexten je andere Nutzungskompetenzen erforderlich werden. Dabei ist die Verteilung der Nutzungsweisen nicht absolut, sie weist unterschiedliche Mobilitätspotentiale sowohl innerhalb des Mediums als auch im Kontext der Teilhabemöglichkeiten außerhalb des Netzes auf.

Andererseits kann nicht übersehen werden, dass es weiterhin Gruppen gibt, die aufgrund ihrer anders gelagerten Interessen bzw. Relevanzstrukturen, Möglichkeiten und Fähigkeiten von der Nutzung bestimmter grundlegender Funktionen des Internet ausgeschlossen sind. Beispielsweise ist hier der Besitz einer Emailadresse zu nennen – die JIM-Studie 2005 spricht hierbei von 22 % der HauptschülerInnen, die keine eigene Emailadresse besitzt gegenüber nur fünf Prozent unter GymnasiastInnen (vgl. JIM 2005: 44)[4].

Inwiefern sich nun diese Hinweise in einem differenzierteren Kontext bestätigen bzw. genauer betrachten lassen, soll im Folgenden anhand eigener empirischer Daten aus der Forschung des KIB untersucht werden.

---

3   Zum allgemeinen Mechanismus vgl. Schütz, Alfred (1971): Zum Problem der Relevanz, Frankfurt/Main; Grundmann, Matthias (1998): Norm und Konstruktion. Zur Dialektik von Bildungsvererbung und Bildungsaneignung. Opladen.

4   Diese Ausdifferenzierung fehlt in der Darstellung der JIM-Studie 2006, doch auch hier wird ausdrücklich festgestellt: „Dreimal so viel Hauptschüler wie Gymnasiasten nutzen die E-Mail-Funktion nicht." (JIM-Studie 2006: 42)

3 Internetnutzung Jugendlicher und digitale Ungleichheit – eine empirische Untersuchung

In Fortführung bisheriger Forschungsarbeiten des Kompetenzzentrums Informelle Bildung (KIB)[5] zur Internetnutzung Jugendlicher wurde im November und Dezember 2006 die Untersuchung „Internetnutzung Jugendlicher und digitale Ungleichheit" durchgeführt[6]. Hierbei handelt es sich um eine repräsentative empirische Untersuchung, die erstmalig darauf abhebt, dass der Bildungshintergrund Jugendlicher für ihre Nutzungschancen im Internet eine zentrale Rolle spielt und dies anhand verschiedener Aspekte nachweisen kann. Die sozial kontextualisierte Analyse von zunächst scheinbar rein individuellen Nutzungsmotiven zeigt hierbei die deutlichen Mobilitätsunterschiede zwischen sozialen Klassen in Hinsicht auf gesellschaftliche und bildungsbezogene Teilhabe innerhalb des Internet. Die Untersuchung konzentriert sich insbesondere auf den zentralen Punkt der Diskussion um *Digitale Ungleichheit* („Digital Inequality"): den Zusammenhang von sozialen und kulturellen Ressourcen der Jugendlichen mit dem konkreten Nutzungsverhalten im informellen Raum des Internet.

Auf dieser empirischen Grundlage können Bildungserfahrungen, soziale Ressourcen und Internetnutzungsweisen miteinander in Beziehung gesetzt und ihre unterschiedliche Relevanz für die Konzeption und Entwicklung von Internetangeboten für Jugendliche, insbesondere unter einer Bildungs- und Beteiligungsperspektive, untersucht werden. Damit werden differenzierte Aussagen über das Nutzungsverhalten unterschiedlicher Gruppen von Jugendlichen und darauf aufbauend über die Entwicklung zielgruppenspezifischer und -sensiver Angebote im Internet möglich.

Für die Erhebung wurde das Offline-Verfahren des CATI-Interviews gewählt, um einen repräsentativen Durchschnitt der bundesdeutschen Jugendlichen zu erreichen und insbesondere verzerrende Effekte von Verfahren der Online-Datenerhebung zu vermeiden. So konnte über die Telefonerhebung ein Selbstrekrutierungseffekt, der zu einer nichtrepräsentativen Verschiebung im Sample führen kann, vermieden und auf diese Weise sowohl Internet-Nicht- oder WenignutzerInnen erreicht als auch eine implizite Überbeteiligung von IntensivnutzerInnen, wie es bei Onlinepanels leicht der Fall ist, verhindert werden. Das Sample von 1.024 Jugendlichen wurde über eine repräsentative Zufallsstichprobenziehung aus der Gesamt-

---

5 vgl. Otto, H.-U./Kutscher, N./Klein, A./Iske, S. (2005); Iske, S. / Klein, A./ Kutscher, N. (2005); Otto, H.-U./Kutscher, N./Klein, A./Iske, S. (2004); Otto, H.-U./Kutscher, N. (Hrsg.) (2004).
6 Mit der Datenerhebung der CATI-Untersuchung („Computer Assisted Telephone Interview") wurde das SOKO-Institut/Bielefeld beauftragt.

bevölkerung der 14-23jährigen bundesweit auf der Basis von sechzehn ausgewählten Kommunen zusammengesetzt[7].

Die Befragung wurde neben deutscher auch in türkischer und russischer Sprache von muttersprachlichen InterviewerInnen durchgeführt, um auch Jugendliche
erreichen zu können, die in der deutschen Sprache nicht hinreichend sicher sind.
Darüber hinaus können auf Grundlage dieses Offline-Verfahrens auch Offliner-
Phänomene („Internetverweigerer") und besonders Drop-Out-Phänomene („Nicht-
mehrnutzerInnen") analysiert werden, für die bislang in Deutschland erst wenig
empirische Daten vorliegen.

Aufgrund der Repräsentativität der Stichprobe und der besonderen inhaltlichen
Fokussierung der Untersuchung können erstmals Aussagen gerade auch in Hinblick
auf differenzierte Bildungs- und Beteiligungsaspekte im Internet getroffen werden,
die über bestehende Erhebungen zum Internetnutzungsverhalten in Deutschland hinausgehen (vgl. JIM-Studien, ARD-ZDF-Onlinestudien, (N)Onliner Atlas).

Im Rahmen dieser Veröffentlichung wird lediglich ein Ausschnitt der Ergebnisse der Untersuchung dargestellt. Aufgrund der generellen Heterogenität des Bil-
dungsbegriffs werden in der vorliegenden Analyse der Bildungsbegriff durch unterschiedliche Operationalisierungen spezifiziert.[8] Vergleichbar den Arbeiten von

---

7 Die Repräsentativität wurde durch
   – *Sample-Point-Verfahren, disproportionale Streuung nach Ortsgrößenklassen*
   Nach dem Schrittziffernverfahren wurden zufällig 16 Städte und Gemeinden (Sample-Points)
   aus einer Datei des Statistischen Bundesamtes gezogen, die alle Städte und Gemeinden zusammen mit ihren Einwohnerzahlen enthält. Mit einem Zufallsgenerator wurden die Städte und
   Gemeinden in eine zufällige Reihenfolge gebracht. Dann wurden die Einwohnerzahlen der am
   Anfang stehenden Gemeinden so lange aufaddiert bis diejenige Stadt/Gemeinde gefunden ist,
   in der der x-te Einwohner lebt. X bedeutet bei einer Personenstichprobe aus der Gesamtbevölkerung (82 Millionen Bundesbürger geteilt durch 16 Städte/Gemeinden= 5.125.000). Nach
   diesem Verfahren mit der Schrittziffer x wurden die 16 Städte und Gemeinden zufällig ausge-
   wählt. Auf diese Weise hat prinzipiell jeder Bundesbürger der Zielgruppe die gleiche Chance,
   in einen ausgewählten Sample-Point zu gelangen.
   – *proportional Ost-West*
   In dieser Untersuchung wurden die Datei mit allen Städten und Gemeinden vor der Zufallszie-
   hung in zwei Gruppen Alte Bundesländer (West) und Neue Bundesländer (Ost) eingeteilt. Es
   wurden vier Städte und Gemeinden in den neuen Bundesländern und 12 in den alten Bundesländern gezogen.
   erreicht. Die Dauer der CATI-Interviews lag im Schnitt bei 15 Minuten.
8 Einen Ausgangspunkt für diese Operationalisierungen bietet das für Deutschland typische formale
   dreigliedrige Schulsystem. Folgende formale Operationalisierungen werden in der Analyse verwendet: Jugendliche nach dem derzeitig besuchten Schultyp; Jugendliche, die eine allgemeinbil-
   dende Schule bereits verlassen haben; Jugendliche nach dem derzeitig besuchten Schultyp bzw.
   dem höchsten erreichten Bildungsabschluss; das „kulturelle Kapital" der Eltern wurde über die
   Variablen 'Besitz von mehr als hundert Büchern' und 'Abonnement einer Tageszeitung' in die
   Analyse einbezogen. In einer Erweiterung dieser Variablen (bildeltern02) wurden zusätzlich die
   Variablen „Besitz eines Computers" und „Internetzugang" einbezogen.

Livingstone et al. (2004) wurden Formen der Internetnutzung hinsichtlich soziodemographischer Variablen analysiert. Hierbei wurden die Kategorien *communicating, peer-to-peer connection, seeking information, interactivity, webpage/content creation* und *visiting political / civic websites gewählt* und für die Analyse der vorliegenden Daten weiterentwickelt:[9]

Sonia Livingstone et al. verwenden in Ihrer Studie „Active participation or just more information?" die oben genannten Kategorien als Indikatoren für *Beteiligung* im Internet. Die Forschungsgruppe des KIB hat diese Kategorien vor dem Hintergrund eines breiten *Nutzungs*begriffs und eines erweiterten Partizipationsbegriffs entsprechend der eigenen Untersuchung weiterentwickelt. So findet sich in der Analyse der Beteiligung des KIB eine Auseinandersetzung mit Lurkern, die bei Livingstone et al. nicht in der Erhebung vorkommen, sowie eine Erweiterung der Frage nach den genutzten Internetseiten. Während bei Livingstone et al. nach klassischen Beteiligungswebsites gefragt wurde, bezog das KIB in seiner Erhebung Internetseiten ein, die Jugendliche als Zielgruppe haben und eine breitere Nutzung – über zivilgesellschaftliche Beteiligung im engeren Sinn hinaus – eröffnen[10]. Die Kategorien des KIB sind wie folgt strukturiert:

–   *Peer-to-peer connection* wird als interaktive Nutzung mit sozialen Konnotationen durch die Nutzungsvariablen „Weblogs besuchen", „Online-Spiele spielen", „Downloaden (z.B. Software, Spiele, Klingeltöne, Musik, Filme etc.)" sowie „Anmelden / bei Internetangeboten registrieren (Chats, Mailprovider, Newsgoups etc.)" abgebildet.

–   *Interactivity* wird als Beteiligung der NutzerInnen, die sie im Netz „sichtbar" macht durch die Variablen „Bei Abstimmungen mitmachen (Votings)", „An die Verantwortlichen/Betreiber von Internetangeboten schreiben (Anmerkungen, Fragen, Kritik etc.)", „Selbst online-Artikel schreiben", „Ein Internetforum besuchen" und „In Internetforen posten" operationalisiert.

–   *Seeking information* wird durch die Nutzungsvariablen „Einfach so ohne bestimmtes Ziel umhersurfen", „gezielt nach Informationen suchen", „Wikis (Internetlexikon) besuchen" spezifiziert.

–   *Communicating* umfasst die klassischen Kommunikationsdienste und wird durch die Nutzungsvariablen „Emails senden und empfangen", „Einen Messenger[11] benutzen" und „einen Chat besuchen" abgebildet.

---

9   Die Kategorisierung der Nutzungsweisen des Internet wurde erweitert durch die Nutzung des Internet zum Einkaufen (Online-Shopping) bzw. zur Teilnahme an Versteigerungen (z.B. Ebay) und „Information und Unterstützung bei persönlichen Problemen suchen" (Support).

10 Eine gesonderte Auswertung hierzu erscheint demnächst von Kutscher/Otto.

11 Instant Messaging ist ein Dienst, der mit Hilfe einer (i.d.R. kostenfreie) Software ermöglicht, mit anderen Personen direkt in Chat-ähnlicher Form zu kommunizieren.

– W*ebpage/content creation* umfasst Aktivitäten im Netz, die mit einer hohen Eigenaktivität verbunden sind und wird durch die Nutzungsvariablen „Eine Website betreuen, die ich selbst erstellt habe" sowie durch Schreiben von Beitragen in Foren, Weblogs, Wikis oder im Chat abgebildet (vgl. unten, Ausführungen zu *Lurkern* und *Postern*).

– V*isiting political/civic websites* wurde ersetzt durch die Frage nach den *Lieblingsseiten* im Internet und erweitert somit den Fokus auf die Nutzungspräferenzen allgemein.

Als zentrale demographische Variablen dieser Untersuchung werden der *formale Bildungshintergrund* der befragten Jugendlichen (s.o.), die *Geschlechtszugehörigkeit*, das *Alter*, die *Herkunft* der Jugendlichen sowie weitere Variablen einbezogen. Weiterhin wurden die *Selbsteinschätzung* der Jugendlichen hinsichtlich ihrer Internetkompetenz und die von den Jugendlichen angegebene *Internetnutzungshäufigkeit* berücksichtigt.

Im Folgenden werden hierzu einige grundlegende Ergebnisse des Surveys dargestellt.

Ins Internet gehen

Bereits auf der allgemeinen Ebene alltäglicher Mediennutzungspraxen wird der Zusammenhang von Internetzugang und -nutzung vor dem Hintergrund von Bildungszusammenhängen deutlich, beispielsweise am Zugang zum Internet über einen eigenen Internetanschluß ($r= -.603^{**}$[12]) bzw. den Zugangsort. Für die Analyse der Nutzung des Internet zur Informationssuche ist festzuhalten, dass bereits der Zugang zum Internet nicht gleichmäßig unter allen Jugendlichen verteilt ist. Die generelle Nutzung des Internet im Freizeitbereich korreliert stark mit unterschiedlichen Operationalisierungen des Bildungshintergrundes (vgl. Tabelle Bildungshintergrund und Internetnutzung): Je höher der erreichte Bildungsabschluss, je höher der besuchte Schultyp unter den befragten SchülerInnen und je höher der erreichte Schulabschluss bei denjenigen, die die Schule abgeschlossen haben, desto häufiger wird das Internet genutzt. Darüber hinaus findet sich ein deutlicher Hinweis auf die Theorie der sozialen Vererbung (Esping-Andersen 2003): Je höher der Bildungshintergrund der Eltern der befragten Jugendlichen ist, desto häufiger nutzen die Befragten das Internet.

---

12 Die mit zwei Sternchen gekennzeichneten Ergebnisse sind jeweils auf dem Niveau von 0,01 (2-seitig) signifikant.

	Häufige Internetnutzung
Derzeit besuchter Schultyp und höchster erreichter Bildungsabschluss: formal hoch	-.342**[13]
Derzeit besuchter Schultyp: formal hohe Bildung	-.289**
Höchster erreichter Schulabschluss: formal hohe Bildung	-.336**
Bildungshintergrund der Eltern: formal hoch	-.409**

Tabelle 1: Soziodemographie und Internetnutzung

Die korrelationsstatistischen Darstellungen verdeutlichen den Zusammenhang des Bildungshintergrundes der Befragten mit der generellen Nutzung des Internet in der Freizeit.

Kommunikative Nutzung

Betrachtet man die einzelnen kommunikationsorientierten Nutzungsweisen, so zeigen sich hier ebenfalls deutliche Unterschiede.

	Intensive Emailnutzung
Internet als Freizeitbeschäftigung	.444**
Häufigkeit Internetnutzung	.410**
Formaler Bildungshintergrund allgemein	-.262**
Angestrebter Schulabschluss	-.241**
Erreichter Schulabschluss	-.307**
Kulturelles Kapital der Herkunftsfamilie (mehr als 100 Bücher im Haushalt)	-.201**
Internetanschluss im elterlichen Haushalt	-.191**
Selbsteinschätzung bezüglich des Internet	-.357**
Internet ist ein wichtiger Begleiter für alle möglichen Fragen und Themen	.299**

Tabelle 2: Emailnutzung und Soziodemographie

---

13 Bei den angegebenen Zusammenhängen handelt es sich um Korrelationen nach Pearson sofern nicht anders angegeben

Eine intensive *Emailnutzung* hängt deutlich mit Internetnutzung als Freizeitbeschäftigung allgemein zusammen (vgl. Tabelle Emailnutzung und Soziodemographie), sowie mit besonders häufiger Internetnutzung. Betrachtet man den soziodemographischen Hintergrund in Zusammenhang mit der Emailnutzung, so finden sich deutliche Hinweise darauf, dass diese Nutzungsweise nicht unabhängig von bestimmten Ressourcen betrachtet werden kann. So korreliert ein hoher allgemeiner formaler Bildungsgrad, ein hoher erreichter Schulabschluss derjenigen, die nicht mehr auf die Schule gehen, der formal hohe angestrebte Schulabschluss derjenigen, die noch SchülerInnen sind sowie das vorhandene kulturelle Kapital der Herkunftsfamilie und ein vorhandener Internetanschluß im elterlichen Haushalt deutlich mit einer häufigen Emailnutzung. Ebenso spielt hier die Selbsteinschätzung als fortgeschrittene/r Nutzer/in sowie die Einschätzung des Internet als „wichtigem Begleiter für alle möglichen Fragen und Themen" eine wichtige Rolle.

	Häufige Chatnutzung
Besuchter Schultyp	.231**
Angestrebter Schulabschluss	.187**
Alter	.115**
Internet als Medium um neue Leute kennenzulernen	.187**

Tabelle 3: Chatnutzung und Soziodemographie

Eine präferierte *Chatnutzung* zeigt deutliche Zusammenhänge mit einem formal niedrigen besuchten Schultyp und tendenziell einem formal mittleren bis niedrigen angestrebten Schulabschluss (vgl. Tabelle Chatnutzung und Soziodemographie). Dieser Unterschied erklärt sich möglicherweise über das Alter, das einen leichten Zusammenhang von Chatpräferenz und eher jüngeren NutzerInnen zeigt. Bei dieser Nutzung steht tendenziell im Vordergrund, „neue Leute kennenlernen" zu wollen. Im Unterschied zwischen der Email- und der Chatnutzung finden sich Indizien für möglicherweise unterschiedliche „Regeln" für Kommunikation beim Mailen bzw. beim Chatten, die eventuell dazu führen, dass unterschiedliche Zielgruppen angezogen werden. Dieser Aspekt eröffnet Fragen, die durch weitere empirische Forschungen zu untersuchen wären.

	Häufige Forennutzung
Internet als Freizeitbeschäftigung	.380**
Intensive Internetnutzung	.366**
Formale Bildung	-.172**
Internet ist ein wichtiger Begleiter für alle möglichen Fragen und Themen	.227**
Internetanschluss im elterlichen Haushalt	-.181**

Tabelle 4: Forennutzung und Soziodemographie

Die Ergebnisse zur *Forennutzung* hingegen zeigen wiederum ein ähnliches Profil wie die zur Emailnutzung (vgl. Tabelle Forennutzung und Soziodemographie): Auch hier spielt Internetnutzung als Freizeitbeschäftigung sowie intensive Nutzung eine Rolle, ebenso wie formal hohe Bildung. Die Einschätzung des Internet als wichtigem Begleiter und ein Internetzugang im Elternhaus scheint hier ebenfalls einen Einfluss zu haben. Beim *Instant Messaging* lässt sich lediglich ein schwacher Zusammenhang mit einem formal hohen besuchten Schultyp (r= -.178**) feststellen.

Insgesamt lässt sich zusammenfassen, dass es deutliche Unterschiede zwischen den formalen Bildungsniveaus hinsichtlich der kommunikativen Nutzungspräferenzen im Internet gibt. So hängt die Email- und Forennutzung deutlich mit einem formal hohen Bildungshintergrund zusammen, die Chatnutzung hingegen tendenziell mit einem formal niedrigeren Bildungshintergrund. Diese Ergebnisse weisen auf Distinktions- und Schließungsprozesse im Netz hin und bestätigen somit bisherige Forschungsergebnisse des KIB, die spezifische Nutzungsweisen als sozial kontextualisiert identifizieren und in der Konsequenz auf differenzierte Internet- und Jugendmedienarbeitsangebote als Bedarf hinweisen.

Informationssuche

Der Nutzung des Internet als Informationsmedium wird in der öffentlichen Diskussion eine besondere Bedeutung zugeschrieben. Zentrale Aspekte bilden dabei das Suchen und das Finden von Informationen im Internet, vor allem durch zielgerichtetes Suchen. Als Gegenpol zur Nutzung des Internet als Informationsmedium wird demzufolge das ziellose Umhersurfen häufig abwertend qualifiziert.

	Gezielte Suche nach Informationen im Internet
Formale Bildung allgemein	-.283**
Besuchter Schultyp	-.216**
Angestrebter Schulabschluss	-.299**
Erreichter Schulabschluss	-.260**
Nutzungshäufigkeit	.221**

Tabelle 5: Gezielte Informationssuche und Soziodemographie

Während im Bereich des „Umhersurfens ohne bestimmtes Ziel" keine spezifischen Zusammenhänge mit Bildungs- oder soziodemographischen Variablen erkennbar sind und insofern von einer über unterschiedliche Nutzergruppen hinweg allgemeinen Nutzungsweise ausgegangen werden kann, besteht im Bereich der „gezielten Suche nach Informationen" ein starker Zusammenhang mit einem hohen formalen Bildungshintergrund sowie mit intensiver Internetnutzung (vgl. Tabelle Gezielte Informationssuche und Soziodemographie). Kein Zusammenhang ist erkennbar beispielsweise mit dem Geschlecht, dem Wohnort oder dem Zeitraum der Internetnutzung. In der Art und Weise der gezielten Informationssuche finden sich unterschiedliche Formen (vgl. Tabelle Formen der gezielten Informationssuche):

	Angaben in Prozent
Suchmaschinen	99,4
Fragen nach Internetadressen	69,3
Direkte (versuchsweise) Eingabe einer Internetadresse im Browser	67,6
Nutzung eines Internetlexikons	55,0
Nutzung von Informationsportalen	25,6

(n = 965)

Tabelle 6: Formen der gezielten Informationssuche

Starke Zusammenhänge mit dem formalen Bildungshintergrund sind vor allem in den Bereichen „Ich benutze eine Suchmaschine, z.B. ‚Google'." und „ich benutze ein Internet-Lexikon" zu erkennen. Zwischen der Nutzung von Suchmaschinen zur gezielten Suche und dem formalen Bildungshintergrund besteht eine Korrelation von r=.317**. Das heißt, je geringer der formale Bildungshintergrund, umso weniger werden Suchmaschinen zur gezielten Suche nach Informationen genutzt.

Während insgesamt der überwiegende Teil der Befragten eine Suchmaschine zur gezielten Suche benutzt (892 Nennungen), zeigt sich in der Gruppe der Befragten, die Suchmaschinen nicht nutzen (83 Nennungen) ebenfalls ein deutlicher Hinweis auf den Einfluss des formalen Bildungshintergrundes: Die Hälfte dieser Nennungen stammen von Jugendlichen mit niedrigem formalem Bildungshintergrund. Unter denjenigen, die nicht auf Suchmaschinen zurückgreifen, ist der hohe Anteil von Personen mit niedrigem Bildungshintergrund auffällig: 28,2 % der Befragten dieser Gruppe nutzen keine Suchmaschinen. Dies legt im Sinne einer differenzierten Nutzung des Internet die These nahe, dass selbst bei so populären Diensten des Internet wie Suchmaschinen (hier am Beispiel von „Google") nicht von einer allgemeinen und gleich verteilten Nutzung ausgegangen werden kann. Die obigen Zusammenhänge verweisen deutlich auf Nutzungsunterschiede aufgrund von Bildungsdifferenzen: Ein großer Teil der Befragten nutzt demnach Suchmaschinen nicht, wenn die gezielte Suche im Vordergrund steht. Dies legt die Vermutung nahe, dass diese Gruppe entweder generell das Internet weniger zur gezielten Informationssuche benutzt (sondern stattdessen z.B. eher zur Kommunikation) oder aber auf andere Arten gezielte Suchen durchgeführt werden.

Die dargestellten Nutzungsunterschiede aufgrund formaler Bildungsunterschiede für den Bereich der Nutzung des Internet als Informationsmedium zeigen sich auch bei der Nutzung von Internet-Lexika (Zusammenhang mit dem formalen Bildungshintergrund: r=.412**) sowie der differenzierten Nutzung von Suchmaschinen.[14]

4 Lurkende und postende Nutzung kommunikativer Angebote

Prinzipiell auf Kommunikation und aktive Beteiligung angelegte internetbasierte Dienste wie etwa Chats oder Foren, aber auch Wikis oder Blogs können auch ausschließlich lesend genutzt werden. In der Literatur wird eine solche Nutzungsweise als „lurken" bezeichnet (vgl. Stegbauer/Rausch 2001, Mayer-Uellner 2003, Nonnecke/Preece 2004). Bislang erfährt diese „schweigende Mehrheit" (Stegbauer/Rausch 2001) kaum bzw. in der Regel eine negative Aufmerksamkeit: Lurkende NutzerInnen gelten als „TrittbrettfahrerInnen", die von der Kommunikationsge-

---

14   z.B. Eingabe *eines* Suchbegriffs; gleichzeitige Eingabe *mehrerer* Suchbegriffe; Eingabe eines zweiten, ähnlichen Suchbegriffs falls ein erste Suchbegriff zu keinen passenden Ergebnissen geführt hat; Auswahl des ersten Treffers in einer Liste mit Suchergebnissen; Auswahl eines Treffers nach dem Lesen der Kurzbeschreibung; Suche nach deutschsprachigen Internetseiten

meinschaft profitieren, in dem sie ihr Wissen nutzen, ohne einen eigenen Beitrag beizusteuern. In der Debatte um die LurkerInnen steht in diesem Sinne mehr das Brechen der Reziprozitätsnorm und das damit einhergehende „Ausnutzen" der Kommunikationsgemeinschaft im Vordergrund als die Gründe und Motive der lurkenden NutzerInnen selbst. Entgegen dieser dominanten Thematisierungsweise haben Jenny Preece et al. (2004: 201) in einer empirischen Studie zu den Motiven der ausschließlich lesenden NutzerInnen von verschiedenen Kommunikationsforen herausgefunden, dass „most lurkers are not selfish free-riders". Vielmehr findet sich bei den lesenden NutzerInnen nicht nur ein breites Spektrum an Begründungen für ihre Nutzungsweise, sondern es sind darüber hinaus auch gerade spezifische soziale Konstellationen innerhalb der virtuellen Kommunikationsgemeinschaft, die von den NutzerInnen als hinderlich für eine schreibende Beteiligung wahrgenommen werden.

In der Auseinandersetzung über die Internetpraxis Jugendlicher spielt diese Nutzungsweise bislang keine Rolle, thematisiert findet sie sich vorwiegend im Rahmen der Debatten um virtuelle Communities. Auch an dieser Stelle können nicht die Motive Jugendlicher, die zu einer ausschließlich lesenden Nutzungsweise führen, dargestellt werden, sondern vielmehr soll zunächst für dieses Thema sensibilisiert werden. Es gibt Jugendliche, die an Chats, Foren und anderen als Kommunikationsdienste konzipierten Angeboten ausschließlich lesend teilhaben. Diese Erkenntnis relativiert bisherige repräsentative Daten zur Internetnutzung Jugendlicher dahingehend, dass mit den Angaben darüber, ob sie bestimmte Dienste nutzen, auf einer grundlegenden Ebene noch nichts darüber gesagt werden kann, *wie* sie diese Dienste nutzen. Nicht jeder, der Chats nutzt, chattet im allgemein unterstellten Sinn, sondern ein Teil derjenigen, die in Chats ‚unterwegs' sind, sieht sich ausschließlich an, was die anderen dort machen. Im Zentrum der nachfolgenden Darstellung steht also die Frage, wie unterschiedliche Jugendliche verschiedene kommunikative Internetdienste nutzen: lesend oder schreibend.

Von den 964 befragten InternetnutzerInnen im Rahmen der KIB-Untersuchung geben 512 Jugendliche (53,2%) an, zumindest selten zu chatten: Bei den SchülerInnen sind es vor allem die Jugendlichen mit mittlerer Bildung, die überproportional häufig zur Gruppe der ChatterInnen gehören (81,7% gegenüber 67,6% derjenigen mit formal niedriger Bildung und 50,8% mit formal hoher Bildung). Bei den „Nicht-Mehr-SchülerInnen" ist es die Gruppe derjenigen mit Hauptschulabschluss bzw. jene ohne Schulabschluss, die den größten Anteil der ChatterInnen stellen (63,2% gegenüber 53,7% mit mittlerer Reife und 38,3% mit (Fach-)Abitur). Wie Jugendliche die Chats nutzen, d.h. ob sie die Beiträge anderer ChatterInnen ausschließlich lesen oder selbst aktiv in das Geschehen eingreifen, steht offenbar nur in geringem Zusammenhang mit soziodemographischen Merkmalen. Erst auf dem Signifikanzniveau von 0,05 zeigen sich Tendenzen von Korrelationen (vgl. Tabelle Schreibende Chatnutzung und Soziodemographie):

	Schreibende Nutzung von Chats
Formale Bildung allgemein	-.161*
Erreichter Schulabschluss	-.137*
Nutzungshäufigkeit	-.097*
Geschlecht	-.090*

Tabelle 7: Schreibende Chatnutzung und Soziodemographie

In absoluten Zahlen ausgedrückt heißt das: Von den 23 SchülerInnen mit niedriger Bildung, die chatten, gibt es keine/n einzige/n, die/der ausschließlich liest. Demgegenüber sind es von den 85 SchülerInnen mit mittlerer Bildung bereits vier und von den 113 Jugendlichen mit hoher Bildung 16 Personen (12,4%), die ausschließlich lesen: Offensichtlich kann zumindest tendenziell gesagt werden, dass wenn Jugendliche mit formal niedriger Bildung diese Angebote nutzen, sie eher schreiben und weniger ausschließlich lesen.

Erwartungsgemäß ist eine lurkende Nutzungsweise in Foren weitaus ausgeprägter als in Chats. Von den 629 befragten Jugendlichen, die Internetforen nutzen, sind 40,5% LurkerInnen. Zusammenhänge zeigen sich hierbei vor allem mit der Nutzungshäufigkeit und der Selbsteinschätzung der Jugendlichen. Von den 82 Jugendlichen, die Foren nutzen und sich als AnfängerInnen bezeichnen, gehört mehr als die Hälfte zu den LurkerInnen, bei jenen, die sich als Fortgeschrittene bezeichnen sind es fast 20% weniger. Mit Blick auf die Nutzungshäufigkeit zeigt sich, dass von jenen 334 Jugendlichen, die „oft" ins Internet gehen und Foren nutzen, 67,4% zu den Postern gehören. Bei den sporadischen NutzerInnen gehört dagegen nur ein Drittel der Jugendlichen zu den Postern. Weblogs (,Blogs') sind unter den befragten Jugendlichen allgemein nicht so sehr verbreitet wie etwa Foren oder Chats. Von den das Internet nutzenden Jugendlichen geben 21,6% an, dass sie selten Blogs besuchen bzw. dort eigene Beiträge schreiben. Differenziert nach Schulbildung zeigen sich nur geringfügige Unterschiede. So nutzen 21,5% der Befragten mit niedriger formaler Bildung Blogs, ebenso wie 17,8% mit mittlerer formaler Bildung und 23,5% mit hoher formaler Bildung. Mit Blick auf die Nutzungsweise der

Blogs sind die Ergebnisse jedoch durchaus überraschend (vgl. Tabelle Schreibende Nutzung von Blogs und Soziodemographie):

	Schreibende Nutzung von Blogs
Angestrebter Schulabschluss	-.280**
Erreichter Schulabschluss	-.364**

Tabelle 8: Schreibende Nutzung von Blogs und Soziodemographie

Anders formuliert bedeutet das, dass während bei den Befragten mit niedriger formaler Bildung knapp die Hälfte angibt, in Blogs auch eigene Beiträge zu schreiben, ist es bei den Jugendlichen mit mittlerer Bildung noch jeder Dritte und bei den Jugendlichen mit hoher formaler Bildung gehören bereits 80% zu den Lurkenden. Diese Ergebnisse weisen auf ein offenes Problem hin, zu dem hier erste Ansätze vorgelegt werden, die auf interessante Zusammenhänge verweisen. Obgleich diese Ergebnisse aufgrund der geringen Fallzahl keinen Anspruch auf Repräsentativität erheben können, sollen sie vor allem aus einem Grund Erwähnung finden: Es ist offenbar nicht haltbar, davon auszugehen, dass Jugendliche mit formal niedriger Bildung prinzipiell nicht im Internet bzw. in Blog schreibend „unterwegs sind". Zumindest tendenziell weisen die hier vorliegenden Zahlen darauf hin, dass sie sich sehr wohl auch schriftlich im Netz und auch in Blogs artikulieren.

Ein Zusammenhang zwischen der formalen Bildung und der Nutzung findet sich ebenfalls bei den so genannten Wikis. Während bei den Jugendlichen mit *niedriger* Bildung der Anteil derer, die *keine* Wikis nutzen, bei über 70% liegt, entspricht dies in etwa dem Anteil derer mit *hoher* formaler Bildung, die Wikis *nutzen*. Wenn man auch hier trotz der kleinen Fallzahlen die Nutzungsweisen betrachtet, offenbaren sich damit interessante Tendenzen: Auch hier gehören die Befragten mit niedriger formaler Bildung – anteilig zu ihrer Nutzung – häufiger zu den Schreibenden als Jugendliche mit hoher formaler Bildung. Letztlich ist jedoch aber unbedingt zu beachten, dass der Anteil der Jugendlichen, die Wikis überhaupt nutzen, sehr stark mit ihrem formalem Bildungshintergrund in Zusammenhang steht. Jugendliche mit formal niedriger Bildung nutzen Wikis signifikant seltener als Jugendliche mit einem anderen Bildungshintergrund. Im Anschluss an die Ausführungen zu milieuspezifischen Präferenz- und Relevanzsetzungen kann damit davon ausgegangen werden, dass die Nutzung von Wikis – qua Definition ein Wissensmanagement-Tool – eher den Präferenz- und Relevanzstrukturen formal hoch gebildeter Jugendlicher entgegenkommt. Zur weiterführenden Interpretation und

Analyse erscheint es jedoch sinnvoll die Nutzung und Nutzungsweisen dieser Dienste eher auf der Basis von Passungsverhältnissen in den Blick zu nehmen als aus der Perspektive ‚substanzieller Argumente', die ausschließlich auf personengebundene und feldunabhängige Kompetenzen und Interessen verweisen.

Auch die virtuelle Suche nach Unterstützung bei persönlichen Fragen und Probleme lässt sich entlang der Nutzungsweisen differenzieren. Dabei scheint die Selbsteinschätzung (Profi– Fortgeschrittene/r–Anfänger/in–Neuling) relevant zu sein: Von den befragten InternetnutzerInnen geben über 45% an, im Internet nach Hilfe und Unterstützung zu suchen: Während von den fortgeschrittenen NutzerInnen fast jede/r Zweite diese Option nutzt, ist es bei den AnfängerInnen noch ein Drittel der Jugendlichen. Doch mit Blick auf die Nutzungsweise zeigt sich, dass die AnfängerInnen nicht nur seltener nach Unterstützung im Internet suchen, sondern auch zudem zurückhaltender hinsichtlich einer schreibenden Hilfesuche sind: Während von den Fortgeschrittenen 38,6% (auch) schreibend Hilfe suchen, ist es bei den AnfängerInnen weniger als jede Vierte. Dennoch ist diese Zahl überraschend hoch und mag letztlich nochmals verdeutlichen, wie sehr das Internet auch unter noch unerfahrenen Jugendlichen bereits zu einem Medium avanciert ist, von dem man sich Hilfe und Unterstützung für persönliche Sorgen und Fragen zu finden verspricht.

Anhand der vorliegenden Auswertung wird deutlich, dass es bei den repräsentativen Daten zur Internetnutzung Jugendlicher und gerade mit Blick auf die verschiedenen Dienste lohnenswert ist, Nutzung differenziert zu analysieren: Chatnutzung ist bereits auf der Ebene der formalen Differenz von Lesen und Schreiben nicht gleich Chatnutzung. Wie Jugendliche solche prinzipiellen auf sozialer und unmittelbarer Interaktivität basierenden Dienste nutzen, ist nicht zuletzt durch ihren Bildungshintergrund, ihre Interneterfahrung, ihre Nutzungshäufigkeit und ihre Selbsteinschätzung vermittelt. All diese Variablen sind jedoch nicht als „substanzielle Kategorien" zu interpretieren, sondern vielmehr als Hinweis darauf, dass die Angebote, in denen sich solche Nutzungsweisen erst realisieren, systematisch hinsichtlich ihres Beitrags zu den jeweils realisierten Nutzungsweisen unterschiedlicher NutzerInnen berücksichtigt werden müssen. Weitere Forschung ist hier notwendig.

5 Digitale Ungleichheit als Herausforderung für die Pädagogik

In den neueren Forschungsarbeiten, die sich mit „Digitalen Ungleichheiten" beschäftigten, herrscht mittlerweile weitgehende Einigkeit darüber, dass sich in der Nutzung des Internet Ungleichheiten niederschlagen, die ihren Ursprung in dem Zugang zu entsprechend verteilten ökonomischen, kulturellen und sozialen Ressourcen außerhalb des Internet haben (vgl. Hargittai 2004, Livingstone et al. 2004 etc.). Dass sich dieses Phänomen bei weitem nicht nur auf erwachsene InternetnutzerInnen beschränkt, sondern sich auch innerhalb der Gruppe der jugendlichen NutzerInnen als der vermeintlich „internet savvy generation" widerspiegelt, verdeutlichen die vorgestellten empirischen Ergebnisse: Auch unter jugendlichen NutzerInnen korrespondieren die klassischen Variablen sozialer Ungleichheit mit Unterschieden in der Nutzung des Internet. Mit einer detaillierten Analyse der Internetnutzungsweisen Jugendlicher wurde auf der Grundlage eines Ansatzes, der die spezifische Erforschung digitaler Ungleichheit in den Blick nimmt, gezeigt, dass signifikante Unterschiede (a) in der Nutzung unterschiedlicher *Angebote* bestehen, sowie darüber hinaus (b) in der unterschiedlichen *Nutzungsweise* gleicher Angebote. Anhand empirischer Daten konnte gezeigt werden, dass die potentiellen Nutzungsoptionen des Internet nicht allen NutzerInnen in gleichem Maße zugänglich sind. Nimmt man das „Großmedium Internet" als Pull-Medium in den Blick, kann diese Einsicht kaum verwundern. Für Pull-Medien ist die Abhängigkeit von den Aufmerksamkeits- und Navigationsentscheidungen der NutzerInnen konstitutiv. Aus dieser Perspektive wird argumentiert, dass innerhalb der neuen Medien eine „kulturelle und soziale Differenzierung gemäß der Interessen und Motivationen der Nutzer" evoziert wird (Lenz/Zillien 2005:250). Innerhalb dieser Argumentationslinie, die einerseits die Interessen und Motive der NutzerInnen und andererseits das Medium „als solches" fokussiert, geraten jedoch wesentliche Aspekte aus dem Blick, die zum Verständnis virtueller Ungleichheit relevant sind. Motive und Interessen der NutzerInnen sind nicht unabhängig von sozialen Kontexten zu verstehen. Vielmehr repräsentieren sie gleichsam die Verwirklichungspotentiale unterschiedlicher Motive und Interessen der NutzerInnen in (virtuellen) Arrangements. Damit muss eine Analyse „Digitaler Ungleichheit" die Unterschiede in der Nutzung derselben Angebote in den Blick nehmen und gleichzeitig immer nach den virtuellen Arrangements fragen, in denen sich diese Nutzungsweisen realisieren.

Vor dem Hintergrund der dargestellten empirischen Ergebnisse steht die Bestimmung des Internet als ausdifferenziertes soziales Feld, innerhalb dessen sich verschiedene Bildungsprozesse vollziehen können, vor einer doppelten Herausforderung: Im Zusammenspiel von Angebot und Nutzung gilt es somit, lebensalltagsbezogene Relevanzstrukturen der Jugendlichen zu erkennen. Es kann nicht darum gehen, alle Jugendlichen zu einer spezifischen Nutzungsweise und inhaltlichen Konformität anzuregen, sondern es gilt hierbei, die Bildungspotentiale im kontextbezogenen Sinn zu entdecken und zu fördern: beispielsweise kann das Chatten die Aneignung von gewissen Handlungskompetenzen (wie z.B. die Kontaktaufnahme mit anderen, informelle Supportkommunikation) befördern. Das Grund-anliegen ist, allen die gleichen Chancen in der Nutzung zu eröffnen. Die Entscheidung, inwiefern sie diese nutzen wollen und inwieweit diese im aktuellen Lebensalltag eine Rolle spielen (sollen) bleibt den Jugendlichen überlassen. Eine grundlegende Ermöglichung hat eine informierte Entscheidung zum Ziel.

6 Qualität informeller und nonformeller Arrangements im virtuellen Raum

Bei der Nutzung des Internet stehen (vgl. Abb.1) Nutzungsmotive im Vordergrund, für die, je nach Kontext, die jeweils individuellen Interessen, Präferenzen aber auch Fähigkeiten den Rahmen und Ausgangspunkt darstellen. Diese erscheinen zwar als subjektiv, sind jedoch durch die den NutzerInnen verfügbaren sozialen (Peergroup, Beziehungen, soziale Unterstützung) und kulturellen (Bildungshintergrund, Wissen, Nutzungskompetenzen) Ressourcen geprägt. Die Aneignung erfolgt in Form informeller[15] Bildungsprozesse, die ggf. auch weitergehend sozial eingebettet sein können wie z.b. die Nutzung eines Chats im Jugendzentrum gemeinsam mit Freunden als Gruppenerlebnis.

Angesichts des Ziels, NutzerInnen soziale Teilhabe und Zugang zu Bildung in einer Wissensgesellschaft zu ermöglichen, stellt sich die Frage, wie dies bei Zielgruppen erfolgen kann, die nicht den Anforderungen selbstgesteuerter, themenbezogener und auf eigenverantwortliche Bildungsaneignung setzender Angebote ohne weiteres entsprechen können oder wollen. Der Bezugspunkt für eine in der (sog. ‚Wissens-‘)Gesellschaft als ‚erstrebenswert‘ definierte Internetnutzung wird häufig durch spezifische Kompetenzen wie beispielsweise kritische Informationssuche, Wissensaneignung etc. definiert. Doch dies entspricht nicht immer den Nutzungsmotiven und der damit verbundenen Aneignungspraxis. Um dieses Spannungsverhältnis aufzulösen, gilt es, soziale Teilhabemöglichkeiten auch im Netz zu eröffnen. Hierbei geht es darum, soziale und kulturelle Ressourcen der NutzerInnen zu erweitern, und gleichzeitig auf Seiten der Angebote die Zugangsmöglichkeiten zu erweitern. Erst durch diese nonformelle[16] Intervention, die nicht alleine ein

---

15 Mit informellen Bildungsprozessen sind hier Aneignungsprozesse gemeint, die auf den individuellen Präferenzen der Handelnden beruhen und nicht in einer zielgerichteten, arrangierten oder gar qualifikationsorientierten pädagogischen Situation sondern in einem „selbstgesteuerten" Kontext (mit allen damit verbundenen Problemen) außerhalb formalisierter Lehr-Lernsituationen stattfinden. Vor dem Hintergrund der jeweils subjektiv verfügbaren Ressourcen kann als informelle Bildung somit auch eine relativ begrenzte Bandbreite an Aneignung beschrieben werden, die u.U. in Hinsicht auf den Grad der „Selbststeuerung" kritisch reflektiert werden müsste.

16 Mit „nonformeller Intervention" sind an dieser Stelle arrangierte Settings und Strukturen gemeint, die im Gegensatz zu formalisierten Bildungskontexten nicht an einem bestimmten Lern-

bestimmtes Qualifikationsziel absolut setzt, sondern *beide* Seiten und insbesondere die Bedürfnisse und Möglichkeiten der NutzerInnen in den Blick nimmt, kann eine Brücke zwischen subjektiver Aneignung und gesellschaftlicher Ermöglichung geschlagen werden (vgl. Kutscher 2006).

Um dies zu ermöglichen, sind nonformelle, d.h. an den Interessen, Möglichkeiten und Präferenzen der Jugendlichen orientierte, zur gesellschaftlichen Teilhabe befähigende Interventionen erforderlich – sowohl innerhalb als auch außerhalb des Netzes. Um diese als fördernde und ungleichheitssensible nonformelle Umgebungen zu gestalten bedarf es der Definition von Qualitätsaspekten, die sowohl die AnbieterInnen- als auch die NutzerInnenseite in den Blick nehmen und somit vor diesem Hintergrund zur Erweiterung von Nutzungsoptionen für unterschiedliche NutzerInnengruppen beitragen[17].

	NutzerIn	**Teilhabe an der „Wissens-" Gesellschaft**
Ziel	Realisierung ‚subjektiver' Nutzungsmotive	Soziale Teilhabe der NutzerInnen
Bezugs- punkt	Interessen/Präferenzen/ Fähigkeiten	Vermittlung von Kompetenzen
Ressourcen	Nutzung der verfügbaren Ressourcen	Erweiterung von Ressourcen durch Intervention
Bildungs- weise	Informelle Aneignung / sozial kontextualisierte Bildungsprozesse	Non-formelle Intervention

(Kutscher 2006)

Abb. 1: Aneignung im virtuellen Raum zwischen Subjekt und Gesellschaft

Relationale Qualität in virtuellen Angeboten

Vor diesem Hintergrund geht es darum, ein komplexes Verständnis der Qualität von Onlineangeboten zu entwickeln, das sowohl die konkreten Nutzungspraxen berücksichtigt, als auch die unterschiedlichen Formen der Angebote, sowie deren komplexes Wechselverhältnis und die grundlegende Struktur des Internet als Pull-Medium reflektiert. Hier liegen zentrale Fragen für weitere empirische Untersu-

---

ziel ausgerichtet sind, sondern sich primär an den Interessen, Fähigkeiten und Möglichkeiten der AdressatInnen orientieren.

17   Erste weitergehende Ergebnisse hierzu siehe Abschlußbericht des KIB für die Bundesinitiative „Jugend ans Netz" (2006).

chungen, die in der Weiterführung der hier dargestellten Ergebnisse Aufschluss über den Zusammenhang von Angebotsstrukturen und Nutzung geben können.

Die Nutzung von Online-Angeboten kann allgemein als das lineare Entfalten eines nicht-linearen Hypertextes aufgefasst werden (vgl. Kuhlen 1991, Iske 2002), wobei generell vielfältige Konkretisierungen der Entfaltung des gleichen Angebotes möglich sind. Konkret bedeutet das, dass der prinzipiell hypertextuell, d.h. wenig vorstrukturierte virtuelle Raum durch die einzelnen Nutzungsschritte und -entscheidungen in linearer Weise durch die NutzerInnen strukturiert wird. Dies erfolgt allerdings, wie oben gezeigt wurde, nicht aufgrund rein individueller Präferenzen, sondern lässt sich in seinen Ausdifferenzierungen vor dem Hintergrund sozialer Kontexte erklären. Daher kann sich Qualität nicht einseitig auf das Angebot beziehen, sondern muss den Prozess der Nutzung mit berücksichtigen: Online-Angebote haben daher keine objektiv-statische, sondern eine relationale Qualität in Bezug zur NutzerInnenperspektive. Damit ist ‚Qualität' ein stets relationales, mit spezifischen Interessen verbundenes und je nachdem auch konfliktäres Konstrukt[18]. Weitgehend unreflektiert bleibt in der verbreiteten Debatte, dass auch zwischen NutzerInnen erhebliche Divergenzen bezüglich der Definition von ‚Qualität' bestehen können. Die Bestimmung von ‚Qualität' ist also nicht nur *zwischen* den verschiedenen Interessengruppen, sondern ebenso *innerhalb* der jeweiligen Interessensgruppen.

Ausgehend von der NutzerInnenperspektive fokussiert die Forschung des KIB Qualitätsanforderungen, die unterschiedliche NutzerInnen an Online-Angebote stellen. Vor dem Hintergrund dieser Forschungsperspektive bewerten die NutzerInnen Online-Angebote aufgrund ihrer bisherigen Nutzungserfahrungen und ihrer Nutzungsintentionen: In einer ersten Annäherung lassen sich somit Angebot, NutzerIn und Nutzungspraxis als die drei bestimmenden Faktoren von Qualität benennen, deren Verhältnis im folgenden näher erläutert wird. Es handelt sich hierbei um ein dynamisches Verhältnis, das durch das „Konzept der Passung und der Passungsverhältnisse" (vgl. Klein 2004, 2005, 2006) analytisch zugänglich gemacht werden kann. Passung und Passungsverhältnisse reflektieren die Bedingungen der Möglichkeiten subjektive Nutzungsinteressen innerhalb spezifischer virtueller Arrangements (weiter) zu entwickeln. In einem dynamischen Verhältnis lassen sich drei Ebenen als mediale, inhaltliche und interpersonelle Passung differenzieren,

---

18 Mit Blick auf die Qualitätsdebatte im Kontext Sozialer Dienstleistungen (zum Überblick vgl. Schaarschuch 2003, Beckmann et al. 2004) lässt sich vor diesem Hintergrund formulieren, dass sich die relationalen Definitionen von Qualität auch bei virtuellen Angeboten in einem grundlegenden Spannungsverhältnis zwischen den Qualitätsdefinitionen unterschiedlicher Interessengruppen bewegen.

die sowohl Nutzung bzw. Nicht-Nutzung als auch Nutzungsweisen beeinflussen können:

Hierbei definiert
- die *mediale* Passung, ob die Formen des Online-Angebots,
- die *inhaltliche* Passung, ob Art und Thematisierung der Inhalte und
- die *interpersonale* Passung, ob weitere Personen, die in das Angebot involviert sind,

den Vorstellungen, Interessen und praktisch realisierbaren Möglichkeiten unterschiedlicher NutzerInnen entsprechen.

Die einzelnen Dimensionen können für konkrete NutzerInnen und ihre Nutzungspraxen in unterschiedlichem Grad dominant sein, unterschiedliche Relevanz besitzen, und daher als akzeptables *Übel* wahrgenommen werden, oder auch als exit-Kriterium (vgl. Hirschman 1970), das zur Nicht-Nutzung führt.

Das Passungsmodell stellt somit eine Vermittlungsebene zwischen Online-Angebot, NutzerInnen und Nutzungspraxen dar.

Um jedoch digitale Ungleichheiten zu überwinden, sind Interventionen sowohl innerhalb des Internet (d.h. über eine zielgruppensensible Angebotsgestaltung) als auch außerhalb des Internet (d.h. über fähigkeitenerweiternde[19] Arbeit mit Jugendlichen in Jugendhilfe und Medienarbeit) erforderlich, um gesellschaftliche und Bildungsteilhabe im Rahmen des Internet zu ermöglichen. Das gilt beispielsweise auch in Zusammenhang mit der Realisierung von öffentlichen Beteiligungsformen. Uwe Bittlingmayer und Klaus Hurrelmann haben in ihrer Expertise für die Bundeszentrale politischer Bildung dargestellt, welche Wege gesucht werden müßten, um zielgruppenadäquate Ausdrucksformen zu beachten und Nutzungsräume dementsprechend zu gestalten (vgl. Bittlingmayer/Hurrelmann 2005, zur Übertragung auf den Bereich der Beteiligung Jugendlicher, auch im Kontext neuer Medien vgl. Kutscher 2007). Entsprechend dem Capabilities-Konzept geht es hierbei darum, Jugendliche zu befähigen, ein Internetleben zu führen das sie wollen – auf der Basis einer grundlegenden Ausstattung mit Kompetenzen und Räumen um sich auszudrücken und ihren Anliegen in der Gesellschaft Gehör zu verschaffen. Kurz, es geht darum, offline und online zu intervenieren, um den NutzerInnen zu ermöglichen, in ihrem lebensweltlichen Kontext erweiterte Chancen zu verwirklichen. Das bedeutet einerseits, bei der Nutzung dessen, was es an Angeboten im Internet gibt, zu unterstützen. Konkret ist hier medienpädagogische Arbeit gefordert, die

---

19   vgl. das Capabilities-Konzept von Amartya Sen (zur Einführung: Robeyns 2003)

die ungleiche Ressourcenausstattung der Zielgruppen beachtet und hier gezielt ausgleichende Angebote entwickelt, die über den in weiten Teilen realisierten Bereich der Medienpädagogik hinausgehen. Hier besteht bislang wie auch im Netz das Problem, dass Angebote für benachteiligte Zielgruppen noch relativ unterrepräsentiert sind. Sie stellen eine besondere Anforderung an die AnbieterInnen. Ähnlich wie in der offenen Jugendarbeit gilt es, für diese Zielgruppen offene, situative Angebotsformen zu entwickeln, die durch eine besondere Sensibilität für ihre Interessen, Anliegen und Möglichkeiten gekennzeichnet sind. Da es hier auch für einen fähigkeiten-erweiternden Ansatz einer Begleitung außerhalb des Internet bedarf, liegt hier ein entscheidender Schwerpunkt. Andererseits wären bislang vorhandene Angebote im Netz auf eine zielgruppensensible Nutzbarkeit hin zu prüfen und zu optimieren (vgl. Kutscher 2005).

Erst vor dem Hintergrund dieser sozial kontextualisierten Perspektive, die die NutzerInnen in ihren Lebenszusammenhängen wahrnimmt, lassen sich Prozesse informeller Bildung im Internet verstehen und über die Verfasstheit der Angebote gestalten. Daher geht es um eine Qualitätsdebatte, die auf der Basis empirischer Erkenntnisse die Gestaltung der Angebote analysiert und damit Bildungs- und Beteiligungsprozesse einer Reflexion zugänglich macht, die den Ausgangspunkt für die Definition demokratischer Bildungsstrukturen im Netz markiert.

Literatur

Baacke, D. (1980): Kommunikation und Kompetenz. Grundlegungen einer Didaktik der Kommunikation und ihrer Medien. München. 3. Auflage.

Beckmann, C. et al. (Hg.) (2004): Qualität in der sozialen Arbeit. Zwischen Nutzerinteresse und Kostenkontrolle. Wiesbaden.

Bittlingmayer, U. und Hurrelmann, K. (2005): Medial vermittelte politische Bildung für Jugendliche aus bildungsfernen Milieus aus soziologischer Sicht. Expertise für die Bundeszentrale für politische Bildung. Manuskript.

Esping-Andersen, G. (2003): Unequal Opportunities and Social Inheritance. Quelle: http://www.progressivegovernance.net/php/print_preview.php?aid=85 (02.02.2004)

Feierabend, S. und Rathgeb, T. (2005): Medienverhalten Jugendlicher 2004. In: Media Perspektiven, 7/2005. 320-332.

Hargittai, E. (2004): Internet access and use in Context. In: SAGE Publications. Vol6(1). London, Thousand Oaks, CA and New Delhi, S. 137–143. URL: www.sagepublications.com

Hirschman, A. O. (1970): Exit, Voice, and Loyalty: Responses to Decline in Firms, Organizations, and States. Cambridge.

Iske, S. (2002): Vernetztes Wissen: Hypertext-Strategien im Internet. Bielefeld: Bertelsmann.

Iske, S., Klein, A. und Kutscher, N. (2005): "Differences in web usage – social inequality and informal education on the internet". Social Work and Society, Volume 3 2005 (2005), Issue 2. URL: www.socwork.de/IskeKleinKutscher2005.pdf (29.10.2006)

JIM 2005: Jugend, Information, (Multik-)Media, herausgegeben von Medienpädagogischen Forschungsverbund Südwest. URL: www.mpfs.de (17.12.06)

JIM 2006: Jugend, Information, (Multik-)Media, herausgegeben von Medienpädagogischen Forschungsverbund Südwest. URL: www.mpfs.de (17.12.06)

Klein, A. (2004): Von Digital Divide zu Voice Divide: Beratungsqualität im Internet. In: Otto, H.-U. & Kutscher, N.: Informelle Bildung Online. Weinheim.

Klein, A. (2005): „Ihr seid vol coll" – Onlineberatung für Jugendliche. In: Schetsche, M. & Lehmann, K.: Die Google-Gesellschaft. Transkript: Bielefeld.

Klein, A. (2006): „Fische im Wasser und Elefanten im Porzellanladen." Vortrag auf der Theorie-AG Dezember 2006 in Bielefeld. In Erscheinen auf www.wiposa.de

Kuhlen, R. (1991): Hypertext. Ein nicht-lineares Medium zwischen Buch und Wissensbank. Berlin u.a.: Springer.

Kutscher, N. (2005): Power to the People? Eine technologische Utopie im Spiegel der Empirie. In: Schindler, W. (Hrsg.): MaC* - Reloaded: Perspektiven aus der Skepis, für *Menschen am Computer. URL: http://www.josefstal.de/mac/days/2004/buch/ (02.01.2007)

Kutscher, N. (2006): Das Netz als Spiegel der Gesellschaft. Soziale Ungleichheit und Bildungschancen in der Internetnutzung von Jugendlichen. URL: http://www.mediendoku.muc.kobis.de/redaxo/ 120-0-dr-nadia-kutscher.html (14.12.06)

Kutscher, N. (2007): Zwischen Interessen, Erwartungen und Lebensalltag – Beteiligung Jugendlicher unter der Perspektive von Zielgruppenadäquatheit. In: Bertelsmann Stiftung (Hrsg.): Kinder- und Jugendbeteiligung in Deutschland – Gegenwärtiger Entwicklungsstand und zukünftige Handlungsansätze. In Erscheinen.

Lenhart, A., Madden, M. und Hitlin, P. (2005): Teens and Technology. Youth are leading the transition to a fully wired and mobile nation. URL: http://www.pewinternet.org/pdfs/PIP_Teens_Tech_July2005web.pdf [21.11.2006]

Lenz, T. & Zillien, N. (2005): Medien und soziale Ungleichheit. In: Jäckel, Michael (Hg.): Mediensoziologie. Wiesbaden: VS-Verlag: 237-254.

Livingstone, S., Bober, M. & Helsper, E. (2004): Active participation or just more information? Young people's take up of opportunities to act and interact on the internet. London. LSE Research Online. URL: http://eprints.lse.ac.uk/archive/00000396/01/UKCGOparticipation.pdf [21.11.2006]

Mayer-Uellner, R. (2003): Das Schweigen der Lurker. Fischer (Reinhard): München.

Medienpädagogischer Forschungsverbund Südwest (2006): JIM Studie 2006. Vorabauswertungen zu den Themenbereichen „Mobiltelefon" und „Chat". September 2006. URL: http://www.mpfs.de/ fileadmin/JIM-pdf/Vorabbericht_JIM_2006.pdf [21.11.2006]

OECD (2006): Are students ready for a technology-rich world? OECD Briefing Notes für DEUTSCHLAND. URL: www.oecd.org (17.12.06)

Oehmichen, E. & Schröter, C. (2006): Internet im Medienalltag: Verzögerte Aneignung des Angebots. In: Media Perspektiven, 8/2006, 441-449.

Otto, H.-U., Kutscher, N., Klein, A. und Iske, S.: „Soziale Ungleichheit im virtuellen Raum: Wie nutzen Jugendliche das Internet?" Forschungsnetz des BMFSFJ 2004. URL: www.familienwegweiser.de/Kategorien/Forschungsnetz/forschungsberichte,did=14282.html überarbeitete Version im Netz von 2005) (31.10.2006)

Preece, J., Nonnecke, B. & Andrews, D. (2004): The top five reasons for lurking: improving community experiences for everyone. In: Computers in Human Behaviour, 20. 201-223.

Robeyns, I. (2003: The Capability Approach: An Interdisciplinary Introduction. URL: http:// www.ingridrobeyns.nl/Downloads/CAtraining20031209.pdf [05.02.2007]

Schaarschuch, A. (2003): „Qualität" sozialer Dienstleistungen – ein umstrittenes Konzept. In: Indikatoren und Qualität sozialer Dienste im europäischen Kontext. Tagungsdokumentation. URL: http:// www.soziale-dienste-in-europa.de/dokumente/Bestellservice/ix_91989_8453.htm. S. 50-56.

Selwyn, N. (2003) ‚Doing IT for the kids: re-examining children, computers and the information society' *Media, Culture & Society*, 25, 3: 351-378.

Stegbauer, C. (2001): Von den Online Communities zu den computervermittelten sozialen Netzwerken. Eine Reinterpretation klassischer Studien. In: Zeitschrift für Qualitative Bildungs-, Beratungs- und Sozialforschung. 2001, 2: 151-174.

Stegbauer, C. & Rausch, A. (2001): Die schweigende Mehrheit – „Lurker" in internetbasierten Diskussionsforen. In: Zeitschrift für Soziologie, 30, 1. 48-64.

Tapscott, D. (1998): Net Kids. Wiesbaden.

TNS Infratest und Initiative D21 (2006): (N)Onliner Atlas 2006. URL: http://www.nonliner-atlas.de/pdf/dl_NONLINER-Atlas2006.pdf [21.11.2006]

Tully, C. J. (2004): Alltagslernen in technisierten Welten: Kompetenzerwerb durch Computer, Internet und Handy. In: Wahler, P./Tully, C.J./Preiß, C. (Hrsg.): Jugendliche in neuen Lernwelten. Wiesbaden: VS-Verlag

van Eimeren, B. & Frees, B. (2005): Nach dem Boom: Größter Zuwachs in internetfernen Gruppen. In: Media Perspektiven, 8/2005, 362-379.

van Eimeren, B. & Frees, B. (2006): Schnelle Zugänge, neue Anwendungen, neue Nutzer? In: Media Perspektiven, 8/2006, 402-415.

Vester, M., von Oertzen, P., Geiling, H., Herrmann, T. und Müller, D. (2001): Soziale Milieus im gesellschaftlichen Strukturwandel. Frankfurt am Main.

Winfried Marotzki

Erinnerungskulturen im Internet

Bildung

Es entspricht einer langen Tradition bildungstheoretischen Denkens, die Orientierung des Menschen in den Mittelpunkt geistes- und sozialwissenschaftlicher Überlegungen zu stellen. Wie der Mensch zu sich und zur Umwelt ein reflektiertes Verhältnis aufbaut, interessiert viele wissenschaftlichen Disziplinen, natürlich auch die Erziehungswissenschaft. Der Bildungsbegriff schließt, das können wir hier abkürzend sagen, im klassischen wie im modernen Sinne den der Orientierung ein. Informationen zu erhalten, ist eben nicht identisch mit Bildung, sondern es bedarf einer inneren Integration dieser Informationen in die Selbst- und Welthaltung der Menschen. Insofern wird häufig Lernen, Information und Wissen auf der einen Seite der Fähigkeit des Menschen, eine orientierende Haltung aufzubauen, entgegengesetzt. Beispielhaft hat dies Jürgen Mittelstraß in seinen Schriften immer wieder getan. So sagt er beispielsweise in seinem Aufsatz „Bildung und ethische Maße": „Je reicher wir an Information und Wissen sind, desto ärmer scheinen wir an Orientierungskompetenz zu werden. Für diese Kompetenz stand einmal der Begriff der Bildung." (Mittelstraß 2002, 154)

Und noch etwas rufe ich an dieser Stelle in Erinnerung, ohne es im Einzelnen auszuführen: Bildung ist, im Sinne Hartmut von Hentigs (1996), ein reflektiertes sich-zu sich-selbst-Verhalten. Bildung ist also ein Begriff, der sich auf die Qualität von Reflexionsmustern bezieht. Eine orientierende Reflexion ist letztlich für die Identität des Einzelnen entscheidend. Das ist der bildungstheoretische Kern. Schaut man sich das Panorama verschiedener Orientierungsformate an, dann können diese in zwei Gruppen eingeteilt werden, nämlich in diachrone und in synchrone. Diachrone sind solche, die den Einzelnen aus seiner individuellen, gemeinschaftlichen, gesellschaftlichen und nationalen Traditionslinie heraus verstehen. Synchrone Orientierungsformate sind solche, die den Einzelnen aus den zum gegenwärtigen Zeitpunkt bestehenden Zugehörigkeits- und Anerkennungsverhältnissen verstehen. Beide gehören zusammen und bedingen sich gegenseitig, können aber analytisch getrennt werden.

Ort der Orientierung sowohl in synchroner als auch in diachroner Hinsicht ist die Lebenswelt, die immer auch eine mediale ist. Neue Informationstechnologien haben die Lebenswelten einzelner erobert und bilden einen nicht zu trennenden Teil von ihr. Es handelt sich, um einen Begriff von Assmann (1999) zu verwenden, gleichsam um eine kulturelle Formation, zu der neue Informationstechnologien, wie das Internet, ganz selbstverständlich gehören. Ein bildungstheoretischer Fokus, der den medialen Aspekt von Subjektkonstitution thematisiert, kann als Medienbildung verstanden werden (vgl. Aufenanger 2000; Marotzki 2004). In diesem Kontext werde ich im Folgenden am Beispiel des Internet beide Dimensionen, diachrone und synchrone) näher erörtern.

Synchrone Orientierungsformate

Fragt man danach, wie sich synchrone Orientierungsformate im Internet herausbilden können, ob dort also Identitätsbildungsprozesse nachzuweisen sind, dann ist auf die klassischen Online-Communities zu verweisen, die – jedenfalls aus meiner Sicht – als gut erforscht gelten können. Die Beiträge in der Online-Zeitschrift „Journal of Computer-Mediated Communication" haben hierfür in den letzten Jahren sicherlich wichtige Beiträge geleistet, um die These vom Kultur- Sozial- und Bildungsraum Internet auszuarbeiten. Zu verweisen ist beispielsweise auch auf auf die Sammelbände von Steve Woolgar „Virtual Society?" (2002) oder von Philip N. Howard und Steve Jones „Society Online. The Internet in Context" (2004), um nur exemplarisch zwei Bände der letzten Jahre zu nennen, die Forschungen in diesem Bereich bündeln. Auch im deutschen Kontext finden wir eine Reihe von wichtigen Arbeiten zu diesem Thema, etwa von Nicola Döring (2003) oder Udo Thiedecke (2004).

Beobachtet man die Entwicklung von Jugendcommunities in den letzten Jahren, dann fällt auf, dass sie im Ausland wesentlich erfolgreicher zu sein scheinen als in Deutschland. Dafür zwei Beispiele:

(1) „Lunarstorm" ist die größte Jugendcommunity in Schweden mit rund einer Millionen Mitglieder. 80% SchwedInnen im Alter von 12-24 Jahren sind dort Mitglied (vgl. http://www.lunarstorm.se/). Im Durchschnitt loggen sich jeden Tag mehr als 360.000 BenutzerInnen ein, um mit Freunden zu chatten, Tagebücher zu schreiben und zu lesen oder um sich Ratschläge zu holen. Alle 24 Stunden werden rund fünf Millionen Nachrichten verschickt. Die Daten zeigen die enorme Aktivität dieser Community. Sie bietet unter anderem Clubs, Verzeichnisse von Klassenkameraden, Listen mit Freunden (und Feinden),

Musik und Filme und ein Reputationssystem, mit dem man Profile anderer BenutzerInnen, Tagebücher und Listen bewerten kann. Nach der Tsunami-Katastrophe im Dezember 2004 wurde Lunarstorm ein wichtiger Treffpunkt für emotionale Unterstützung und Planung von Aktionen. Während tausende SchwedInnen im Katastrophengebiet vermisst waren, nutzten die Menschen zu Hause Lunarstorm, um Informationen und Emotionen auszutauschen sowie Spendenaktionen zu organisieren.

(2) Cyworld (vgl. http://cyworld.nate.com/main2/index.htm) erreicht in Südkorea 90 Prozent aller Jugendlichen (15 Mio. User) und ist nach dem MySpace-Prinzip mit den üblichen Userprofilen, Blog-, Kontakt- und Verbindungsmöglichkeiten ausgestattet. Das besondere hier ist, dass man einen eigenen virtuellen „Miniroom" hat, den man mit (käuflich zu erwerbenden) Gegenständen ausstatten kann. Der Fernsehsender 3sat kommentierte diese Commuity am 26. Juli 2005 mit den Worten: „Der Anbieter Cyworld hat mit seiner Plattform einen regelrechten Boom ausgelöst. Praktisch jeder hat seine eigene Cyworld-Seite. Auf der Cyworld-Seite wird das eigene Leben präsentiert mit Rubriken, Photos oder den kleinen Cyworld-Figürchen. Die Mini Homepages sind interaktiv. Man besucht sich gegenseitig, schickt Kommentare."[1]

So weit die beiden Beispiele. Die relativ gute Erforschung von Kommunikationsstrukturen, Interaktionsverhalten und -typiken, von Aushandlungsprozessen, Ausprägung von Zugehörigkeit, von Vergemeinschaftungsprozessen, Partizipationskulturen u.ä. erlaubt die Aussage, dass unter dem Aspekt synchroner Orientierungsformate Online-Communities im hohen Maße bildungsrelevant sind (vgl. Marotzki 2003). In dieser Arbeit werde ich mich überwiegend mit diachronen Orientierungsformaten beschäftigen, und zwar mit einem spezifischen Aspekt, nämlich dem der Erinnerungsarbeit, weil dieser Aspekt in der bisherigen Internetforschung nicht in der Breite erforscht worden ist wie die eben genannten Aspekte.

Diachrone Orientierungsformate

Diachrone Orientierungsformate beziehen ihre Kraft daraus, dass der einzelne sich eingebettet in eine geschichtliche, historische, gesellschaftliche, gemeinschaftliche oder biographische Kontinuität verstehen kann. Solche Bildungslinien können individuell sein, nämlich dann, wenn der einzelne an seiner biographischen Kontinuität arbeitet (biographische Wurzeln), sie können – oft damit verbunden – auch

---

1   http://www.3sat.de/3sat.php?http://www.3sat.de/neues/sendungen/spezial/81682/index.html

gemeinschaftsorientiert (Gemeinschaftswurzeln) sein, nämlich dann, wenn der einzelne sich selbst darüber vergewissert, aus welchen Zugehörigkeiten er sich zu dem entwickelt hat, der er jetzt ist. Auf jeden Fall ist es Aufgabe von Biographisierungsprozessen, die Teile der Vergangenheit zu einem Ganzen zu fügen. Biographiearbeit hat also immer etwas mit der Herstellung von diachronen Bildungslinien zu tun, ist also zu großen Teilen Erinnerungsarbeit.

Erinnerungsarbeit als Facette eines diachronen Orientierungsformats

Betrachtet man die Diskussionen der letzten Jahre oder Jahrzehnte im Hinblick auf Gedächtnis- und Erinnerungstheorien, dann finden wir im Werk Paul Riceurs[2] wichtige Hinweise für unsere Perspektive. Der zentrale Aspekt der Erinnerungsarbeit, den ich herausheben möchte, heißt: Erinnerungsarbeit ist zugleich immer auch biographische Aufarbeitung eines Verlustes. Damit meint Ricoeur, dass Vergangenheit, eben weil sie nicht mehr ist, per se einen Verlust darstellt, insofern Erinnern immer Trauerarbeit ist, um einen Begriff von Freud zu verwenden, auf den sich Ricoeur auch bezieht. Zum anderen sind aber natürlich damit auch reale Verluste, z.B. von Menschen, gemeint.

Ricoeur bezieht sich bei der Exposition dieses Gedankens auf die dafür einschlägigen Schriften von Sigmund Freud, nämlich zum einen auf „Erinnern, Wiederholen und Durcharbeiten" (Freud 1914) und zum anderen auf „Trauer und Melancholie" (1917). Er sieht eine grundlegende Verwandtschaft zwischen Erinnerungsarbeit und Trauerarbeit. Trauer ist gemäß der bekannten Definition von Sigmund Freud die Reaktion auf einen Verlust[3]. Der Übergang von der Trauer zur Melancholie ist fließend. Freud nimmt eine klare analytische Unterscheidung vor, indem er sagt, dass bei der Trauer die Welt verarmt und leer, bei der Melancholie dagegen das Ich niedergeschlagen sei. Dabei ist auch ihm klar, dass es fließende Übergänge in beide Richtungen gibt. Unter den Spuren der Identität, die in der Erinnerungsarbeit freigelegt werden, würden sich auch Verletzungen und Kränkungen, manchmal auch Traumata finden. Sie sind nach Freud die Ursachen dafür, dass Erinnerungsarbeit im Verdrängen oder im Agieren gefangen gehalten werden kann. Verlust, Verletzungen, Kränkungen und ggf. auch Traumata müssen in ir-

---

2   Ich werde mich durch Überlegungen von Paul Ricoeur leiten lassen, genauer durch sein Spätwerk, nämlich durch Schriften, die im Umkreis seines Hauptwerkes „Gedächtnis, Geschichte, Vergessen" erschienen sind (vgl. Ricoeur 2004; 2004a).

3   „Trauer ist regelmäßig die Reaktion auf den Verlust einer geliebten Person oder einer an ihre Stelle gerückten Abstraktion wie Vaterland, Freiheit, ein Ideal usw." (Freud cit. Ricoeur 2004, 104)

gendeiner Form bearbeitet werden. Aber in welcher Form werden sie im Rahmen biographischer Arbeit bearbeitet? Und warum muss überhaupt erinnert werden? Nach Ricoeur muss die Vergangenheit auf Distanz gebracht werden. Er spricht deshalb auch davon, dass es in der Erinnerungsarbeit um die Eroberung der zeitlichen Distanz gehe. Gelinge es nicht, Vergangenheit in diesem Sinne zu distanzieren, beeinträchtige sie mein Vermögen, Zukunft zu entwerfen. Freud würde davon sprechen, dass agiert werde (also Wiederholung) und dadurch die Lebenskraft des Menschen eingeschränkt werde, weil ein Teil der Energie für das Agieren benötigt werde und insofern nicht anderweitig zur Verfügung stehe. Die Vergangenheit werde zur Last für die Gegenwart und Zukunft.

Erinnerungsarbeit, um Lebenskraft zu gewinnen, wird also immer dann wichtig, wenn uns die Vergangenheit gleichsam Energien geraubt hat, so dass sie uns für das Leben nicht zur Verfügung stehen. Das Auf-Distanz-Bringen der Vergangenheit ist nicht Vergessen, sondern die Distanz ermöglicht es uns, eine Haltung zu ihr einzunehmen. Das ist eine wesentliche Funktion dessen, was wir *reflektierende Orientierung* nennen. Erinnern, Durcharbeiten und Reflexion sind nicht identisch, aber sie liegen dicht beieinander und bedingen sich. Durch Erinnerung muss Vergangenheit präsent gemacht werden, damit Durcharbeiten und Reflexion ermöglicht wird. Erst durch erinnernde Reflexion kann Orientierung in dem oben genannten Sinne erreicht werden. Das ist die Strukturlogik diachroner Orientierungsformate.

Erinnerungskulturen im Cyberspace

Erinnerungskulturen gibt es viele. Das Totengedenken ist eine der ursprünglichsten und in den verschiedenen Gesellschaften am weitesten verbreitete Erinnerungskultur. Der Tote lebt in der Erinnerung der Nachwelt weiter. In diesem Sinne sagt Jean Paul Sartre in seinem Hauptwerk „Das Sein und das Nichts" (1943/1993), dass ein Mensch zweimal sterben könne: Einmal wenn er körperlich sterbe und zum anderen, wenn er aus der Erinnerung seiner sozialen Umgebung verschwinde, wenn er also vergessen werde, wenn die Erinnerung aus seinem sozialen Umfeld verschwindet. Im Folgenden frage ich also, welche Erinnerungskulturen wir – am Beispiel des Totengedenkens – im Internet finden. In den letzten Jahren haben sich mit erstaunlich steigender Tendenz verschiedene Formen des Erinnerns etablieren können. Die Palette ist groß. Schauen wir uns einige Beispiele an.

1. Zunächst ist die Vielzahl *virtueller Tierfriedhöfe* auffallend. Nahezu für jede Haustierart, ob Katze, Hunde, Vögel, Reptilien, Kleintiere oder Großtiere (z.B. Pferde), gibt es solche virtuelle Gedenkstätten. So heisst es beispielsweise auf der

Eingangsseite von http://www.virtueller-tierfriedhof.de/: „Der virtuelle Friedhof bietet Ihnen die Gelegenheit Ihrem Liebling einen würdigen Abschied zu bereiten." Dort finden sich auch Gräber prominenter Tiere wie z.B. Daisy Moshammer (gest. 24.10.2006), Braunbär Bruno (gest. 26.06.2006) mit entsprechenden Kondolenzbüchern. Ein Grabbesuch beispielsweise bei dem Kater Felix (geb. am 10.3.1996, gest. am 7.10.2006) zeigt uns einen Rahmen, der von zwei schmaleren Rahmen flankiert wird. In dem linken schmalen Rahmen sehen wir untereinander drei Bilder von Felix, einem schwarzweißen Kater. Der mittlere große Rahmen zeigt mit zunächst, dass ich der 810. Besucher bin. Darunter sehen wir ein Grab mit Grabstein, Umrandung und Blumen; links daneben folgenden Text: „Lieber Felix, vor 10 Jahren hattest Du mich erwählt, Dein Herrschen zu sein. Du hattest Deinen eigenen Willen, aber dennoch wurdest Du für mich ein treuer und liebevoller Begleiter. Leider musste ich Dich nun von Deinen Leiden erlösen. Ich werde Dich nie vergessen und immer lieben. R.I.P." Im rechten schmalen Rahmen befindet sich das Kondolenzbuch mit vier Texteinträgen (Stichtag: 19.2.2007) und drei Blumen. Dieses ist sicherlich nicht der größte virtuelle Friedhof, aber er beinhaltet immerhin Gedenkstätten für 188 Katzen, 158 Hunde, 15 Vögel, 4 Reptilien, 135 Kleintiere und 18 Großtiere. Da die Zahl virtueller Tierfriedhöfe steigt, so kann vermutet werden, ist auch das Bedürfnis, den eigenen Verlust öffentlich zu dokumentieren und dem Haustier ein virtuelles Weiterleben, ein Präsentsein in einer Gemeinschaft zu ermöglichen, gewachsen. Natürlich können auch andere Ursachen zu diesem Anwachsen geführt haben, aber ich vermute, dass es das Bedürfnis ist, dem toten, geliebten Tier einen bleibenden Platz im öffentlichen Raum zu geben.

2. Neben den Gedenkseiten für Tiere gibt es die für verstorbenen Menschen. Zunächst ist eine nahezu unüberschaubare Zahl von momorial sites bekannter und berühmter Persönlichkeiten zu nennen. Allein die Gedenkseiten für Prinzessin Diana sind kaum zu überschauen. Im deutschsprachigen Raum ist es beispielsweise die Seite http://www.prinzessin-diana.de/, die dem Besucher alle Informationen zu Dianas Leben bietet. Das internationale Kondolenzbuch beinhaltet 2665 Einträge. Die registrierten 2225 User haben die Möglichkeit, Filme und Fotos zu betrachten, im Forum sich auszutauschen, an regelmäßigen Diana Umfragen teilzunehmen, News als RSS-Feed zu abonnieren und sich in der Diana Bibliothek herumzutummeln. Ziel dieser Bibliothek ist es, sämtliche Medienberichte über Prinzessin Diana zu sammeln und von allen Besuchern bewertet zu lassen. Neben Büchern, Sonderheften, CD-ROMs gibt es auch Software rund um das Leben von Diana.

3. Interessanter und weniger spektakulär sind die memorial sites, die Privatpersonen ins Netz stellen, wenn sie einen Verlust erlitten haben. In der Regel sind dies persönliche Trauerseiten, wenn beispielsweise ein Kind, der Partner, Vater oder

Mutter oder auch Freunde gestorben sind. Auch hier ist es nicht möglich, allein im deutschsprachigen Raum diese Seiten vollständig zu recherchieren. Es dürften Tausende sein. Das Gedenken erfolgt durch Texte, Photos, Bilder und kleine Videos. Auch hier finden wir in der Regel ein Kondolenzbuch, in das Bekannte und Freunde ihre Erinnerungen schreiben können. Die Seite memory-of.com vereinigt, um weitere Beispiele zu nennen[4], 41.000 Einträge (Toten-Profile) und 1.646.697 virtuelle Kerzen. Ähnlich sind „http://gonetoosoon.co.uk/", mit über 4.200 Einträgen und „http://www.last-memories.com" mit über 1300 Einträgen strukturiert. Das Prinzip der Seiten ist gleich: Es gibt es die Möglichkeit, ein Profil für einen Verstorben anzulegen und anschließend u.a. virtuelle Kerzen für diesen anzuzünden, Erinnerungen in ein virtuelles Kondolenzbuch einzutragen und sogar Fotos, Audio- und Video-Dateien hochzuladen. Bei „http://gonetoosoon.co.uk/" kann man sich sogar per SMS informieren lassen, wenn ein neuer Kondolenzbuch-Eintrag im Profil eines Verstorbenen gemacht wurde. Durch die Aktivitäten verschiedener Hinterbliebener kann sich so auch ein Besucher der jeweiligen Profil-Seite, der den Toten nicht kannte, ein annähernd lebendiges Bild des Verstorbenen machen.

4. Ein weiterer Typ von memorial sites wird von Institutionen ins Netz gestellt, beispielsweise von Holocaust-Organisationen (Shoa Foundation oder Yad Vashem). Die zentrale israelische Gedenkstätte Yad Vashem in Jerusalem stellt die eigenen Aktivitäten auf ihrer Homepage ausführlich vor, und auszugsweise ist das dort archivierte Material online verfügbar, so dass ein kleiner Teil der Erinnerungsarbeit virtuell geleistet werden kann, auch wenn dort keine förmliche, virtuelle Gedenkstätte errichtet wurde. Ein Bestandteil der virtuellen Gedenkstätte Yad Vashem (http://www.yadvashem.org/) ist beispielsweise die „Halle der Namen", die die so genannten „Seiten der Aussagen" (Pages of Testimony) beherbergt. Dabei handelt es sich um von Freunden oder Verwandten erstellte Erinnerungsseiten mit den Namen, Daten und persönlichen Informationen ermordeter Juden, deren Andenken so auf eine persönliche Weise bewahrt werden soll. Ein halbes Dutzend von ihnen ist stellvertretend für die vielen anderen Papierdokumente via Internet einzusehen. Sie sollen als symbolische Grabsteine dienen. In naher Zukunft sollen alle Dokumente ermordeter Juden online verfügbar gemacht werden. Schon jetzt sind Exponate aus den Fotoarchiven abrufbar. Mit ihnen wird nicht nur die Verfolgung dokumentiert, gleichzeitig wird die Biografie der dort abgebildeten Verfolgten dokumentiert und den Menschen gleichsam ein Gesicht gegeben. Der Versuch der Nazis, alles auszulöschen, auch die Erinnerung an die Menschen, nicht nur ihre physische Existenz, dieser Versuch wird nachträglich zumindest ein Stück weit

---

4   Ich danke Benjamin Rücker für hilfreiche Hinweise.

revidiert. Die Rettung des einzelnen Schicksals vor der Logik der Macht kann also auch durch das Internet stattfinden.

Kirstin Foot und Barbara Warnick haben in ihrer Arbeit „Web-based Memorializing after September 11" (2005) die Memorialsites untersucht, die nach dem 11. September 2001 ins Netz gestellt worden sind. Nach den Angaben der Autorinnen sollen es tausende solcher Seiten sein. Es sind überwiegend persönliche Gedenken, die hier ins Netz gestellt wurden, um den Opfern Präsenz zu verleihen, um auch in diesem Fall den Toten einen Platz in der Gemeinschaft zu erhalten.

Ähnliches gilt auch für die Inszenierung der Erinnerung an die Gefallenen und Vermissten des Vietnamkrieges durch den Vietnam Veterans Memorial Fund (VVMF). Ausgangspunkt ist eine reale Mauer in Washington D.C., in die 58.000 Namen von Toten oder Vermissten des Vietnamkrieges eingeschrieben sind. Am 10. November 1998 wurde die Virtual Wall im Rahmen einer feierlichen Zeremonie durch den damaligen U.S. Vize-Präsidenten Al Gore offiziell ins World Wide Web gestellt. Angela Summner hat in ihrer Arbeit „Kollektives Gedenken individualisiert: Die Hypermedia-Anwendung ‚The Virtual Wall'" (2004) im Rahmen des Gießener Sonderforschungsbereiches „Erinnerungskulturen" diese virtuelle Gedenkstätte untersucht. Bei der Virtual Wall können sogenannte „remembrances" hinzugefügt werden. Eine remembrance ist eine Datei, die einen (oder allen) der Gefallenen bzw. Vermissten gewidmet ist. Es können sowohl Textnachrichten als auch Audio- oder Bilddateien hinterlegt werden. Im Mai 2003 waren 52.400 remembrances eingestellt, im November 2003: 88.536, im Januar 2004: 90.917 und im Januar 2006 156.797. Diese Daten zeigen, dass die Seite nicht als einmaliges Dokument, das als einmaliger Trauerakt zu bewerten ist, verstanden werden kann. Vielmehr wird hier Trauerarbeit über Jahre hinweg gleichsam kontinuierlich betrieben.

5. Schauen wir uns eine letzte Gruppe von memorial sites an. Allen genannten Seiten ist bisher gemeinsam, dass Toten – bezogen auf ihr Offline-Leben – eine virtuelle Gedenkstätte gegeben wird. Nun ist es bei den eingangs erwähnten Communities aber so, dass Menschen neben ihrer Offline-Existenz auch eine Online-Existenz leben. Die letzte Gruppe von memorial sites, die ich vorstellen möchte, bezieht sich auf diese Online-Existenzen. Die Seite MyDeathSpace (http://www.mydeathspace.com) ist ein Ort für verstorbene Mitglieder von Myspace. Auf der Startseite heißt es: „Welcome to MyDeathSpace.com. Your global resource for MySpace.com member obituaries. MyDeathSpace.com is an archival site, containing news articles, online obituaries, and other publicly available information. We have given you the opportunity to pay your respects and tributes to the recently deceased MySpace.com members via our comment system. Please be respectful."

Auch hier finden wir eine ähnliche Logik. Es findet sich eine Seite für den Toten, die einen Link auf seine MySpace-Seite, also sozusagen auf seine Online-Existenz, enthält. Neben dem üblichen Kondolenzbuch finden wir umfangreiche Foren und Diskussionsmöglichkeiten.

Schlußbetrachtung

Ich sagte eingangs, dass Erinnerungsarbeit nach Ricoeur biographische Arbeit eines Verlustes ist. In diesem Sinne sagt er: „Die Trauerarbeit ist der Preis der Erinnerungsarbeit, und die Erinnerungsarbeit ist der Gewinn der Trauerarbeit." (Ricoeur 2004, 106) Erinnern hat die Funktion, uns zu ermöglichen, eine Haltung zur Vergangenheit einzunehmen. Indem die Vergangenheit durch Erinnerung präsent gemacht wird, kann sie auf Distanz gebracht werden und damit wird sie der Reflexion zugänglich. Der Aufbau einer solchen Haltung bedeutet den Aufbau einer Orientierung.

Maurice Halbwachs betont in seinem Hauptwerk „Das Gedächtnis und seine sozialen Bedingungen" (1925/1985) die sozialen Rahmen von Erinnerung. Seine Zentralthese ist, dass die Erinnerungen der Menschen sich an einem sozialen Zusammenhang orientieren; Gedächtnis wird also als ein soziales Phänomen interpretiert. Wenn etwas in der Gegenwart keinen sozialen Bezugsrahmen hat, wird es vergessen. Wie wir gesehen haben, ist die Tendenz der letzten 15 Jahre, einen solchen sozialen Bezugsrahmen vermehrt im Internet zu suchen; sicherlich nicht nur, aber immer mehr. Das ist ein weiterer Beleg für die generelle These, dass das Internet als Kulturraum betrachtet werden kann (vgl. Marotzki 2003a).

Zwar ist es richtig, wie Angela Sumner in ihrer Arbeit „Kollektives Gedenken individualisiert" (2004) betont, dass im Falle der Virtual Wall Gedenken höchst individualisiert ermöglicht wird, aber es ist nicht zu unterschätzen, dass durch die remembrances gleichsam das Netz der sozialen Beziehungen aufgespannt wird und jeder Freund oder Bekannter den Verstorbenen aus seiner Perspektive würdigt. Auf diese Weise findet gleichsam eine (Wieder)Einbettung in ein soziales Netz, in eine Gemeinschaft statt. Angehörige finden in virtuellen Gedenkstätten Sichtweisen auf ihren Verstorbenen, die ihr Bild von ihm erhalten oder auch modifizieren können. Das Bewußtsein sozialer Zugehörigkeit beruht auf der Teilhabe an einem gemeinsamen Wissen und einem gemeinsamen Gedächtnis. Beides wird hier in bescheidenem Rahmen medial hergestellt.

Kultur – um einen Begriff von Assmann wieder zu verwenden – ist ein Komplex medial vermittelter Gemeinsamkeit, eine „kulturelle Formation" (vgl. Assmann 1997, 139)[5]. Unspektakulär und leise verändert das Internet unsere kulturelle Formation. Die Identität des Einzelnen wird immer stärker in diachroner und synchroner Perspektive durch das Internet konstituiert. Dadurch verändern sich nicht die Grundkoordinaten menschlicher Identität, wohl aber die Form der kulturellen Praktiken.

Literatur

Assmann, J. (1997): Das kulturelle Gedächtnis. Schrift, Erinnerung und politische Identität in frühen Hochkulturen. Dritte Auflage 2000. München (C.H.Beck).

Assmann, A. (1999): Erinnerungsräume. Formen und Wandlungen des kulturellen Gedächtnisses. München (C.H. Beck).

Aufenanger, St. (2000): Medien-Visionen und die Zukunft der Medienpädagogik. Plädoyer für Medienbildung in der Wissensgesellschaft. In: Medien praktisch. Zeitschrift für Medienpädagogik, 24, 2000, Heft 1, S. 4-8.

Döring, N. (2003): Sozialpsychologie des Internet. Die Bedeutung des Internet für Kommunikationsprozesse, Identitäten, soziale Beziehungen und Gruppen. 2. überarbeitete und erweiterte Auflage. Göttingen (Hogrefe).

Foot, K.; Warnick, B. (2005): Web-based Memorializing after September 11: Toward a Conceptual Framework. Journal of Computer-Mediated Communication: Volume 11, Issue 1, October 2005. http://jcmc.indiana.edu/vol11/issue1/foot.html

Freud, S. (1914): Erinnern, Wiederholen und Durcharbeiten. In: Sigmund Freud Studienausgabe Ergänzungsband: Schriften zur Behandlungstechnik. Frankfurt a.M. (Fischer). S. 205-215.

Freud, S. (1917): Trauer und Melancholie. In: Sigmund Freud: Studienausgabe Bd. III (Psychologie des Unbewußten). S. 193-212.

Halbwachs, M. (1925/1985): Das Gedächtnis und seine sozialen Bedingungen. Frankfurt/Main (Suhrkamp).

Hentig, H. von (1996): Bildung. München und Wien (Hanser).

Howard, Ph. N.; Jones, St. (Eds.) (2004): Society Online. The Internet in Context. Thousand Oaks, California (Sage).

Marotzki, W. (2003): Online-Ethnographie – Wege und Ergebnisse zur Forschung im Kulturraum Internet. In: Bachmeier, B.; Diepold, P.; de Witt, C. (Hrsg.) (2003): Jahrbuch Medienpädagogik 3. Opladen (Leske + Budrich). S. 149-166.

Marotzki, W. (2003a): Bildung und Internet. In: J. Beillerot/Ch. Wulf (Hrsg.): Erziehungswissenschaftliche Zeitdiagnosen: Deutschland und Frankreich. Münster u.a. (Waxmann). S. 126-141.

Marotzki, W. (2004): Von der Medienkompetenz zur Medienbildung. In: Brödel, R.; Kreimeyer, J. (Hrsg.) (2004): Lebensbegleitendes Lernen als Kompetenzentwicklung. Analysen – Konzeptionen – Handlungsfelder. Bielefeld (wbw Bertelsmann Verlag). S. 63-74.

Mittelstraß, J. (2002): Bildung und ethische Maße. In: Killius, N.; Kluge, J.; Reisch. L. (Hrsg.) (2002): Die Zukunft der Bildung. Frankfurt a. M. (Suhrkamp). S. 151-170.

Ricoeur, P. (2004): Gedächtnis, Geschichte, Vergessen. München (Fink).

Ricoeur, P. (2004a): Das Rätsel der Vergangenheit. Erinnern – Vergessen – Verzeihen. Vierte Auflage. Essen (Wallstein).

---

5   „Die kulturelle Formation ist das Medium, durch das eine kollektive Identität aufgebaut und über Generationen hinweg aufrecht erhalten wird." (Assmann 1997, 139)

Sartre, J.-P. (1943/1993): Das Sein und das Nichts. Reinbek bei Hamburg (Rowohlt).

Sumner, A. M. (2004): Kollektives Gedenken individualisiert: Die Hypermedia-Anwendung „The virtual Wall". In: Erll/Nünning (Hrsg.) (2004): Medien des kollektiven Gedächtnisses. Konstruktivität – Historizität – Kulturspezifität. Berlin, New York (Walter de Gruyter). S. 255-276.

Thiedeke, U. (Hrsg.), 2004: Soziologie des Cyberspace. Medien, Strukturen und Semantiken. Wiesbaden (Verlag für Sozialwissenschaften).

Woolgar, St. (Ed.) (2002): Virtual Society? Technology, Cyberbole, Reality. Oxford, New York (Oxford University Press).

Gustavo S. Mesch

Social Diversification: A Perspective for the Study of Social networks of Adolescents Offline and Online

Current academic and policy debates on the social implications of gaps in the ad-option of information and communication technologies have focused on the "digital divide" concept to describe the uneven social distribution and use of the Internet (Anderson et al., 1995; Fong, Wellman, Kew and Wilkes, 2004). Information and communication technologies (ICT's) are conceived as an agent of change in society because they support the rapid creation, diffusion and access of information, the formation of social networks, and the accumulation of social capital (Lin, 2001; DiMaggio et al., 2001). In this sense, many suggest that ICT's can reduce social inequalities by lowering the cost of information and enhancing the ability of socially marginal groups to gain human capital, compete for good jobs, and enhance their life chances (Anderson, et al., 1995). At the same time, many scholars are concerned that the Internet is creating a post-industrial society of information haves and have-nots that exacerbates rather than alleviate existing inequalities (DiMaggio and Hargittai, 2001). Reducing the digital divide has become a concern of social activists, non-profit organizations, political activists, and governments.

In exploring the implications of the digital divide, it is a common practice to distinguish between aspects of access (owning a computer, having access to the Internet and a broadband connection) and dimensions of use (general cultural literacy, degree of computer literacy, and differences in type of use) and the ability to evaluate the quality of information (DiMaggio, et al., 2001; Van Dijk, 2005). It can be argued that while physical access to computers and to the Internet is becoming increasingly universal, at least in western countries, the types of use differ and these differential patterns of use can lead to either two social outcomes: a reduction of social inequalities or its amplification. Use diversity is dramatically important because Internet network skills and digital literacy are acquired mainly by informal training (Van Dijk, 2005). The diffusion, contagion and adoption perspective argue that over time the gaps between social categories will shrink relatively and the digital divide in access and in use will be dramatically normalized

(Van Dijk, 2005). Others suggest that because Internet skills and kinds of use are soft skills, associated mainly with material wealth, income disparity, and the cultural capital of the household, the rate of information and online literacy skills will continue to accumulate differentially for those who have skills and those who do not. Therefore, the effect of differential acquisition of computer skills, online use, and Internet experience can produce a dramatic digital divide in the future (Van Dijk, 2005).

The focus of the research on Internet and social networks has been restricted mostly to the study of the effect of this technology on network size. The central question shaping the research agenda for many years has been whether the number of friends, family members, and neighbors with whom we are engaged is higher, lower, or the same for Internet users and non-users. (Kraut, et al., 1998.;Katz & Rice 2002). One neglected area in the study of the digital divide is the role of adoption of ICT'S on the structure and composition of social networks. One frequent use of ICT's is for the formation of new ties and the maintenance of existing ties as individuals use this channels of communication to search for individuals with shared interests and to maintain and develop family, personal and business associations. The argument of this chapter is that the extensive use for communication purposes among adolescents might lead to a change in the structure of the social networks exposing them to non similar individuals, overcoming the limitations of proximity, age and gender. This exposure to individuals with similar interests but different social background leads to a diversification of the adolescent's social network that might facilitate access to resources, information and knowledge, representing an investment in social capital and reducing social inequalities.

Internet Sociability and Social Diversification

At the center of the diversification approach is a conceptualization of ICT's as a space of activity and social interaction. The Internet is not only about communication with existing ties. Although is true that many adolescents are using the Internet as another channel of communication with existing relationships, the innovative aspect of the Internet is to provide opportunities for activities that induce social interaction resulting in providing a space for meeting new individuals, and in that sense the social use represents more than a communication channel, in many cases a space of social activity. Playing interactive games is more than playing games in a group of online members, and like in any game, groups are formed, interaction is recurrent and names and phone numbers are exchanged. Teenager forums are used for advice, social support and information search creating opportunities for social interaction and involvement. It is not uncommon that teens that know each other, introduce friends or family members to other friends and family members creating opportunities to socially interact with new acquaintances. The implication of this view is that the focus of inquiry are the motivations for online friendship formation, the differences between online and offline ties and the effect of online ties for the structure of adolescents' social network.

Societies are characterized by varying levels of social segregation. In societies that reward individuals differentially according to income, prestige, and power, stratifications systems result in a differential ability of individuals to gain access to jobs and residential locations. As a result, individual social associations tend to be with individuals of similar social characteristics such as age, gender, marital status, ethnicity, religion, and nationality. Studies on the formation, development, maintenance, and dissolution of close social relationships have emphasized the importance of homophily (McPherson, Smith-Lovin & Cook, 2002), which maintains that "contact and friendship formation between similar individuals occurs at a higher rate than among dissimilar individuals" (McPherson et al., 2002). Homophily is the result of the opportunity structure for interaction that emerges from the social structuring of activities in society. Feld (1981) uses the concept of foci of activity, defining them as "social, psychological, legal or physical objects around which joint activities are organized." Whether they are formal (school) or informal (regular hangouts), large (neighborhood) or small (household), foci of activity systematically constrain choices of friends. From this perspective, association with others is the result of a two-step process: foci of activity place individuals in proximity (for example, they provide opportunities for frequent meetings), which causes individuals to reveal themselves to each other. According to Feld (1982), whatever the basis of their initial association with a focus, it may be difficult, costly, and time consuming not to associate with certain individuals who share the same foci. For all these reasons, individuals' association with particular foci of activity may have unintended social consequences for them. Specifically, people tend to choose their friends from the set of people available through these foci.

Among adolescents, proximity is important for friendship formation because it establishes the boundaries within which they choose friends. Each individual occupies several separate but overlapping social worlds, each one is a potential sphere for association. A key location for meeting and making friends is school, where adolescents spend a large part of their waking hours. But other settings may be important as well. Adolescents spend their free time in neighborhood hang-outs that they frequent after school. In shopping malls, video arcades, and movie theaters, usually in the neighborhood or nearby, groups of adolescents get to know others who live in the same neighborhood but do not attend the same school (Cotterell, 1996).

I argue that unlike other groups that are geographically more mobile and exposed to more diverse foci of activity, adolescents lack geographic mobility and are trapped in social relationships that involve individuals similar to them. Consequently, an important motivation for adolescents to form online relationships is to diversify their social network and identify other individuals who share their interests, concerns, or problems but are not part of their social circle. Online social formation is thus not a general need, as not all the adolescents are involved in this activity, and is not the result of insufficient relationships with parents or friends, but merely the need to find other individuals with similar interests, not available in the social network because of its deterministic similarity. Thus diversification of social ties rather than needs for company and lack of social skills motivate online relationship formation. Although most adolescents are restricted geographically and dependent on public transportation, segregation in relationships with similar individuals varies according to social characteristics.

Diversification is a concept that can be linked to social capital. Although there are several accepted definitions and operationalizations of this concept, it is agreed that social capital refers to network ties that provide mutual support, shared language, shared norms, social trust, and a sense of mutual obligation from which people can derive value (Huysman &Wulf, 2004). The definition emphasizes the central role of the size, structure, composition, and trust in social networks. Based on these qualities, networks provide differential access to resources that include opportunities, skills, information, social support, and sociability. In the diversification perspective, the Internet is conceived as a social arena of shared activities. Therefore, social context mold relationship formation and not merely individual motivations and preferences. Social relationships are established in social contexts that bring individuals together for purposes that create opportunities for social interaction and expose individuals to each other. The context of friendship includes everything apart from the most immediate characteristics of the relationship itself. In this sense, a central concept that captures the social context of relationship formation is foci of activity that refers to any "social, psychological, legal and physical entity around which joint activities are organized" (Feld, 1981). Foci of activity can take many forms including the work place, school, neighborhood, voluntary organizations and the Internet. The common characteristic is that these are institutional arrangements that bring a relatively set of individuals together in repeated interactions around the focused activities. School is a social arrangement that brings individuals segregated according to age, to engage in learning, play and social interaction during an extended period in life (from childhood to adolescence). The Internet can be seen in the same way, as many adolescents participate in this space playing interactive games, participating in forums with specific or general topics, conducting homework together, exchanging files or information. As focus of activity, the Internet bring individuals to perform certain activity, social interaction develops and friendship formation is a "focused choice" a constrained choice that reflects social structure that systematically constrain choices to form and maintain relationships. In our example of the Internet, one structural characteristic is Internet access and it is obvious that individuals that do not have Internet access their friendships will reflect participation in other social settings. For all these reasons, the association of an individual with a particular foci may have unintended consequences for him or her. Specifically, people tend to choose friends from among those with whom they have regular contact, in one or another focused activity and the set of people who are available through these foci tends to direct their choices to individuals with particular characteristics.

Social Similarity and Friendship Formation among Adolescents

Prior to the Information age, adolescent's social choices were very restricted. Their lack of geographical mobility and belonging to a group age that is expected to attend school, structurally reduced their social circle to friends that were met in the neighborhood, school and extracurricular activities. Thus, proximity was a central social constrain for relationship formation. The structural constrain of opportunities for social interaction in a reduced number of foci of activity, resulted in high levels of friendship similarity. Living in the same neighborhood and attending the same school transpires in a high level of homophily, a notion that indicates that "contact and friendship formation between similar individuals occurs at a higher rate than among dissimilar individuals" (Mc Pherson, et al., 2002). Yet at the same time, friendship similarity has its costs, a lack of diversity that reduces the likelihood of finding peers when a new interest develops.

The cost of similarity, namely lack of individuals that can provide information and company when new interests develops results from the social embeddness of associations. A relationship between any two people is accompanied by relationships of those two people to many others who are themselves related to one another. Thus, a friendship that is embedded within such a set of relationships among the others is affected by the entire set of relationships. In that sense, the individual becomes trapped not only in the cultural and social similarity of his/her friends but in the similarity of friends of friends. In adolescents this embeddedness is clear, as society constrains their foci of activity to the neighborhood and school in which the relationships are embedded in social networks with a high similarity. The Internet, as a space of social interaction, as new foci of activity provides to teens a new venue for searching of like minded individuals with whom they can share activities and interests that are not represented in the extremely homogeneous offline social networks. Thus, individuals that report being linked to others that are similar to them, may be motivated to diversify their social circle by participating in activities in cyberspace. In other words, for individuals that are surrounded by friendships of individuals that are similar to them, that are geographically restricted, that their foci of activity are made of adolescents that are similar to them in their main characteristics, we expect that for them the internet appeals to find others that are different from them at least demographically. This expectation I have named the diversification hypothesis: I expect that for individuals that report having networks that are characterized by similarity the motivation to go out there and find new friends is driven by a motivation for diversity, for change, for meeting others that are different.

A second hypothesis related to the diversification perspective is social in nature. In the context of the Israeli society one should know that the major cleavage is between Jews and Arabs. This cleavage has cultural, religious and national roots resulting in a high level of residential segregation and most of the Arab and Israeli populations reside in different residential environments. Being more traditional, the Arab population is not only segregated from the Israeli population but is organized around patriarchal extended families that restrict the access to social networks. This social organization of the Arab villages leads to a high homogeneity in social networks that are mainly local, belonging to the same extended family and through gender lines. This high similarity in social networks is expected to be a motivation for making online friends, as through online friends it is possible to diversify the composition of the social network. In addition, and following the same argument we expect the existence of a high motivation for online friendship formation for other groups of adolescents.

Age is an important characteristic to consider for various reasons. First, studies have shown that gender segregation, this is the likelihood to associate with others from the same gender category is higher at the elementary and middle school and decreases in high school and apparently reflects a process of gender socialization. Second, age segregation in friendship has been extensively documented as a reflection of the age segregation that schools impose in their classrooms. Following our conceptualization of the Internet as a new space of activity and social interaction, in our study is expected that younger adolescents will report a higher motivation to take advantage of the Internet to diversify their social network.

Friendship is created in contexts of social activity. Proximity enforces similarity. During adolescence the most traditional contexts are school and the neighborhood in which the age grade structure of education facilitates the formation of friendships that are similar in age. Thus we expect that adolescents whose friends are similar in age and place of residence will be more motivated for friendships formation. The motivation for diversification of the friendship circle when the Internet is conceived as a space of activity and interaction provides structural oportunities that should be expected to be higher for individuals that report having a more homogeneous network. Two features in particular are expected to be important. First, the extent that friends reside in the same location is an indicator of similarity and adolescents seeking to diversify their social network will be more motivated to online friendship formation. Second, gender composition of the network should provide a motivation as well, as taking advantage of the features of the Internet facilitates friendship formation of cross gender associations.

Thus, different from studies that were concerned with ICT's access and use and whether ICT use decrease, increase or does not change the social and community involvement of individuals, the current study focus on the study of the consequences of ICT use on the structure of social networks. In particular whether Internet users reporting online friends have a more heterogeneous network than the ones that report not having met online friends.

Data

Survey data were collected in 2004. The survey covers a representative sample of 1,000 households in Israel. We began with a random sample of 60 localities with a population of 2,000 or more. Next, we selected neighborhoods-, according to the size of the adolescent population in each settlement. The survey includes items on social and demographic characteristics of the youths, socio-demographic characteristics of their closest friends, channels of communication, types of resources exchanged, and the extent of perceived closeness to each friend. The survey asked each adolescent for the names of six close friends. Respondent provided information about each friend's age, gender, place of residence; whether they met the friend for the first time at school, in the course of extracurricular activities, in the neighborhood, or online. The adolescents were also asked to indicate the length of time they have known the friend, the extent of closeness and trust they felt toward the friend, and whether they would ask for help from each of the friends listed. The analysis of the data in the current chapter is restricted to the first friend that was named by the respondent.

The surveys provide information about the amount (average hours) spent on the Internet, the frequency of use, and the type of Internet use interviewees used. The survey also included an open-ended question asking adolescents to indicate the average number of daily hours they were connected to the Internet. In addition, in the multivariate analysis we controlled for each adolescent's age, gender, number of siblings, and nationality (0=Arab Israeli and 1=Israeli Jew) and for mother's education.

Sample Description

Of the 1000 adolescents contacted, 987 agreed to participate in the study. Respondents' average age was 15.52 years (S.D. 1.66); girls and boys were almost equally represented (52% were boys). In terms of religious denomination, 79% were Israeli Jews. In terms of socioeconomic status, average father's education was 12.63 years (S.D. 3.50) and average mother's education was 12.52 years (S.D. 3.37). Regarding family status, 86.8% reported that their parents were married and 13.2% of parents were separated or divorced.

In the first step of data analysis we investigated the origin of the friends mentioned by Israeli adolescents. In the study was found that from the first friend named, 10.4 percent were met online, 63.3 percent at school, and 26.5 percent at the neighbourhood. In other words, around 10 percent of the adolescents that report using the Internet reported that at least one friend was met online. An interesting question is the link between online and offline friends. This question can be studied looking at the distribution of the friends named by the respondent according to the origin of the relationship and place of residence. Table 1 present the results.

The results show, as can be expected, that the vast majority of friends that were met at school and the neighbourhood reside in proximity to the adolescent. According to the results almost 92 percent of the friends that were met at school and 91 percent of the friends that were met in the neighbourhood live in the same neighbourhood or city. On the other side, friends that were met online are both local and non local. Almost 75 percent reside locally and a quarter resides in another city. Thus having online friends increases the diversity of residence of the members of the adolescent social network.

Table 1: Distribution of the place of residence of friends by origin of relationship

Place of residence	Origin of Relationship		
	Online	School	Neighborhood
Same neighborhood	24.6% (17)	39.11% (167)	64.0% (114)
Same city	50.7% (35)	52.0 (222)	27.0% (48)
Other city	24.6% (17)	7.7% (33)	7.9% (14)
Other country	0%	1.2% (5)	1.1% (2)
	100% (69)	100% (427)	100% (178)
n			674

The diversification framework implies that Internet users that have included online friends in their social network will report a more diverse composition of the network. Of importance is the extent of social network diversification according to characteristics such as age, gender and place of residence. Table 2 present the proportion of similar friends according to the origin of the relationship.

Table 2. Diversification according to age, gender and place of residence

	2004		
	School	Neighborhood	Online
Proportion same age	90.2	80.1	77%
Proportion same gender	92.0	88.2	69%
Proportion same residence	93.2	93.7	74.8

According to Table 2 the proportion of friends from the same age, gender category and same residence differs according to the place in which the friend was met. Adolescents having an online friend in their social network report the lowest proportion of friends that are from the same age, from the same gender category and from the same place of residence. Thus, adolescents having met a friend online, have a more diversified social network in terms of age, gender and place of residence.

The final question to be explored in this paper is what the motivations for online friendship formation are. The hypothesis derived from the diversification framework implies that is not loneliness, social isolation or low self esteem the factors that are driving online friendship formation but the need for diversification of social network. In other words, individuals that report a higher similarity in terms of age, gender and place of residence will report a higher likelihood of friendship formation. The results of a logistic regression predicting having at least one friend that was met online was conducted and the results are presented in Table 3.

The central results support the hypothesis that online friendship formation is particularly appealing to individuals who report an homogeneous social network of peers. These individuals are more likely to create online social relationships. According to the results, Arab Israeli adolescents were more likely to make online friendships. The conditions of the Arab Israeli society that is residentially segregated to their villages and cities in which the social organization is based on the identification with the extended family, results in restrictions in the kind of social relationships that are created. Social relationships in the Arab village are based on the intersection of a number of characteristics: Propinquity, relationship formation along gender lines and high social control. Propinquity means that individuals are exposed in their residential environment mainly to members of the extended family and opportunities for association are structurally restricted, as the likelihood of association is higher with other adolescents that belong to the same extended family. An important role of the extended family is to make use of space to enforce segregation in friendships according to gender lines, in order to protect any contact between family and non family members and among members of the same family before a wedding has been arranged or agreed. Space in the context the arab village represents a powerful instrument to reproduce the type of relationships that is accepted by the society and culture.

In addition, more empirical support for the diversification hypothesis is provided by the effect of gender and residential proximity. In the survey respondents reporting a high degree of gender similarity with their friends and a high similarity in place of residence were more likely to make friends online. On the other side, the effect of age similarity was non-significant.

Discussion

In this chapter we investigated extent to which Internet use is associated with changes in the structure of social relationships. To this end we focused on one well-known characteristic of social networks: homophily, a principle stating that social contacts between similar individuals occur at a higher rate than among dissimilar people (McPherson, Smith-Lovin & Cook, 2002). Homophily means that cultural, behavioral, or material information flows through networks of similar individuals providing advantages to some and disadvantages to others according to the composition of the social network. A distinction should be made between status and value homophily. Status refers to similarity based on ascribed status such as age, gender, or ethnicity, whereas value homophily is based on values, attitudes, and beliefs The two types are not entirely distinct, as social status at least partially shape values, attitudes, and beliefs. The focus in this chapter is on status homophily.

Table 3. A logistic regression prediciting the likelihood of Making friends online:

Variable name	Parameter Estimate	Odds Ratio
Age	-.142 (.111)	.868
Gender (1=boy)	.270 (.346)	1.310
Nationality (1=Jew)	-.905 (.543)	.404**
Mother's Education	.052 (.054)	1.054
Parental Status (1=Married)	-.174 (.354)	.840
Child Parent Conflict	-1.113 (.629)	.329
Self Esteem	-.034 (.181)	.967
Family Time	.413 (.203)	1.511**
Spending Weekends Alone	.288 (.420)	1.334
Closeness to Friends	.103 (.090)	1.108
Daily Internet use	.038 (.042)	1.039
Internet Use for Social Purposes	.162 (.097)	1.176
Internet Use for Instrumental purposes	.059 (.064)	1.061
Place of Residence Similarity	-1.512 (.368)	.221*
Gender Similarity	2.009 (.553)	7.456*
Constant	5.883* (2.091)	
-2 Log Likelihood (initial)	288.992	
-2 Log Likelihood (Final)	239.898	
Neglerke R Square	.340	
*p<.01, **p<.05		

The tendency toward homophily in social relationships is more intense among adolescents, a group that is restricted in physical mobility and spaces of social interaction, and therefore in the contexts in which friends can be met (Berndt & Ladd, 1989). The Internet has changed social interactions by providing all of us, and adolescents in particular, with a new space for social interaction.

Because this new space is not limited by similarity, the question arises to what extent the similarity of the social network differs for individuals that have met friends online and the ones that did not

We have seen that for some users, the Internet is becoming another location to meet and socialize and relations created there tend also to migrate to other settings (Wolak, J., et al, 2003; Mesch and Levanon. 2003). As individual are less controlled by social traditional authorities, they can go beyond their local groups' boundaries, using all kinds of media (Wellman, 2001). As the Internet provides the informational space and collective organization for social interaction, through time ties that were created online become new social ties that are integrated in the social life of the adolescent (Parks and Floyd, 1996; McKenna, Green and Gleason, 2002). We found that having online friends diversified the composition of the social network according to age, gender and place of residence. We also found support for the diversification framework implying that social similarity is a main motivation for online friendship formation. Future studies should inquiry whether social diversification of social networks that results from the use of ICT's can reduce social inequalities by lowering the cost of accesing information and enhancing the ability of socially marginal groups to gain human capital, compete for good jobs, and enhance their life chances (Anderson, et al., 1995).

The diversification approach represent a more sociological way of looking at the association between Internet use and social interactions, as it is not restricted to the investigation of network size. The evidence found for network diversification should motivate future studies that take a closer look at the resources exchanged and the long term effects of increased network heterogeneity for social capital formation. It is very likely that network diversification contributes to the reduction of social inequalities in society, through the acquisition of resources for members of disadvantaged groups that through electronic communication are able to reach resources and information that were not previously available to them.

References

Anderson, Robert, Tora Bikxon, Sally Ann Law and Birdger Mitchell. (1995). Universal access to E-mail: Feasibility and Social Implications. Santa Monika, CA: Rand Foundation.

Cotterell, John. (1996). Social Networks and Social Influences in Adolescence. London: Routledge.

DiMaggio, Paul and Eszter Hargitai. (2001). From the Digital Divide to the Digital Inequality. Working Paper: Princeton University.

Feld, Scott. (1981). "The Focused Organization of Social Ties." American Journal of Sociology 86: 1015-1035.

Feld, Scott. (1982). "Social Structural Determinants of Similarity among Associates." American Sociological Review 47: 797-801.

Fong, Eric, Barry Wellman, Melissa Kew and Rima Wilkes.(2001). "Correlates of the Digital Divide: Individual, Household and Spatial Variation." Report to Office of Learning Technologies, Human Resources Development Canada, June, 84 pp.

Katz, James, E. and Ronald E. Rice.(2002). Social Consequences of Internet use. Access Involvement and Interaction. Cambridge, MA: MIT Press.

Kraut, Robert, Micahel Patterson, Vicki Lundmark, Sara Kiesler, Tridas Mukopadhyay and William Scherlis. (1998). "Internet Paradox: A Social Technology that Reduces Social Involvement and Psychological Well-Being?" American Psychologist 53: 1011-1031.

Lin, Nan. (2001): Social Capital: A Theory of Social Structure and Action. Cambridge, Cambridge University Press Horton,

McPherson, Miller, Lyn Smith-Lovin and James M. Cook. (2002). "Birds of a Feather: Homophile in Social Networks." Annual Review of Sociology 27: 415-444.

McKenna, Katelin., Amie .S. Green and Marcie .E.G. Gleason. 2002. "Relationship Formation on the Internet: What is the Big Attraction?" Journal of Social Issues 58: 9-31.

Mesch, Gustavo S. and Yael Levanon.(2003). "Community Networking and Locally-Based Social Ties in Two Suburban Localities." City and Community 2: 335-351.

Parks, Malcom R. and Kory Floyd. 1996. "Making Friends in Cyberspace." Journal of Communication 46: 80-97.

Van Dijk, Jan. (2005). The Deepening Divide: Inequality in the Information Society. London: Sage Publications

Wellman, Barry. (2001). "Computer Networks As Social Networks." Science 293: 2031-2034.

Wolak, Janis, Mitchell Kimberly.J. and David Finkelhor (2003). "Escaping or Connecting? Characteristics of Youth Who Form Close Online Relationships." Journal of Adolescence 26: 105-119.

**Use Differences and Social Inequality in the
Internet / Nutzungsdifferenzen und Soziale
Ungleichheit im Internet**

*Eszter Hargittai**

A framework for studying differences in people's digital media uses

Introduction

Information technologies have become a staple of adolescents' lives with young people among the most connected in countries that have seen high levels of Internet and cell phone diffusion by the first decade of the 21st century (Livingstone and Bober 2004; National Telecommunications and Information Administration 2004). However, merely knowing various digital media's rates of use says little about how young people are incorporating IT into their everyday lives. Ignoring nuanced measures of use, it is difficult to determine whether digital media are leveling the playing field for youth or whether they are raising new barriers for some while advantaging the societal positions of others. While many have suggested that we must move past the binary classification of haves and have-nots when it comes to information technology uses, few have offered a detailed conceptual framework for such an undertaking, one that can then inform empirical studies of usage differences. This chapter considers the various domains in which users of the Internet may possess different levels of know-how. In addition to presenting the conceptual framework, it also draws on unique data about a diverse group of young people's Internet uses to illustrate existing diffe-rences along the lines of the discussed dimensions.

Refined approaches to the digital divide

Initial work looking at differences in the Internet's diffusion looked at the so-called "digital divide" focusing on a binary classification of haves and have-nots regar-

* The author would like to thank Brigid Barron, Greg Duncan, Karen Mossberger and Connie Yo-well for helpful conversations on this topic, Ann Feldman and Tom Moss for supporting the study at UIC, and Laurell Sims, Dan Li, Vanessa Pineda and Erika Priestley for assistance with data collection and data entry. The author is also grateful to the John D. and Catherine T. MacArthur Foundation, the Northwestern University Research Grants Committee, the Northwestern School of Communication Innovation Fund and the Northwestern Department of Communication Research Fund for their support.

ding digital technologies (for a review, see DiMaggio et al. 2004). Findings from the first investigations showed that while the Internet was diffusing to an increasing number of users, the spread of the medium happened at unequal rates depending on the population segment (Bimber 2000; Bucy 2000; Hargittai 2003; Hargittai 2004b; Loges and Jung 2001; NTIA 2000; 2004; Norris 2001; Wilhelm 2000). Moving the agenda forward, recent work has increasingly broadened the research program to focus on refined measures of access and use including quality of access, context and intensity of use, types of utilization and user abilities (Attewell 2001; Bonfadelli 2002; Bunz 2004; DiMaggio et al. 2004; Hargittai 2002; Hargittai 2004b; Howard, Rainie and Jones 2001; Katz and Rice 2002; Mossberger, Tolbert and Stansbury 2003; van Dijk 2005; Warschauer 2003; Wellman et al. 2002). In these investigations, the differences are no longer considered as a dichotomous property; rather, they exist on a spectrum. In fact, DiMaggio et al. (2004) advocate the use of the term "digital inequality" instead of "digital divide" to reflect more accurately the varying levels of use and their potential social implications. In this chapter, I continue the tradition of exploring refined measures of digital inequality. In particular, I focus on ways in which differences in users' understanding of online tools and services may encourage or hinder the extent to which people can optimally benefit from their use of digital media.

Refined data about average users' online behavior show that while some activities are nearly universal (e.g. the majority of users say they have sent or received email), many activities are a much less common practice (Madden 2003). Even activities in which a large proportion of users engages are not distributed equally among people depending on their background characteristics. For example, on the aggregate, one study found that eighty percent of American users have looked for some type of health-related information online (Fox 2005). However, once this activity is broken down by type of user, we find that 87 percent of those with a broadband connection at home sought some health information on the Web, while only 72 percent of those with a home dial-up connection did so. Also, Internet veterans (in the case of Fox's study people who have been online for six or more years) are considerably more likely to have engaged in such an activity (86%) compared to those who have 2-3 years of online experience (66%). These figures suggest that certain attributes of users' Internet-related experiences (i.e. quality of connection, history of Web use) influence the types of activities they pursue online.

Of course, more refined analyses are necessary to draw conclusions about the independent effect of any particular factor on people's online engagements. In the above case, those who started using the Internet later and who do not have high-speed connections at home may differ from others in various ways (e.g. lower income, lower education), which may then be related to their propensity to search for health information in the first place. Nonetheless, these relationships are important to note and suggest that growth in basic user statistics does not necessarily mean that everybody is taking advantage of the medium in similar ways. Since those who have become users in the recent past are not equivalent in demographics to early adopters, uses by veteran status may differ not only due to different levels of experience, but as a result of differences in user attributes as well.

As the amount of information online has grown exponentially over the years, the need for tools to sift through the material and keep track of updates has gotten larger. Search engines and portal sites have evolved to meet some of the needs of users in this more complex environment (Hargittai 2004a), nonetheless, they still require a certain level of understanding and skill for efficient uses (Hargittai 2002). Although, the Internet offers information on every imaginable topic, it is easy to get lost in the vastness of resources and not always trivial to find that special nugget of material of particular interest to the user. If those in need of certain types of material are unable to find it, the mere availability of the content will not aide them. Moreover, increases in volume have also meant the rising presence of incorrect information (whether inaccurate intentionally or not) and scams. Evaluating the credibility of online content itself poses a challenge to the utility one might be able to derive from time spent online.

Thus, people's ability to find desired types of information and their capacity to evaluate the credibility of the material they come across compose an important part of the medium's potential to contribute to people's everyday needs and well-being, and ultimately improve their life chances. Conversely, the lack of ability in these domains may disadvantage others. A nuanced approach to digital inequality takes a critical look at how people are able to benefit from digital media once they have gained access to them. The following section breaks down the realms in which advanced know-how is necessary for informed participation in the digital world.

Informed User Participation

Differential know-how and practices have the potential to fragment users and perpetuate existing social inequalities. As discussed above, nuanced measures of use are necessary to delineate exactly how different people may benefit to varying degrees from their engagement with digital media. In order to know what differences to observe and track empirically, it is important to have a conceptual framework for the types of ways in which digital media uses may diverge across users.

This section presents an eleven-item list that encompasses numerous ways in which people's online activities and know-how may differ. All of these aspects of use may contribute to differences in online abilities and thereby hinder those who lack them and advantage those who possess them.

The following items contribute to users' ability to make the most of their time spent online. While these categories are not mutually exclusive, they fall into various substantively distinct domains that are worthy of investigation on their own. Studies can focus on just one or two of these dimensions, or they may attempt to encompass most or all of them. The latter approach allows for comparisons across the domains. The focus on just a few enables more in-depth investigations, however, so both may lead to valuable insights.

The description of each point below is not meant to be an exhaustive elaboration of what types of activities fall under the respective headings. The examples are just meant as illustrations to guide the reader in understanding the various domains of know-how. Moreover, while cases mainly focus on use of the Internet on a personal computer, they also apply to the use of other digital media such as PDAs and cell phones, platforms that are becoming increasingly common for communicating with others as well as accessing and sharing content. Finally, while many of these factors are relevant with respect to the use of other media as well, the focus here is on developments of the last decade in the digital landscape.

1. Effective and safe ways of communicating with others

While basic email communication may seem simple, a sophisticated approach to exchanging messages with others involves more than simply knowing how to compose and send a note to another user. Rather, issues from professionalism to privacy all have to be taken into consideration when managing one's email exchanges. Potential concerns range from writing a clear subject line that maximizes chances of receiving a response to not divulging too much information in certain types of interactions.

One particular feature of email that is unknown to many is the option to copy multiple recipients blindly – or "bccing" a list of people – when sending out a note. There are occasions when one might want to send out the same message to several people, but it is not advisable for everyone to see all other people's names on the list. An example of such a situation may concern applicants to a job who are being emailed in bulk. It is not possible to maintain confidentiality in such a case if all recipients are included in the "cc" line, the one that makes all addresses visible to all others on the list. Nonetheless, such mistakes are common and lead to embarrassment on behalf of both the sender and some of the recipients.

2. Knowledge of how to contribute to group conversations and share content

One of the unique aspects of online communication as compared to more traditional media is that users can contribute their own opinions and content much more easily than in many other domains. Such contributions can best be grouped into two relatively distinct although not necessarily mutually exclusive categories: (1) commenting in response to material created and shared by others; and (2) posting one's own content for others to access. While the Internet makes such contributions much more straight forward than other media, effective communication and participation still presupposes some skills.

Some recent developments in Internet services are good examples of this point. Users may read blogs, but it is an additional step to know that leaving a comment is an option. Also, users may consult sites that are compiled by numerous people (e.g. wikis like Wikipedia), but knowing how to edit a page on such a site is a whole other step in the process with which many are not familiar.

It is also possible to take a more active role in this realm, but only for those who possess certain necessary skills. For example, users may create mailing lists or entire Web sites with adjoining forums dedicated to a topic of interest. There are lots of opportunities for this online (whether within a particular site such as the photo-sharing site Flickr or less structured out on the open Web through, for example, Yahoo! Groups or Google Groups), but different users are not equally aware of them nor would they necessarily know how to navigate such services.

3. Knowledge about and use of tools

In addition to services such as blogs and wikis that all have their own particular systems, there are additional tools available to users nowadays that allow more efficient navigation of online content (and beyond). From feed readers (e.g. Bloglines) to social bookmarking sites (e.g. del.icio.us), new tools are allowing sophisticated users to employ a multitude of approaches to finding and following online content. Similarly, additions to software (in some cases free software, e.g. Firefox) also improve considerably upon certain navigational practices. For example, extensions to the Firefox browser program make all sorts of functionalities accessible at the click of a button. For example, a user can create an image snapshot of the entire Web page on the screen for archiving purposes – as opposed to an image of simply what is viewable in the browser window –, or a user can render Web pages differently from their original layout, but many of these functionalities do not come bundled with the software and so users need to know how they can find extensions of interest and what they have to do to the program to implement them.

4. Knowledge of what is available online

When encountering a question in everyday life, how likely is a user to realize that answers to the question are likely available online? While some users may automatically turn to the Web no matter the type of information, others may only think to look for answers online in particular instances. These queries can range from factual information to opinion pieces, from contact information to free tools and services. For example, would it occur to all users that sophisticated photo-editing programs exist online that can be obtained free legally (e.g. Gimp)? Do users know about alternate licensing schemes for content that allows non-commercial use of material for free (e.g. Creative Commons licenses)? Would all users think to look online for legally free copies of entire books (e.g. Alice in Wonderland) before proceeding to purchase a copy in a store (whether online or not)? These questions all concern a user's know-how about what is even possible before taking the next step of searching for it.

5. Ability to find content

Once a user recognizes that it is worth looking online for a particular type of content, the next step concerns finding this content in the chaos of billions and billions of Web pages. Although search engines have improved over the years tremendously, they are far from being able to guess the exact intentions of a user and therefore particular skills are required on the part of the user to find the sought after content, especially on topics that are less mainstream. For example, finding the email address of a person is not always trivial, especially if it is for a person whose name is fairly common and the person is less prominent online.

6. Efficiency in Web navigation

Being able to find material on the Web is one thing, doing so efficiently is another. Many people lead busy lives that do not allow for much time in front of the computer. When that is the case, a user cannot spend too much time on any one query. If relevant results do not start showing up in response to various initial clicks and queries, the user might abandon the task and may seek the desired information using another method altogether (e.g. going and talking to someone) that may or may not result in a satisfactory outcome and may take even longer to achieve. Refined information-seeking skills are necessary to find content quickly. For example, knowing how to exclude terms from a search can be important in the case of ambiguous queries (i.e. where the term may have multiple meanings), but few people know that typing a hyphen right before a word (no spaces) will yield such a result.

7. Ability to assess source and message credibility

With the growing potential to make money online, more and more content providers – and in some cases outright scammers – have flooded the network. On occasion intentionally, in others by accident, the content a user encounters is not necessarily correct. There are several steps involved in dealing with such a situation. First, users have to recognize that cases of misinformation exist online and they should not take for granted material they see on the Web. After recognizing that online content may not always reflect quality content, users need to know how to collect information about the source of material to determine whether it is legitimate. This is not always a trivial undertaking.

These skills are important not only while users are out on the open Web, but also while they are checking their email. Lots of scams come through on email and people must recognize that email messages cannot be trusted inherently either. From requests for help originating across the globe to notifications about a necessary password change on the user's account, users are often bombarded with deceitful messages. One indication of many users' inability to stop and consider email content is the prevalence of people forwarding chain messages that contain nothing but hoaxes and often unnecessary and unsubstantiated rumors about situations supposedly in need of assistance. Both the belief that these are real crises and the assumption that forwarding an email will help such a situation suggest a lack of critical approach to messages on behalf of users.

8. Understanding of privacy issues

Online services have become increasingly sophisticated in tracking the actions of their users. But to what extent do people realize these practices and are they aware of the particular types of technologies that are making their actions ever-more trackable? Do people consciously think about not divulging too much information while they surf the Web? This issue raises concerns not only in the realms of financial life (e.g. the loss of one's credit card information), but also in the realm of political and religious expression and the domain of health, just to name a few.

Options certainly exist for restricting the amount of information that sites and companies collect about users, but one has to possess a certain level of know-how to (1) recognize that there is an issue that needs to be addressed; and (2) know where to turn – what tools or actions – to protect oneself. While there are a myriad of ways in which unwanted junk mail may end up in users' mailboxes, some of the reasons can be traced back to users' actions easily. However, not being aware of how these things happen, users continue to engage in actions that do not serve their best interests.

In another example, many users seem to have a false sense of anonymity while online. People have been known to lose jobs over divulging too much information in settings where anonymity was assumed incorrectly. While users can take steps to minimize the traceability of their online actions, how many are aware of the necessary steps to do this well and how many realize that being completely anonymous is nearly impossible?

9. Understanding of security issues

Related to the previous point is the question of security. Not divulging too much information is essential to maintaining the security of sensitive information. Do users stop to think about the context of, for example, a message that requests confidential information from them? If everyone was aware of these issues and careful as a consequence then phishing emails – messages that pretend to be from a reputable source to extract confidential information from users – would not lead to people giving up their passwords to Web sites that contain private information such as bank accounts.

10. Knowledge of where and how to seek assistance with questions

No matter one's level of user sophistication, it is unlikely that users exist who do not, at least on occasion, require some assistance with an online service, a search, or a tool to contribute to conversations. Lots of options exist on the Web to seek assistance from other users, however, these opportunities are not always obvious. From the serious to the trivial, communities have come together to offer insights on each others' queries. Some of these are more reliable than others. But many provide valuable information often for free. Examples include Yahoo! Answers for any topic imaginable to a very specialized site solely focusing on the use of one spreadsheet application, MrExcel.com. But in order to benefit from others' know-how, users have to either know about these options or have the ability to realize such communities exist (see #4 above) and know how to find them (as per #5 above).

11. Customization

More and more services are allowing customization by users. This feature has been around since the early days of the Web with one prominent example the personalized home pages that big portals provided to their users. One could get weather, stock, sports, movie information plus quick access to one's email account on just one page. These services have continued to expand and many others nowadays give users the option of creating customized rules to meet their particular needs. For example, mail applications allow users to configure spam filters or filters to organize incoming email messages upon their arrival. Feed readers are another example, giving users the opportunity to follow numerous sources of information through just one interface. While available to all users, many of these services have not seen mass diffusion. As with every other dimension mentioned here, certain levels of skill are necessary to take advantage of these services so those who lack them are much less likely to adopt them and benefit from their assistance.

Some of the above areas have seen considerable investigation by scholars (e.g. on information seeking) while others remain largely unexplored. Moreover, many related studies limit their scope to convenience samples of college students leading to results with limited generalizability. Additionally, many such projects do not collect detailed data on users' background characteristics making it impossible to consider how observed variation about online abilities relates to users' attributes. These shortcomings of the existing corpus of work in this realm limit our understanding of how skill factors relate to questions of social inequality, which is why gathering data on these dimensions in conjunction with user background characteristics is essential. The next section draws on precisely such data to illustrate briefly the types of differences by user attributes that we find regarding some online abilities.

Differences in Young People's Internet Uses

To illustrate that users do, in fact, differ on the usage dimensions discussed above, this section provides empirical evidence from a unique data set. Findings presented here are based on data collected by the author in February-March, 2006. A survey was administered to a diverse group of students at the University of Illinois, Chicago, an urban public research university in the United States. Participating students were all enrolled in the one required class on campus: the First-Year Writing Program. Given that this course is required of all students, surveying this group poses no selection bias concerning the university's student population.

College students offer the ideal population to study differential IT uses given their high – often 100 percent – connectivity levels and frequent uses of the medium. Does ubiquitous connectivity mean ever-increasing skills and intense participation or do differences in abilities and contributions remain even when we control for access to the medium? This data set allows us to address these questions and illustrate differential know-how regarding some of the skill dimensions discussed in the previous section.

The data presented here represent 1,160 first-year students who took the survey. Table 1 includes some descriptive statistics about the demographics of the group suggesting considerable diversity in socio-economic background and academic achievements while largely controlling for age. Table 2 includes some information about the sample's IT access and uses. The figures in Table 2 clearly suggest that this is very much a wired generation given the number of years the average user has been online, how frequently students use the Internet, the number of locations of access and high levels of computer and cell phone ownership. Consequently, nuanced measures of use are especially relevant since basic measures of use may obfuscate very real differences in actual usage and skill and do not allow us to distinguish too much among sample respondents. Looking at such a wired group of users allows us to control for basic access to digital media and focus on details of use and know-how instead.

Previous work has shown that measures of a respondent's self-perceived online ability is not an optimal proxy for actual skills (Hargittai 2005) with particular concerns about the gender bias in such measures (Hargittai and Shafer 2006). Therefore, in addition to presenting figures about self-perceived skill, we also look at other variables that indicate various levels of online know-how.

When asked what level of expertise they consider themselves to possess, 6.4 percent of the sample indicated to be not at all or not very skilled, 52.2 percent claimed to be fairly skilled, 33.0 percent believed themselves to be very skilled and the remaining 8.5 percent thought of themselves as experts. While not an optimal proxy for actual skills, these measures do give us an idea of how college students think about their online abilities. Insofar as attitude influences activity, this measure is worthy of note since it suggests that some people approach their online activities with much more confidence than others. Self-perceived Internet skill is positively correlated, at a statistically significant level, with parental education and performance on the college entrance exam (as measured by the American College Testing score).

Attitudinal differences may translate into variations in online behavior especially regarding what types of activities a user may attempt. In that sense, it is valuable to note that there is considerable variance in how students perceive their Internet user skills and that this perception is not randomly distributed among study participants. In particular, those from less privileged backgrounds and with lower academic aptitude are more skeptical about their online abilities potentially disadvantaging them with respect to how they embrace digital media and the extent to which they derive benefits from them.

Next, let us consider students' level of understanding regarding various Internet-related items. It is valuable to split these terms into two categories signifying different types of familiarity with the Internet: (1) terms about basic Internet use; (2) terms describing more recent Web developments. By considering these two constructs separately, we can disaggregate a more general type of familiarity with the Internet from a higher-level understanding that concerns recent developments. Both are measured here using an index variable that was constructed from several items. These items ask respondents to rank their level of understanding of various terms on a 5-point scale from no understanding to full understanding. These measures were derived from methods developed in earlier work on proxies for actual skill measures (Hargittai 2005).

The index measure of basic Internet terms contains the following items: frames, preference settings, pdf, spam, jpg, bookmark, newsgroup, mp3, and browser. Cronbach's alpha for this construct is .88. Not surprisingly, the resulting index is somewhat skewed with the majority of people scoring high. This is expected since the terms making up this variable will be familiar to many long-time users, which is characteristic of this sample's majority. The value of this index ranges from 9-48. Its mean is 32 with 75 percent of respondents scoring a 26 or above. Nonetheless, some differences are apparent. Moreover, these differences are statistically significantly related to some user attributes. In particular, students with lower reported grades, with lower reported college entrance exam scores and with lower parental educational backgrounds indicate lower levels of understanding even regarding the understanding of very basic Internet terms. This suggests that even at the level of basic Internet use, a one hundred percent wired group is not on the same footing when it comes to basic know-how.

The second construct includes terms focusing on more recent Web developments: bookmarklet, feed reader, malware, mashup, phishing, podcasting, RSS (real simple syndication), social bookmarking, tabbed browsing, torrent, tagging, Web feeds, widget, and wiki. Cronbach's alpha for this index is .91. This index is also skewed, although this time in the other direction with the majority of users claiming low levels of understanding. This measure ranges from 14-70 with a mean of 28. In this case, more than 75 percent of respondents got less than half the maximum score with a value of 34 at the 75th percentile. Similarly to the other variable, we find a statistically significant positive relationship between this score and some background variables, namely: parents' educational background and college admissions test score. Students whose parents have higher educational degrees and students who score higher on the ACT exam report a higher level of familiarity with recent Web developments. Similarly to observations presented in the previous paragraph, these findings again suggest a better position with respect to the Internet for those who are already more privileged.

Conclusion

The goal of this chapter has been to offer a framework for thinking about and studying user abilities in our digital world. There are multiple dimensions along which users may differ and studying each is imperative for a more holistic picture of where inequalities may lie with respect to the new opportunities offered by information technologies. The following are the dimensions described in detail in this piece, all pertaining to actions performed online:

1. Effective and safe ways of communicating with others
2. Knowledge of how to contribute to group discussions and share content
3. Knowledge about and use of tools
4. Knowledge of what is available
5. Ability to find content
6. Efficiency in Web navigation
7. Ability to assess source and message credibility
8. Understanding of privacy issues
9. Understanding of security issues
10. Knowledge of where and how to seek assistance with questions
11. Customization

These eleven areas all pose both challenges and opportunities to users. Those who possess a high level of familiarity and understanding of each dimension of use described here will be in a considerably better position to derive benefits from digital media than those who lack expertise in these domains. In fact, depending on the extent to which certain users may not appreciate some of the nuances of usage, they may even suffer negative consequences due to scams and fraud.

As the Internet has matured and has made way for an increasing number of opportunities, it has also opened up possibilities for deception. The options are limitless; both in the realm of the good and in the realm of the bad especially while traditional institutions such as legal systems take time to catch up with many new developments. While technical improvements and government policy may address some of the above issues, those interventions take time necessitating the need for an informed user base. Whether "Cyberworld Unlimited" turns out to be beneficial for all people, and all youth in particular, will depend on more than mere usage. Different dimensions of skill will influence the outcome. And since skill seems to mirror a student's existing societal position, it is unlikely that benefits will be distributed equally on their own. Rather, training intervention may be necessary to provide an equal playing field so all youth have a chance to avoid the pitfalls of the digital terrain, and instead, have a chance to reap its benefits.

Table 1. Descriptive statistics about the sample

	Percentage
Female (N=1,157)	59.9
Age (N=1,160)	
18	67.2
19	30.1
20 and older	2.7
Parental education (N=1,145)	
Neither parent has high school degree	7.7
Both parents have no more than high school degree	25.1
One parent has college degree, other does not	23.5
Both parents have at least a college degree	27.1
Grades (N=1,138)	
Mostly As	20.1
As and Bs	33.3
Mostly Bs	18.2
Bs and Cs or lower	28.4
ACT scores (N=930) – analyzed as a continuous variable	
16-19	11.2
20-23	39.1
24-27	40.4
28 and higher	9.3

Table 2. Basic IT access & use statistics for sample participants

	Percentage
Number of years online (N = 1,156)	
1-4	10.1
5	22.8
6 or more	67.0
Number of Internet access locations (N = 1,160)	
1-2	13.4
3-4	37.8
5 or more	48.9
Number of Internet use locations (N = 1,160)	
1	20.0
2	42.2
3 or more	37.8
Regular access location has high-speed connection (N = 1,093)	95.2
Uses chat (N = 1,152)	82.3
Uses VoIP (N = 1,160)	17.2
Goes online more than once a day (N = 1,158)	83.7
Owns a computer (laptop or desktop or both) (N = 1,160)	98.0
Has cell phone (N = 1,158)	96.6

References

Attewell, P. 2001. "The first and second digital divides." Sociology of education 74:252-259.

Bimber, B. 2000. "The Gender Gap on the Internet." Social Science Quarterly 81:868-876.

Bonfadelli, Heinz. 2002. "The Internet and Knowledge Gaps. A Theoretical and Empirical Investigation." European Journal of Communication 17:65-84.

Bucy, E. 2000. "Social Access to the Internet." Harvard International Journal of Press/Politics 5:50-61.

Bunz, Ulla. 2004. "The Computer-Email-Web Fluency Scale: Development and Validation." International Journal of Human-Computer Interaction 17:477-504.

DiMaggio, Paul, Eszter Hargittai, Coral Celeste, and Steven Shafer. 2004. "Digital Inequality: From Unequal Access to Differentiated Use." Pp. 355-400 in Social Inequality, edited by Kathryn Neckerman. New York: Russell Sage Foundation.

Fox, Susannah. 2005. "Health Information Online." Washington, D.C.: Pew Internet and American Life Project.

Hargittai, Eszter. 2002. "Second-Level Digital Divide: Differences in People's Online Skills." First Monday 7.

–. 2003. "The Digital Divide and What To Do About It." in The New Economy Handbook, edited by Derek C. Jones. San Diego, Calif: Academic Press.

–. 2004a. "The Changing Online Landscape: From Free-for-All to Commercial Gatekeeping." in Community Practice in the Network Society: Local Action/Global Interaction, edited by Peter and Doug Schuler Day: Routledge.

–. 2004b. "Internet Access and Use in Context." New Media & Society 6.

–. 2005. "Survey Measures of Web-Oriented Digital Literacy." Social Science Computer Review 23.

Hargittai, Eszter, and Steven Shafer. 2006. "Differences in Actual and Perceived Online Skills: The Role of Gender." Social Science Quarterly.

Howard, Philip N., Lee Rainie, and Steve Jones. 2001. "Days and Nights on the Internet: The Impact of a Diffusing Technology." American Behavioral Scientist 45:383-404.

Katz, J.E., and R.E. Rice. 2002. Social Consequences of Internet Use: Access, Involvement and Interaction. Cambridge, MA: MIT Press.

Livingstone, Sonia., and Magdalena Bober. 2004. "UK Children Go Online." Pp. 1-61: Economic & Social Research Council.

Loges, William E., and Joo-Young Jung. 2001. "Exploring the Digital Divide: Internet Connectedness and Age." Communications Research 28:536-562.

Madden, Marry. 2003. "America's Online Pursuits." Washington, D.C.: Pew Internet and American Life Project.

Mossberger, Karen, Caroline J. Tolbert, and Mary Stansbury. 2003. Virtual Inequality: Beyond the Digital Divide. Washington, D.C.: Georgetown University Press.

National Telecommunications and Information Administration. 2000. "Falling Through the Net: Toward Digital Inclusion." Washington, DC: NTIA.

–. 2004. "A Nation Online: Entering the Broadband Age." Washington, D.C.: NTIA.

Norris, P. 2001. Digital Divide: Civic Engagement, Information Poverty and the Internet in Democratic Societies. New York: Cambridge University Press.

van Dijk, Jan A.G.M. 2005. The Deepening Divide. London: Sage Publications.

Warschauer, M. 2003. Technology and Social Inclusion. Cambridge, Mass: MIT Press.

Wellman, B, A.Q. Haase, J. Witte, and K Hampton. 2002. "Capitalizing on the Internet: Social Contact, Civic Engagement, and Sense of Community." Pp. 436-455 in The Internet in Everyday Life, edited by B. Wellman and H. Haythornthwaite. Oxford: Blackwell.

Wilhelm, Anthony G. 2000. Democracy in the Digital Age: Challenges to Political Life in Cyberspace. New York: Routledge.

Heinz Bonfadelli/Priska Bucher

Alte und neue Medien im Leben von Jugendlichen mit Migrationshintergrund

Im vorliegenden Beitrag werden der theoretische Hintergrund sowie empirische Befunde aus einer *quantitativen Studie* zum Stellenwert von alten und neuen Medien im Leben von Jugendlichen mit Migrationshintergrund, die am IPMZ – Institut für Publizistikwissenschaft und Medienforschung der Universität Zürich durchgeführt worden ist, präsentiert und diskutiert. Die Untersuchung ist Teil eines Schweizerischen Nationalfondsprojekts; sie umfasst zudem einen *qualitativen Teil*, der von der Pädagogischen Hochschule Zürich realisiert worden ist und auf Leitfadengesprächen und Beobachtungen türkischer Familien basiert.

1. Ausgangslage

1.1 Gesellschaftliche Ebene

Migration ist ein Phänomen, das für die meisten industrialisierten Länder Europas speziell seit dem Wirtschaftswachstum nach dem II. Weltkrieg charakteristisch ist. In der Schweiz gehört heute jeder dritte Einwohner zu einer Migrationsgruppe oder hat einen durch Immigration geprägten Familienhintergrund. Die Migrationsbewegungen und die daraus resultierende Koexistenz zwischen der sog. „einheimischen" Bevölkerung und den vielfach als „Fremden" betrachteten Migranten schaffen soziale Probleme wie Bildungsbenachteiligung, Wertkonflikte oder gar Rassismus. Und diese Konflikte wiederum haben in letzter Zeit in der Öffentlichkeit vermehrt zu Diskussionen über die Fähigkeit und den Willen zur Integration verschiedener Einwanderungsgruppen geführt. Jüngste Anlässe und Beispiele für solche Konflikte sind und waren etwa die Jugendunruhen in den Pariser Vorstädten, die Ermordung des Filmemachers Theo van Gogh in Holland, die Gewalt rechtsradikaler Gruppen gegen Ausländer oder das nicht automatisch an ausländische Jugendliche der zweiten und dritten Generation verliehene Bürgerrecht in der Schweiz.

1.2   Medien

Neben Schule und Familie spielen nicht zuletzt die Massenmedien eine wichtige
Rolle für das Zusammenleben in der heutigen multikulturellen Gesellschaft. Sie
sind von Relevanz für die soziale und kulturelle Integration von ethnischen Minoritäten, indem sie beispielsweise eine wichtige Quelle der Information und der
Orientierung über die (nationale) Gesellschaft und deren kulturelle Identität, aber
auch über das aktuelle politische Geschehen sind. Massenmedien vermitteln zudem ein gemeinsames Wissen über Normen und Wertvorstellungen und ermöglichen so auch den ethnischen Minoritäten, sich an der Gesellschaft des Aufnahme-
landes zu beteiligen. Auf diese Weise schaffen Medien eine gemeinsame Basis für
politische Partizipation, für die kulturelle Teilhabe sowie für alltagsrelevante interpersonale Anschlusskommunikation.

Medientechnische Innovationen wie Video, Satelliten-TV oder Internet stellen
jedoch die bis anhin postulierte *positive Integrationsfunktion der Medien* zunehmend in Frage, weil sie es ermöglichen, durch ausschließliche Nutzung von Medi-
en des Herkunftslandes und in der Herkunftssprache weiterhin mehr oder weniger
ausschließlich der Herkunftssprache und -kultur verhaftet zu bleiben. Ein solcher
Medienumgang kann so zur Stabilisierung oder gar Verstärkung einer sogenannten
„Ghetto-Situation" von ethnischen Minoritäten beitragen. Bezüglich gleichen Bil-
dungs- und Teilhabechancen stellt sich für Heranwachsende aus Familien mit Migrationshintergrund zudem die Frage nach den Zugangsmöglichkeiten zu den neu-
en Informations- und Kommunikationstechnologien IuKT (Digital Divide).

2.   Theoretischer Hintergrund

Die Kommunikationswissenschaft hat sich seit den 1960er Jahren verstärkt mit der
Beziehung zwischen Massenmedien und ethnischen Minoritäten befasst, und zwar
meist in einer interdisziplinären Perspektive. Hauptsächlich wurden hierbei Medieninhalte (d.h. die Darstellung der ethnischen Minoritäten und ihrer Kultur in der
Medienrealität) untersucht, wobei speziell die *verzerrte Repräsentation* in Form
von negativer Stereotypisierung immer wieder kritisiert worden ist (vgl. Poole 2000;
Müller 2005; Bonfadelli 2007). Dies geschah nicht zuletzt vor dem Hintergrund
der Hypothese, dass die Präsenz negativer Stereotypen in der Medienrealität sich
ungünstig auf die soziale Integration der ethnischen Minoritäten auswirken könnte. Aus der Perspektive der Medienproduktion war zudem die *ethnische Diversität*

in den Medienorganisationen selber immer wieder ein Thema der Forschung und der öffentlichen Auseinandersetzung.

Was die *Mediennutzung* ethnischer Minderheiten anbelangt, wurden bis anhin erst wenige Studien durchgeführt (u.a. Anker/Ermutlu/Steinmann 1995 in der Schweiz; Trebbe/Weiss 2001 in Deutschland oder d'Haenens u.a. 2002 und d'Haenens 2003 in den Niederlanden; zusammenfassend zum Forschungsstand Müller 2005). Weil aber die Medien nur dann einen Einfluss auf die gesellschaftliche Integration ethnischer Minoritäten haben können, wenn sie auch genutzt werden, ist eine genauere Beschäftigung mit der Mediennutzung von ethnischen Minoritäten unerlässlich. Dabei können zwei Linien der Forschung unterschieden werden (vgl. Abb. 1):

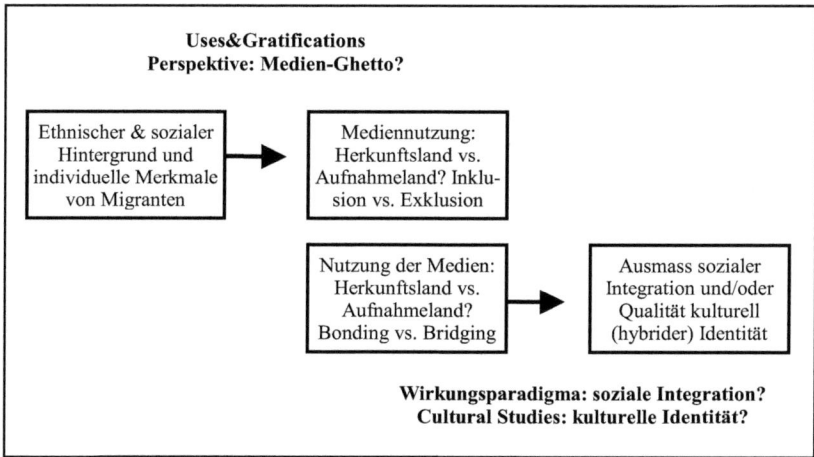

Abb. 1: Theoretische Perspektiven zur Mediennutzung ethnischer Minoritäten

Auf der einen Seite kann die Mediennutzung von ethnischen Minoritäten als *abhängige Variable* ins Zentrum der Forschung gerückt werden. Die zentrale Forschungsfrage lautet dann: Gibt es tatsächlich ein „Medien-Ghetto"? – Oder allgemeiner gefragt: Welche Muster prägen die Mediennutzung von Jugendlichen oder Erwachsenen mit Migrationshintergrund? Und darauf bezogen: *Welche Faktoren* erklären den Medienumgang von ethnischen Minoritäten? Im Folgenden wird dieses Forschungsfeld unter dem Label „Mediennutzungs-Perspektive" zusammengefasst.

Auf der anderen Seite kann die Mediennutzung der ethnischen Minoritäten auch als *unabhängiger Faktor* betrachtet werden. In diesem Fall wird beispielsweise quantifizierend im Rahmen des klassischen *Medienwirkungsparadigmas* (z.B. Weiss/ Trebbe 2001) oder qualitativ in der Tradition der *Cultural Studies* (z.B. Barker 1997; Ogan 2001; Grixti 2006) gefragt, inwiefern der Medienumgang sowohl zur sozialen Integration als auch zur kulturellen Identität von ethnischen Minderheiten beiträgt.

2.1   Perspektive der Mediennutzung

Im Rahmen dieser Forschungstradition wurde die simple „Medienghetto-These" im Verlauf der Zeit ergänzt bzw. ersetzt durch differenziertere Muster des Medienumgangs. Man geht heute davon aus, dass es nicht nur eine Polarität zwischen separatistischer Bindung an die Medien des Herkunftslandes und integrativer Adaption der Medienangebote des neuen Kulturkontextes gibt, sondern im Sinne des „Sowohl-als-Auch" ebenso eine verbindende dualistische Mediennutzung, bei der sowohl Medienangebote der Herkunftskultur als auch jene der neuen Aufnahmekultur genutzt werden (z.b. Ogan 2001; d'Haenens/ Beentjes/ Bink 2005).

Neben der *„ Ghetto-These"* wird in Forschungsübersichten (z.B. Müller 2005) immer wieder die Dominanz des Fernsehens – insbesondere in Familien aus der Türkei oder Ex-Jugoslawien – erwähnt. Neuere Studien, wie auch die unsere, untersuchen darüber hinaus den Stellenwert der Printmedien im Medienmenu von Jugendlichen mit Migrationshintergrund und gehen auch der Frage nach, ob eine *bildungsrelevante Exklusion* bei den neuen Medien wie Computer und Internet im Sinne eines „Digital Divide" besteht.

Außer diesen Differenzierungen im Bereich der Mediennutzung als abhängiger Variable interessieren auch die weiteren unabhängigen Einflussfaktoren, welche die Mediennutzung der Jugendlichen mit Migrationshintergrund beeinflussen.

Während ethnische Minderheiten in älteren Studien meist als homogene Gruppe betrachtet wurden, und deren Medienverhalten mit jenem der „Einheimischen" verglichen wurde, werden heute verstärkt auch die Unterschiede innerhalb der ethnischen Minoritäten selbst betont, indem *komplexere Erklärungsmodelle* des Medienverhaltens formulieren werden. Neben dem *Hauptfaktor der ethnischen Zugehörigkeit* werden nun stärker auch mediatisierende Faktoren wie der Bildungshintergrund, Sprachkompetenzen, politisches Vertrauen oder das soziale Kapital als Eingebundenheit in soziale Netzwerke untersucht (vgl. Weiss / Trebbe 2001).

2.2   Medienwirkungs- / Cultural Studies Paradigma

Im Rahmen des *Medienwirkungsparadigmas* steht vor allem die soziale Integrationsfunktion der Medien im Zentrum. Die meisten funktionalistischen Theorien gehen davon aus, dass die Medien ungeplante langfristige Integrationsfunktionen im Sinne von positiv gewerteter Sozialisation und Akkulturation für die Gesellschaft leisten (Geißler/Pöttker 2004).

Allerdings betonen kritische Kommunikationswissenschafter auch verstärkt negative oder dysfunktionale Wirkungen, insofern ethnische Minderheiten in der Medienberichterstattung ausgeblendet oder nur als soziales Problem thematisiert werden. Qualitative Analysen weisen hier auf Framing-Mechanismen oder Metaphern wie „das Boot ist voll" oder der „Islam als rückständige Kultur" hin (Poole 2000; Schiffer 2000).

Im Unterschied zum Medienwirkungsparadigma gehen die *Cultural Studies* stärker vom aktiven Mediennutzer aus und betonen den Beitrag der Medien zur Herausbildung einer kulturellen Identität. Medienumgang wird als aktive Konstruktion von kulturellen Bedeutungen und sozialer Identität verstanden. Mittlerweile gibt es dazu eine Vielzahl vor allem qualitativer Studien. Während ältere Studien untersuchen, wie ethnische Minoritäten durch Nutzung von Medieninhalten aus ihrer Herkunftskultur im Sinne eines sog. „Bondings" sich vom neuen kulturellen und politischen Umfeld abschließen, konzentrieren sich neuere Studien stärker dafür, wie durch eine gemischte Mediennutzung im Sinne eines „Bridgings" neue sog. *hybride Identitäten* (Eickelpasch/Rademacher 2004: 21ff.) entstehen, welche auf flexible und reflexive Weise zwischen den verschiedenen Kulturen zu vermitteln helfen (vgl. d'Haenens u.a. 2002).

3.   Eigene Studie: Fragestellung, Methode, Stichprobe Zielsetzung

Fragestellung: Im Rahmen unserer quantitativen Befragung wurde der Frage nachgegangen, inwiefern sich in der Mediennutzung von Jugendlichen mit und ohne Migrationshintergrund Gemeinsamkeiten und Unterschiede feststellen lassen. Dabei interessierte uns in medialer Hinsicht neben den alten Medien (Fernsehen, Printmedien) besonders der Umgang mit neuen Medien bzw. IuKT (Computer, Internet). In erklärender Hinsicht stand vor allem die Frage im Vordergrund, welche Bedeutung der Migrationshintergrund im Vergleich zu den Faktoren soziale Herkunft, Bildungsniveau und Geschlecht für die Erklärung von Varianz im Mediennutzungsverhalten hat.

Methode: Die Befunde basieren auf einer schriftlichen Befragung im Klassen-verband mit einem standardisierten Fragebogen mit Fragen zum Medienbesitz, zur Mediennutzung und zu präferierten Medieninhalten. Daneben wurden weitere Daten erhoben, etwa zu den Sprachfertigkeiten, zur kulturellen Orientierung, zur politi-schen Einstellungen und auch zu persönlichen Zukunftsplänen. Die quantitativen Daten wurden durch 40 Leitfadengespräche speziell zum Thema Internet vertieft

Stichprobe: Im Sommer 2004 wurden insgesamt 1468 Zürcher Jugendliche im Alter von 12-16 Jahren befragt, davon ein Drittel aus Schweizer Familien und zwei Drittel aus Familien mit Migrationshintergrund. Untersucht wurden die letzte Klasse der Primarschule sowie die drei folgenden obligatorischen Schulstufen der Ober-stufe, wobei drei Bildungsniveaus berücksichtigt wurden. Aufgrund des geringen Anteils an Schülern mit Migrationshintergrund wurden Gymnasien nicht in die Stichprobe aufgenommen.

4.   Befunde

4.1   Strukturelle Benachteiligungen

Bevor im Folgenden auf den Medienumgang eingegangen wird, zunächst einige Befunde zur bestehenden strukturellen Benachteiligung von eingewanderten Fa-milien und ihren Kindern und Jugendlichen.

Ein Blick in unsere Daten zeigt, dass Jugendliche mit Migrationshintergrund im Vergleich zu ihren Schweizer Kameraden stärker in statustieferen und bild-ungsferneren sozialen Milieus aufwachsen. Dies hat zur Folge, dass diese Jugend-lichen selbst wiederum schulisch benachteiligt sind. Darüber hinaus haben es die Jugendlichen aus Migrationsfamilien auch bei gleichem Bildungsniveau der El-tern (Abb. 2) auch noch schwerer, in Schweizer Schulen Erfolg zu haben.

Anteile in %			Bildung der Schüler		
			tief	mittel	hoch
Bildung der Eltern	hoch	Schweizer	0	29	**71**
		Migranten	**20**	42	38
	mittel	Schweizer	4	52	**44**
		Migranten	**22**	49	19
	tief	Schweizer	7	52	**44**
		Migranten	**34**	49	17

Abb. 2: Bildungsniveau der Schüler in Abhängigkeit der Bildung der Eltern

Dies trifft aber nicht für alle Herkunftsländer gleichermaßen zu, wie der Vergleich zwischen Jugendlichen mit Eltern aus Italien, der Türkei oder Ex-Jugoslawien zeigt: Während durch die Berechnung *partieller Korrelationen* (unter Kontrolle des Bildungsniveaus der Eltern) für Jugendliche italienischer Herkunft im Vergleich zu Schweizern eine signifikante Benachteiligung von +0.10 festgestellt werden kann, liegen diese Zusammenhänge für Jugendliche aus der Türkei mit +0.29 und für Jugendliche aus Ex-Jugoslawien mit +0.34 sogar noch deutlich höher.

4.2   Medienausstattung: Familie

Da die Nutzungshäufigkeit und Nutzungsdauer von Medien immer davon abhängig ist, welche Medien überhaupt zugänglich sind, soll zunächst ein Überblick über den Medienzugang zu Hause außerhalb des eigenen Zimmers, aber auch über den Medienbesitz im eigenen Zimmer der befragten Jugendlichen gegeben werden:

genannt (%)	Schweiz	Migrations-hintergrund	Italien	Türkei	Ex-Jugo-slawien
Radio	77	68	74	66	63
Zeitungs-Abo	89	61	64	63	55
Zeitschriften-Abo	65	46	48	56	45
TV	89	85	99	99	97
Satelliten TV	24	61	56	71	74
Video	85	80	84	74	78
Stereoanlage	70	63	65	53	59
Computer	81	52	60	40	38
Internet	80	49	57	34	38

In den ersten zwei Spalten sind Schweizer Jugendliche (N=499) und solche mit Migrationshintergrund (N=969) ausgewiesen; zudem sind innerhalb der Gruppe der Migrationsjugendlichen noch drei größere ethnische Gruppen gesondert dargestellt: Befragte aus Italien (N=163), der Türkei (N=135) und Ex-Jugoslawien (N=350).

Abb. 3: Medienbesitz zu Hause (ohne eigenes Zimmer)

Generell zeigen die Befunde einen *medialen Versorgungsgrad auf hohem Niveau.* Im Nationenvergleich sind die Schweizer Familien nur im Bereich der *Printmedien* deutlich besser ausgestattet. Für Migrationsfamilien ist hingegen die bessere

Versorgung mit *Satellitenantennen* typisch, was wohl mit der Möglichkeit zusammenhängt, auf diese Weise in Verbindung mit der Herkunftskultur bleiben zu können. Auffallend ist generell die *hohe Verbreitung von PC und Internet*, wobei hier der Zugang in Schweizer Familien leicht besser ist. Ein Vergleich mit der Gesamtbevölkerung zeigt, dass im Jahr 2004 nur zwei Drittel der Personen ab 18 Jahren Zugang zum Internet hatten; Haushalte mit schulpflichtigen Kindern weisen also eine deutlich bessere IuKT-Ausstattung auf.

4.3   Medienausstattung: im eigenen Zimmer

Ein etwas anderes Bild zeigt sich, wenn man die Medienausstattung im eigenen Zimmer betrachtet (Abb. 4), gibt es doch eine medienspezifische Verteilung auf die Kinderzimmer einerseits und Räume andererseits, die von der Familie gemeinsam genutzt werden. Dies trifft nach unseren Daten zum einen auf das Fernsehgerät und zum anderen auch auf die Informations- und Kommunikationstechnologien IuKT zu.

genannt (%)	Schweiz	Migrations-hintergrund	Italien	Türkei	Ex-Jugoslawien
Radio	**89**	74	78	69	72
Zeitschriften-Abo	**24**	17	11	10	**21**
TV	32	**46**	**50**	39	**52**
Satelliten TV	6	6	8	5	8
Video	18	**23**	**25**	**22**	**25**
Stereoanlage	**87**	78	83	81	74
PC	45	**56**	51	**68**	**61**
Internet	30	**49**	40	**64**	**56**
DVD	27	**39**	36	**46**	**44**
Playstation	25	**37**	40	**43**	**41**
Ø Anzahl Bücher	**37**	23	22	24	16

Abb. 4: Medienzugang im eigenen Zimmer

Während einerseits für Jugendliche mit Migrationshintergrund der geringere Besitz von Printmedien auch hier klar ersichtlich ist, kann andererseits eine deutlich *bessere Ausstattung mit elektronischen Medien* im eigenen Zimmer als unter Schweizer Kindern festgestellt werden. Dies weist darauf hin, dass in eingewanderten

Familien die neuen Medien Computer und Internet häufig speziell für die Kinder angeschafft werden, ohne dass die Eltern diese Medien ebenfalls mitnutzen würden. Allerdings zeigen weitergehende Auswertungen (Abb. 5), dass nicht nur der Migrationshintergrund von Bedeutung für den Internetzugang ist: Ein sog. „Digital Divide" besteht ebenfalls bezüglich der Faktoren Geschlecht, Alter und Bildungsniveau der Jugendlichen selbst, aber auch bezüglich des sozioökonomischer Status (SES) der Eltern. So besitzen beispielsweise Knaben und ältere Jugendliche bedeutend häufiger Zugang zum Internet im eigenen Zimmer als Mädchen und jüngere Kinder. Interessant ist, dass bei Jugendlichen aus bildungsfernen Familien, wenn sie überhaupt Zugang zum Internet haben, der Zugang in ihrem eigenen Zimmer ist, während in den privilegierten Familien der Internetzugang, weil auch von den Eltern genutzt, nicht im Zimmer der Kinder selber ist.

Zugang zum Internet (%)		im eigenen Zimmer	in der Familie	Kein Zugang
Total		42	47	11
Migrations-hintergrund	nein	30	**62**	8
	ja	**49**	38	13
Geschlecht	Knaben	**47**	44	9
	Mädchen	37	49	**14**
Alter	12-13 J.	34	**55**	11
	14 J.	41	48	11
	15 J.	**45**	46	11
	16-18 J.	**48**	40	12
Schicht-hintergrund der Familie	hoch	40	**53**	7
	mittel	40	**49**	10
	tief	**48**	34	**18**
Bildung: nur Befragte der Oberstufe	hoch	41	**54**	4
	mittel	**46**	42	12
	tief	**46**	32	12

Abb. 5: Dimensionen des Digital Divide

4.4   Dauer und Häufigkeit der Mediennutzung

Was die Dauer und die Häufigkeit der Mediennutzung anbelangt, so gibt es vergleichsweise wenig Disparitäten zwischen den verschiedenen kulturellen Gruppen; entscheidend sind viel stärker die jugendkulturellen Gemeinsamkeiten im Unterschied zu den Erwachsenen.

Trotzdem bestehen aber einige Unterschiede, etwa dass Schüler mit Migrationshintergrund weniger oft und weniger lange Radio hören; umgekehrt ist ihr TV-Kon-
sum aber deutlich höher. Speziell bei der Internetnutzung zeigt sich, dass der Anteil
an Nicht-Nutzern unter den Migrantenkindern etwas höher ist als unter den Schweizer Jugendlichen. Werden aber nur die User betrachtet, so sitzen die Schüler mit
Migrationshintergrund signifikant länger vor ihrem PC. Die Kluft zwischen Internet-
nutzern und solchen, die keine Erfahrung damit haben, ist demnach unter den Schülern mit Migrationshintergrund ausgeprägter als unter den Schweizer Schülern.

Betrachtet man die *Nutzung der Medien* noch etwas genauer, so lässt sich fol-
gendes Bild zeichnen:

Als *jugendkulturelle Gemeinsamkeit* gilt, dass *Musik und Fernsehen* nach wie
vor die wichtigsten Medien im Leben der heutigen Heranwachsenden sind. Rund
70% nutzen diese täglich. Im Vergleich dazu werden *Zeitungen* und *Bücher*
eher in einem wöchentlichen Rhythmus genutzt. Gut ein Drittel nutzt noch kaum
Zeitungen und fast die Hälfte der heutigen Jugendlichen lebt „Buch abstinent".
Gut 15% der Jugendlichen nutzen täglich den Computer und mehr als 30%
loggen sich täglich ins Internet ein.

Vergleicht man die Schweizer Jugendlichen mit Jugendlichen aus Migrationsfamilien, so zeigen sich im Medienumgang aber auch bestimmte *Unterschiede:*

Vor allem Jugendliche aus südeuropäischen Familien sitzen deutlich häufiger,
aber auch länger vor dem *Fernseher* als ihre Kollegen aus der Schweiz; in
Schweizer Familien wird umgekehrt aber deutlich mehr in *Büchern* gelesen.

Häufigkeit in %	Computer		Internet	
	Schweizer	Migranten	Schweizer	Migranten
Täglich	16	**21**	31	**39**
Mehrmals	37	38	37	31
Einmal pro Woche	17	16	12	10
Weniger	26	17	13	10
Nie	4	**8**	7	10
Dauer in Std./Wo.	4.7	**6.0**	7.9	**10.3**
Computer: Summe aus Schreiben, Grafik, Spielen, Programmieren. Internet: Summe aus Mailen, Surfen, Chatten.				
Genannte Funktionen der Internetnutzung in %	Zur Information		Zur Unterhaltung	
	Schweizer	Migranten	Schweizer	Migranten
	60	56	58	52

Abb. 6: Häufigkeit der Nutzung von Computer und Internet

Neue Medien werden von Migrationsjugendlichen überraschenderweise häufiger und auch länger genutzt (vgl. Abb. 6). Dies ist vermutlich eine Folge davon, dass die digitalen Medien in den Migrationsfamilien viel häufiger in den Zimmern der Jugendlichen selber stehen. In funktionaler Hinsicht wird das *Internet* sowohl von Schweizer Jugendlichen aber auch solchen aus Migrationsfamilien etwa gleich häufig zur Information wie zur Unterhaltung genutzt. Überraschenderweise gibt es somit auf den ersten Blick kaum Tendenzen der Exklusion.

Partielle Korrelation	Herkunft 4=CH, 3= Ital., 2= Türk,1=Yug	SES 1=tief 2=mittel 3=hoch	Bildung 1=tief 2=mittel 3=hoch	Alter Anz. Jahre	Geschlecht 1=Frau 2=Mann
Internet- Zugang zu Hause	-0.00 ns	+0.07 *	**+0.17** **	-0.02 ns	+0.07 *
Internet- Zugang im Zimmer	**-0.18** **	+0.05 ns	**+0.11** **	+0.02 ns	**+0.10** **
Internet- Nutzung	**-0.09** **	-0.07 *	**+0.10** **	+0.09 *	-0.03 ns
PC- Nutzung	-0.07 *	-0.00 ns	+0.02 ns	-0.02 ns	**+0.20** **
Lesehäufigkeit	+0.07 *	+0.09 **	**+0.10** **	-0.10 **	-0.20 **
Fernsehnutzung	**-0.10** **	**-0.10** **	+0.02 ns	+0.08 *	+0.08 *
Es handelt sich um Partielle Korrelationen, jeweils kontrolliert für die übrigen 4 Dimensionen.					

Abb. 7: Einfluss des Migrationshintergrunds im Vergleich zu anderen Faktoren

Vergleicht man allerdings den Faktor „Migrationshintergrund" mit weiteren Einflussfaktoren, so wird deutlich, dass es neben den jugendkulturellen Gemeinsamkeiten auch Unterschiede gibt, wobei je nach Medium andere Faktoren von Relevanz sind.

Beim *Zugang zum Internet* spielt der ethnische Hintergrund nur bezüglich des Standorts des Computers eine Rolle; wichtig ist außerdem der Bildungshintergrund der Jugendlichen. Weiter lässt sich auch feststellen, dass männliche Jugendliche eher Zugang zum Internet haben als weibliche. Die *Nutzung des Internets* wiederum liegt, wie bereits erwähnt, bei den Jugendlichen mit Migrationshintergrund höher; wichtig ist aber auch hier das persönliche Bildungsniveau sowie das Geschlecht. Bezüglich *Buchlesen* zeigen sich insbesondere geschlechtsspezifische Unterschiede; auch dem Bildungsniveau kommt aber eine wichtige Bedeutung zu. Was schliesslich das Fernsehen angelangt, so lässt sich ein signifikanter Effekt des Migrations- und Schichthintergrundes feststellen.

4.5   Inhaltliche Präferenzen

Auf die offenen Fragen nach beliebten TV-Sendungen, Zeitschriften und Internetseiten antworteten Schweizer Schüler und solche mit Migrationshintergrund
interessanterweise ganz ähnlich; fremdsprachige Sendungen, Titel oder Internetseiten wurden relativ selten und eher zusätzlich genannt.

Spitzenreiter im Bereich Fernsehen sind einerseits Serien, wobei von den Mädchen häufiger Titel wie „Marienhof" oder „Gute Zeiten, schlechte Zeiten"; von den
Knaben oftmals Trickfilmserien wie „Futurama", „Spongebob" etc. genannt werden. Bei beiden Geschlechtern sehr beliebt sind Musiksender wie „MTV" und
„Viva".

Beliebteste Internetsites sind einerseits Suchmaschinen wie „google" oder „al-
tavista", andererseits aber auch Messenger- und E-mail-Anbieter wie „msn" oder
„hotmail". Darüber hinaus sind es individuell unterschiedliche Homepages von
Stars aus dem Musik-, Sport- oder Filmbereich, die häufig und gerne besucht werden, und als letzte wichtige Kategorie von Websites sind Anbieter von Games genannt worden.

Bei den Zeitschriften sind es Jugendmagazine wie „Bravo" oder „Young Miss",
die – unabhängig vom kulturellen Hintergrund – vor allem von Mädchen erwähnt
wurden, Sport- und Computer-Magazine werden häufig von Jungen genannt. Mu-
sikzeitschriften hingegen wurden von beiden Geschlechtern etwa gleich häufig
angegeben.

Zusammenfassend gibt es im Unterhaltungsbereich homogene jugendkulturell
geteilte Präferenzen, in denen sich aber immer auch persönliche Vorlieben äußern.
Im Informationsbereich hingegen zeigen sich gewisse Unterschiede, insofern
Schweizer Jugendliche deutlich häufiger Info-Angebote des Schweizer Fernsehens
bevorzugen, während jugendliche Migranten sich Nachrichtensendungen vorzugs-
weise bei deutschen Privatsendern sowie bei Euronews anschauen.

4.6   Sprachliche Orientierung im Medienumgang

Kabel- und Satellitenfernsehen oder das Internet machen es möglich, Medieninhalte
aus verschiedenen Ländern und in verschiedenen Sprachen zu nutzen. Es stellt
sich darum die Frage, in welcher Sprache jugendliche Migranten, die in der Schweiz
zur Schule gehen, Medien nutzen.

Printmedien werden von den meisten Jugendlichen mit Migrationshintergrund
in deutscher Sprache genutzt. Berücksichtigt man allerdings die Tatsache, dass die

Printmedienausstattung in den Migrantenhaushalten tief ist, so liegt der Schluss nahe, dass der Umgang mit der Kulturtechnik Lesen vor allem in der Schule – also in Deutsch – eingeübt wird.

Bezüglich *TV* lässt sich festhalten, dass Migrantenkinder zu 50% (auch) in der Herkunftssprache fernsehen. In gleichem Masse werden auch Medien, die dem interpersonellen Kontakt dienen, in der Herkunftssprache genutzt.

%	Deutsch	Herkunftssprache	Beides
Radio	77	7	16
Zeitung	80	5	15
Zeitschriften	80	5	15
Bücher	80	5	15
Surfen	63	10	27
E-mail	59	12	29
Chat	59	11	30
TV	49	11	40
Video	58	10	32
DVD	62	9	29
Telefon/Handy	45	13	42
SMS	49	11	40

Abb. 8: Mediennutzungssprache (nur Jugendliche mit Migrationshintergrund)

In einem weiteren Schritt wurde untersucht, wie die *kulturelle Orientierung* der Kinder und ihren Eltern aus Migrationsfamilien aussieht (Abb. 9), wobei besonders interessierte, inwiefern die kulturelle Orientierung mit der Mediennutzungssprache zusammenhängt. Grundsätzlich ist der *Anteil der Schweiz-Orientierten* mit etwa 40% bei allen drei betrachteten Gruppen sehr ähnlich, wobei auffällt, dass die Eltern unabhängig vom Herkunftsland stärker herkunfts-orientiert sind als ihre Kinder. Wie vermutet lassen sich zudem starke Korrelationen zwischen der kulturellen Orientierung und der *Sprache, in der Medien genutzt werden* feststellen: Bei einer Orientierung an der Schweiz werden signifikant häufiger auch Medien in deutscher Sprache genutzt, während die Gruppe der Herkunftsorientierten Medien in deutscher Sprache eher meidet und dafür Medien in der Herkunftssprache bevorzugt.

Anteile in %	Schweiz-Orientierung	Dualis-mus	Herkunfts-Orientierung	Un-gebunden
Ex-Jugoslawien, Kinder	41	27	25	7
Ex-Jugoslawien, Eltern	18	35	45	2
Italien, Kinder	41	23	29	7
Italien, Eltern	20	30	48	4
Türkei, Kinder	41	28	24	7
Türkei, Eltern	10	31	57	2

Abb. 9: Kulturelle Orientierung von Kindern und Eltern

5.   Fazit

Bezüglich *Medienzugang* konnte festgestellt werden, dass jugendliche Migranten einerseits ein Printmediendefizit aufweisen: Vor allem Bücher, aber auch Zeitschriften sind im Haushalt und im Kinderzimmer weniger präsent als bei Schweizer Familien. Bezüglich PC und Internet fällt andererseits auf, dass diese Geräte bei Migrantenfamilien häufiger als in Schweizer Familien im Kinderzimmer stehen.

Die *Mediennutzung* der Jugendlichen mit und ohne Migrationshintergrund unterscheidet sich bezüglich dreier Merkmale von derjenigen ihrer Schweizer Kollegen: Jugendliche mit Migrationshintergrund hören deutlich seltener und weniger lang Radio, verbringen mehr Zeit vor dem Fernseher und weisen bezüglich Internetnutzung eine größere Kluft zwischen Nicht-Usern und Vielnutzern auf als Schweizer Jugendliche. Verglichen mit ihren Schweizern Kollegen nutzen jugendliche Migranten PC und Internet jedoch intensiver.

Was präferierte *Medieninhalte* angeht, so kann festgestellt werden, dass globalisierte Medieninhalte unter Jugendlichen beliebt sind und dass sich im Unterhaltungsbereich kaum Differenzen feststellen lassen. Im Bereich der Information durch Medien lassen sich nur insofern Unterschiede ausmachen, als jugendliche Migranten mehr als ihre Schweizer Kollegen Kurzinformationen auf Privatsendern und in Gratiszeitungen nutzen.

Insgesamt wird deutlich, dass sehr viele jugendkulturelle Gemeinsamkeiten die Jugendlichen mit und ohne Migrationshintergrund verbinden, dass aber auch Unterschiede im Zugang und in der Nutzung der Medien bestehen. Allerdings zeigen unsere Analysen auch, dass die Migrationsjugendlichen als Gruppe genauso wenig wie Schweizer Jugendlich homogen sind und dass neben dem Faktor „Migrationshintergrund" die soziale Herkunft und das eigene Bildungsniveau sowie das Alter und Geschlecht ebenfalls einen wichtigen Einfluss auf den Medienumgang haben.

Literatur

Anker, Heinrich/Ermutlu, Manolya/Steinmann, Matthias (1995): Die Mediennutzung der Ausländerinnen in der Schweiz. Ergebnisse einer schriftlichen Umfrage in der ganzen Schweiz vom März/ April 1995. Bern 1995.

Barker, Chris (1997): Television and the reflexive project of the self: soaps, teenage talk and hybrid identities. In: British Journal of Sociology, 48(4), S. 611-628.

Bonfadelli, Heinz (2007): Die Darstellung ethnischer Minderheiten in den Massenmedien. In: Bonfadelli, Heinz / Moser, Heinz (Hg.): Medien und Migration. Europa im multikulturellen Raum. Wiesbaden, S. 95-118.

Eickelpasch, Rolf/Rademacher, Claudia (2004): Identität. Bielefeld.

Geißler, Rainer/Pöttker, Horst (2004): Mediale Integration von Migranten. Ein Problemaufriss. Beitrag zur Internationalen Tagung der Universität Siegen „Welche Rolle spielen Medien bei der Integration von Migranten?" am 24./25. Juni 2004.

Grixti, Joe (2006): Symbiotic transformations: youth, global media and indigenous culture in Malta. In: Media, Culture and Society, 28(1), S. 105-122.

d'Haenens, Leen (2003): ICT in multicultural society. The Netherlands: A context for sound multiform media policy? In: Gazette, 65(4-5), S. 401-421.

d'Haenens, Leen/Beentjes, J.W./Bink, S. (2000): The media experience of ethnic minorities in the Netherlands. A qualitative study. In: Communications 25(3), S. 325-41.

d'Haenens, Leen u.a. (2002): Ownership and use of old and new media among ethnic minority youth in the Netherlands. The role of the ethno-cultural position. In: Communications 27(3), S. 365-393.

Müller, Daniel (2005): Die Darstellung ethnischer Minderheiten in Deutschland. In: Geißler, Rainer / Pöttker, Horst (Hg.): Massenmedien und die Integration ethnischer Minderheiten in Deutschland. Problemaufriss, Forschungsstand, Bibliographie. Bielefeld, S. 83-126.

Müller, Daniel (2005): Die Mediennutzung der ethnischen Minderheiten. In: Geißler, Rainer / Pöttker, Horst (Hg.): Massenmedien und die Integration ethnischer Minderheiten in Deutschland. Problemaufriss, Forschungsstand, Bibliographie. Bielefeld, S.359-387.

Ogan, Christine (2001): Communication and Identity in the Diaspora. Turkish Migrants in Amsterdam and Their Use of Media. Lanham/Boulder/New York/Oxford.

Poole, Elisabeth (2000): Framing Islam: An Analysis of Newspaper Coverage of Islam in the British Press. In: Hafez, Kai (Hg.): Islam and the West in the Mass Media. Fragmented Images in a Globalizing World. Cresskil, N.J., S. 157-179.

Schiffer, Sabine (2000): Der Islam in deutschen Medien. In: Aus Politik und Zeitgeschichte, Heft 20. Auf: www.bpb.de/popup/popup_druckversion.html?guid=PEULKO

Weiss, Hans-Jürgen/Trebbe, Joachim (2001): Mediennutzung und Integration der türkischen Bevölkerung in Deutschland. Ergebnisse einer Umfrage des Presse- und Informationsamts der Bundesregierung. Potsdam.

Horst Niesyto

Medienpädagogik, Mediensozialisation und soziale Benachteiligung

Handlungsorientierte Medienpädagogik ist eng mit dem Anspruch verknüpft, Medienbildung zu einem integralen Bestandteil von Bildung und Erziehung zu machen. Trotz zahlreicher Anstrengungen auf unterschiedlichen Ebenen sind wir in Deutschland von der Realisierung dieses Anspruchs noch relativ weit entfernt. Es gibt verschiedene Konzepte und Modellprojekte, „allerdings bleibt die Umsetzung in der notwendigen Breite eine bedeutsame Aufgabe für die Zukunft" (Tulodziecki 2006: 55). Zwar gelang es seit den 1980er Jahren vor allem im außerschulischen Bereich, viele Kinder und Jugendliche in praxisbezogenen Medienprojekten zu erreichen; öffentliche Mittelkürzungen in der Jugend- und Sozialarbeit gefährden jedoch diese Teilerfolge und führten an vielen Orten bereits zur Streichung medienpädagogischer Aktivitäten. An Schulen mangelt es nach wie vor an einer soliden medienpädagogischen Grundbildung der pädagogischen Fachkräfte; im Bereich der Primarstufe und der Sekundarstufe I besteht ein besonderer Entwicklungsbedarf, insbesondere für Kinder und Jugendliche aus Hauptschul- und Migrationsmilieus.

Befunde der Medienforschung belegen, dass Medien nicht die großen Gleichmacher sind, sondern sehr unterschiedlich genutzt werden. Vor allem für Jugendliche haben Medien im Sozialisationsverlauf neben Gleichaltrigengruppen eine zentrale Orientierungs- und Lebensbewältigungsfunktion. Mit der Mediennutzung und Mediensozialisation sind Ressourcen und Risiken verbunden (Süss 2004), die in der medien- und kulturtheoretisch orientierten Forschung der letzten zwei Jahrzehnte zu wenig beachtet wurden. Der folgende Beitrag arbeitet anhand ausgewählter Problemfelder Aspekte sozialer Benachteiligung im Medienbereich heraus und entwickelt hieraus Überlegungen für die weitere medienpädagogische Forschung und Praxis.

1   Medien und soziale Benachteiligung

Aktuelle Beiträge über soziale Ungleichheit und Benachteiligung[1] betonen, dass
jenseits einer zu konstatierenden Pluralisierung von Lebensstilen nach wie vor
unterschiedliche soziale Lebenslagen und Milieus eine prägende Kraft für die Bil-
dungs- und Entwicklungschancen von Menschen haben. Aufgeschreckt durch empirische Befunde im Rahmen der PISA-Studien (PISA-Konsortium 2004) und
weiterer Analysen (u.a. Becker/Lauterbach 2004), die Zusammenhänge zwischen
sozialer Herkunft und Bildungschancen belegten, sowie durch wachsende Integra-
tionsprobleme insbesondere an Hauptschulen, entwickelte sich in den letzten Jahren in der gesellschaftlichen und politischen Öffentlichkeit eine größere Bereitschaft, Fragen der sozialen Ungleichheit und Benachteiligung zu thematisieren.

Im medienpädagogischen Bereich waren diese Fragen lange Zeit kein beson-
deres Thema. Eigene Bemühungen, im Rahmen eines *sozialästhetischen* Ansatzes
soziokulturelle Unterschiede und Formen sozialer Benachteiligung in der Medienpädagogik stärker zu thematisieren (u.a. Niesyto 2000) wurden in der scientific
community zunächst mit Zurückhaltung aufgenommen – der Mainstream segelte
auf der großen Welle jugend- und kulturtheoretisch inspirierter Medienrezeptionsstudien, betonte die Ausdifferenzierung von Jugendkulturen im Medienumgang
und setzte sich nur am Rande mit Fragen der sozialen Benachteiligung auseinander. Inzwischen hat sich das Blatt gewendet und das Interesse an der sozialen Frage in der Medienpädagogik hat sowohl im praktischen wie im theoretischen Bereich zugenommen.[2]

So wird in Zusammenhang mit aktuellen Internet- und Onlinestudien von mehreren Autor/innen betont, dass sich mit dem Themenfeld „Digitale Ungleichheit"
kein technisches, sondern ein soziales Problem verbindet und dass soziale Probleme primär soziale Lösungen erfordern. Viele der sog. „bildungsfernen" Jugendlichen – so die Diagnose aus zahlreichen Beobachtungen und Befunden – fühlen
sich von der Gesellschaft ausgegrenzt und können durch technologieorientierte

---

1   Siehe u.a. der 32. Kongress der Deutschen Gesellschaft für Soziologie zum Thema „Soziale Un-
     gleichheit, Kulturelle Unterschiede" (Rehberg 2006) sowie der 20. Kongress der Deutschen Ge-
     sellschaft für Erziehungswissenschaft, der vom 20.-22. März 2006 zum Thema „Bildung – Macht
     – Gesellschaft" an der Johann Wolfgang Goethe-Universität in Frankfurt am Main stattfand (URL:
     http://www.dgfe2006.uni-frankfurt.de/).
2   Siehe in diesem Zusammenhang die Medienprojekte „Medienkompetenz sozial benachteiligter
     Kinder und Jugendlicher" (gefördert von der Landesanstalt für Medien NRW; URL: http://www.lfm-
     nrw.de/medienkompetenz_neu/infos_projekte/; Erfahrungsbericht: Hoffmann 2006) sowie das
     Projekt „Lernen, Migration und digitale Medien – Potenziale für Jugendliche mit Migrationshin-
     tergrund" (gefördert von der Bundesinitiative Schulen ans Netz e.V.; URL: http://www.lift-web.de).
     Für den Bereich „Filmbildung in bildungsbenachteiligten Milieus": Maurer (2006); Rüsel (2006).

„Medienoffensiven" und zeitlich begrenzte „Medienkampagnen" nicht oder nur unzureichend erreicht werden. Überhaupt erscheint es schwierig, bildungsmäßig und sozial benachteiligte Gruppen durch institutionelle Angebote, die top down organisiert sind, zu erreichen. Bundesweite Internetportale können Kontakte und pädagogische Arbeit im sozialen Nahraum nicht ersetzen. Ungleichheiten – so Bonfadelli auf der internationalen Fachtagung „Grenzenlose Cyberwelt? Digitale Ungleichheit und neue Bildungszugänge für Jugendliche" (Bielefeld 2006) – gingen mehr in Richtung sozialer und kommunikativer Klüfte. Medienpädagogik scheint gut beraten zu sein, diese Klüfte stärker zu beachten. Worin bestehen die damit verbundenen Problemlagen? Inwieweit drücken sie eine soziale Benachteiligung aus? Was bedeutet dies für die medienpädagogische Praxis und Forschung?

1.1 Gesellschaftliche Medienentwicklung und soziale Benachteiligung

Die massenhaft eintretende Individualisierung in den westlichen Gesellschaften im Laufe der zweiten Hälfte des 20. Jahrhunderts (Beck 1986) schaffte zwar neue Lebenschancen jenseits von traditionell zugeschriebenen Rollenbildern, Berufs- und Lebenswegen. Traditionelle Milieus wurden brüchig, Lebensstile differenzierten sich aus, Konsum- und Medienkulturen forcierten die Prozesse kultureller Selbständigkeit, Kinder und Jugendliche erhielten über Medien neue, eigene Weltzugänge. Die mit der „digitalen Revolution" einhergehenden Prozesse der Globalisierung von Ökonomie, Kultur und Kommunikation eröffneten im kulturell-kommunikativen Bereich nicht nur neue Formen interkulturellen Austauschs und Lernens – die kapitalistisch dominierte Weltgesellschaft und die „neoliberale Revolution" beschleunigt die technologischen und ökonomischen Konzentrationsprozesse und forciert unter Hinweis auf „Globalisierungszwänge" Ausgrenzungsprozesse von sehr vielen Menschen. Unter dem Primat einer profitorientierten Marktwirtschaft werden Menschen massenhaft „wegrationalisiert", öffentliche Bildung für ein marktkonformes „Output"-Denken instrumentalisiert, bestimmte Schulen de facto zu „Aufbewahranstalten" von jungen Menschen degradiert, die deutlich spüren, dass sie in dem enorm beschleunigten und flexibilisierten „Turbo-Kapitalismus" so gut wie keine Chance haben.

Bei der Frage „Was ist soziale Benachteiligung?" spielen Ressourcen eine große Rolle. Der französische Kultursoziologe Pierre Bourdieu (1970) sprach in diesem Zusammenhang von unterschiedlichen Formen sozialen, kulturellen und ökonomischen Kapitals. Soziales Kapital meint – vereinfacht ausgedrückt – die Ressourcen, die in einer Gesellschaft den jeweiligen Individuen zur Verfügung stehen, um ein Netz sozialer Beziehungen zu knüpfen. Kulturelles Kapital umfasst wesentlich Bildungsressourcen, die Kenntnis und den differenzierten Umgang mit verschiedenen Kulturgütern, auch die Kenntnis und den Umgang mit spezifischen Codes für die Kommunikation. Allgemein lässt sich formulieren, dass *soziale Benachteiligung* dann vorliegt, wenn bestimmten sozialen Gruppen der Zugang zu gesellschaftlich relevanten Ressourcen, zum Beispiel höheres Einkommen, soziale Sicherheit (Arbeitsplatzsicherheit, Gesundheitsvorsorge), aber auch Bildung, durch Schichtgrenzen und/oder Diskriminierung verwehrt bleibt oder erschwert ist. Bezogen auf *Medienbildung* kann man sagen: Benachteiligung liegt zum Beispiel dann vor, wenn durch pädagogisch-didaktische Konzepte, die einseitig kognitiv-planerische Arbeitsformen ansprechen, Kinder und Jugendliche ausgegrenzt werden, die mit diesen Arbeitsformen Probleme haben (z.B. durch eine zu starke Orientierung auf ein ausführliches Erstellen von Drehplänen, bevor Kinder/Jugendliche erste Filmaufnahmen machen). Benachteiligung ist also nicht nur ein materieller Faktor, z.B. zu wenig Geld, um sich bestimmte Geräte kaufen oder sich bestimmte Dienste leisten zu können. Benachteiligung hängt auch mit der Art und Weise zusammen, *wie* Bildung realisiert, mit welchen Konzepten gearbeitet wird. Auch dies kann zu einem Faktor von Benachteiligung werden.

Benachteiligung verweist als *strukturelle* Kategorie auf bestimmte Lebenslagen, muss aber nicht für jedes Mitglied der betreffenden Gruppe zutreffen.[3] Sozial und bildungsmäßig benachteiligte Gruppen sind nicht homogen. Es besteht vielmehr die Gefahr einer Stigmatisierung ganzer Gruppen, wenn übersehen wird, dass stets individuell unterschiedliche Verarbeitungsweisen von Benachteiligung möglich sind. Dieser Aspekt kommt auch ein Stück weit in den Begriffen „benachteiligt" und „benachteiligend" zum Ausdruck. „Benachteiligt" ist relativ statisch, „benachteiligend" akzentuiert eher das Prozesshafte, die Möglichkeiten, die eine bestimmte Situation für den Einzelnen haben kann, aber nicht determinierend haben muss. Die Verarbeitungsweisen von Benachteiligung sind mit Werten, Deutungs- und Verhaltensmustern verbunden. In diesem Zusammenhang ist es wichtig, schichtspezifische Werte und Muster zu unterscheiden und eine Hierarchisierung zwischen ihnen zu vermeiden. Unterschiede und Andersartigkeiten sind wahrzunehmen, zu respektieren und im Sinne einer subjektorientierten Sichtweise zum Ausgangspunkt des eigenen pädagogischen Handelns zu machen. Der Begriff „bildungsfern" ist in diesem Zusammenhang insofern sehr problematisch, weil er ein Bildungsverständnis nahe legt, das

---

3   In soziologischen Diskursen wird in diesem Zusammenhang zwischen Differenztheorien und Ungleichheitstheorien unterschieden (u.a. Schwinn 2004). Differenztheoretische Analysen unterscheiden horizontale, vertikale, funktionale und soziale Differenzierungen und beanspruchen eine „genauere Erfassung der unterschiedlichen Kontexte und Lebensbereiche, deren institutionelle Leitkriterien darüber bestimmen, welcher Aspekt von sozialer Ungleichheit hier zählt" (Schwinn 2006: 1295).

Bildungsinhalte und bildungsbezogene Lernformen einseitig an institutionell etablierten Bildungseinrichtungen und -standards koppelt und zu wenig vorhandene Bildungsmotivationen und informelle Bildungsprozesse der Subjekte im Blick hat. Beispiel: Medienbildung. Die Medienwelten von Hauptschülerinnen und Hauptschülern unterscheiden sich deutlich von denen ihrer Lehrerinnen und Lehrer. Eine Abwertung der Medienwelten dieser Kinder und Jugendlichen, etwa im Stil: „Alles Klischee, alles Hollywood!" versperrt jegliche Zugänge zu einem sinnvollen medienpädagogischen Handeln. Der andere Weg ist: versuchen zu verstehen, welche Bedürfnisse und Themen Kinder und Jugendliche mit Medienangeboten verbinden, was für sie interessant, was langweilig oder abstoßend ist.

Hieraus ergeben sich Anknüpfungspunkte für lebendige Formen der Medienreflexion, die gesellschaftliche Medienangebote auf eigene Bedürfnisse und Themen beziehen, im kommunikativen Austausch inhaltliche und ästhetische Qualitätskriterien entwickeln und die Fähigkeit zu einer selbstbestimmten und sozial verantwortlichen Medienauswahl und Medienbewertung fördern. Die kritische Auseinandersetzung mit Medien ist untrennbar mit einer kritischen Auseinandersetzung mit gesellschaftlichen Entwicklungen und der Frage verknüpft, inwieweit Medien und Gesellschaft die eigene Orientierung und Entwicklung beeinflussen. Hier zeigt sich die Janusköpfigkeit der Mediennutzung für Jugendliche: einerseits bieten sie Chancen für kulturelle Freisetzungsprozesse und Formen selbständigen Wissenserwerbs, andererseits offerieren sie Deutungsmuster und Identifikationsangebote (z.B. bestimmte Rollenbilder und Konsumangebote), die mitunter in deutlicher Diskrepanz zu eigenen Ressourcen und Realisierungsmöglichkeiten stehen. Unter dem Aspekt sozialer Benachteiligung ist pädagogisch eine „medienpessimistische", pauschale Abwehrhaltung fatal, weil sie Kinder und Jugendliche nicht darin unterstützt, Medien für die eigene Persönlichkeitsbildung aktiv und differenziert zu nutzen. Jenseits „medieneuphorischer" und „medienpessimistischer" Grundhaltungen ist eine pädagogische Begleitung gefragt, die nicht nur kognitive, ästhetische und technische Medienkompetenzen fördert, sondern dies stets mit einer kritischen Reflexion inhaltlicher, normativer und wertbezogener Aussagen verknüpft.

1.2 Medienpädagogik und soziale Benachteiligung

Anhand der Entwicklung der Medienpädagogik in verschiedenen Handlungsfeldern und unter Einbeziehung von Befunden zur Mediennutzung lässt sich die Relevanz sozialer Fragen und sozialer Benachteiligung verdeutlichen. Hier einige Beispiele:

In der Filmerziehung der 1960er und 1970er Jahre dominierten lange Zeit *bewahrpädagogische* sowie *ideologiekritische Ansätze*, die in populären Film- und Kinoangeboten vor allem eine Verrohung des Geschmacks und eine moralische Verwahrlosung der Jugend (Bewahrpädagogik) bzw. eine affirmative Integrationskultur der Kulturindustrie (Kritische Theorie) erblickten. Mit diesen Grundhaltungen war es nicht möglich, Kinder und Jugendliche aus Arbeitermilieus zu erreichen. Ein zusätzliches Hindernis markierten die einseitig sprachorientierten Formen der Filmnachbereitung (Filmanalysen, Filmgespräche).

Vor dem Hintergrund gesellschaftlicher Pluralisierungsprozesse rückte die Förderung *ästhetisch-kultureller Ausdrucksformen* mit Medien in den 1980er und 1990er Jahren immer mehr in den Vordergrund. In deutlicher Abgrenzung von einem elitären Kulturverständnis und einem pauschalisierenden Begriff von ‚Masse‘ akzentuierten rezipientenorientierte Medienstudien die Aneignungs- und Auswahlleistungen der Subjekte (Leitfrage „Was machen die Menschen mit Medien?"). Im Mittelpunkt steht eine multiperspektivische Analyse und Kritik, die medien- mit rezipienten- und kontextbezogenen Dimensionen verknüpft (Cultural Studies). Gleichzeitig verstärkten sich in der außerschulischen Medienpädagogik Formen *handlungsorientierter Medienarbeit*, die besonders durch sozialästhetische Ansätze Kindern und Jugendlichen anschauliche und assoziativ-intuitive Möglichkeiten des medialen Selbstausdrucks bieten (u.a. Niesyto 1991, Röll 1998). Lebenswelt-, Erfahrungs- und Handlungsorientierung waren und sind wesentliche Leitprinzipien, die jenseits einer institutionell-normativen Medienerziehung die Subjektperspektive betonen und für Kinder und Jugendliche symbolische Probe- und Handlungsräume mit Medien erschließen.

In der *schulischen* Medienpädagogik entwickelten sich parallel zu medienerzieherischen und medienkritischen Überlegungen Konzeptionen zur informationstechnischen Grundbildung, die insbesondere von Tulodziecki (1997) entlang der Leitidee „sachgerechtes, selbstbestimmtes, kreatives und sozialverantwortliches Handeln" zusammengeführt wurden. Die medienpädagogische und mediendidaktische Wirklichkeit hinkt vielerorts hinter den formulierten – und zwischenzeitlich ausdifferenzierten und modifizierten – Leitideen her. Dies betrifft sowohl die faktische Verwendung von Computern im Unterricht (PISA-Konsortium 2004) als auch die geringen Erfahrungen, die insbesondere Grund- und Hauptschüler/innen mit Formen aktiver Medienarbeit haben (Medienpädagogischer Forschungsverbund 2005). Hinzu kommen *Medienklüfte* zwischen Schüler/innen und Lehrenden, auf die vor allem Kommer (2006) im Rahmen einer medienbiografischen Studie aufmerksam machte: bei einer großen Zahl der untersuchten Lehrpersonen war „ein derart ‚oberflächlich-kritischer‘, nicht die eigene Milieu-Verortung reflektierender Habitus vorhanden", der eine pädagogisch sinnvolle Annäherung an die Medienwelten Jugendlicher verhindere (ebd., S. 176f.). Ähnliche Befunde finden sich in einer Studie von Billes-Gerhart (2006) sowie in den Analysen von Buckingham zu der sich vergrößernden Kluft zwischen Popularkultur und Schulkultur.[4]

Der *E-Learning-Boom*, der Ende der 1990er Jahre einsetzte und in den letzten zwei bis drei Jahren von deutlicher Ernüchterung gekennzeichnet ist, thematisierte nur am Rande Fragen sozialer Benachteiligung. Mediendidaktische Überlegungen zu *digitalen Medien* beziehen sich aktuell mehr auf die Integration lebensweltorientierter und medienbildnerischer Aspekte (u.a. Schelhowe 2006). Auch die Bielefelder Studie über „Digitale Ungleichheit und formaler Bildungshintergrund" (Iske u.a. 2004; Otto/Kutscher 2004) betont die Notwendigkeit, stärker auf den lebensweltlichen, soziokulturellen Hintergrund der Jugendlichen zu achten. Als ein zentraler Befund wird festgehalten, „dass die Möglichkeiten der Internetnutzung stark mit den Ausgangsbedingungen der NutzerInnen und deren sozialem Kontext im „real life" zusammenhängen [...]. Nutzung, Beteiligung und Bildungsprozesse ergeben sich nicht zwangsläufig durch ein vorliegendes, zur Verfügung stehendes Angebot, sondern erfordern eine entsprechende Berücksichtigung der unterschiedlichen Ressourcen von jugendlichen Nutzern" (Iske et al., 22f.). Entgegen einer medienfixierten Argumentation untermauern die Ergebnisse der genannten Studien die Relevanz einer *lebensweltorientierten* Herangehensweise, die nach den vorhandenen Bedürfnissen, medialen Aneignungsweisen und zur Verfügung stehenden Ressourcen bei Kindern und Jugendlichen aus sog. bildungsfernen Milieus fragt. Dies impliziert einen Absage an Medienkompetenz-Modelle und Kriterienkataloge, die top down von „Experten" festgelegt werden, ohne die pragmatischen Nutzungsbedürfnisse und das mediale Können der Jugendlichen entsprechend zu würdigen und differenziert zu bewerten.

Aktuelle Studien aus dem Bereich *„Medien und Migration"* hinterfragen die These von der digitalen Kluft. So verweisen sowohl Moser (2006) als auch Niesyto/Holzwarth (2005) auf komplexe Medienaneignungs- und Identitätsbildungsprozesse bei Kindern und Jugendlichen aus Migrationskontexten, die sich sowohl medialen Elementen der Herkunftskultur (Eltern), der Medienangebote der Aufnahmegesellschaft als auch der globalen Medienkulturen bedienen. Treibel (2006) konnte keine durchgängige Kluft zwischen einheimischen Jugendlichen und solchen mit Migrationshintergrund feststellen; allerdings gebe es unterschiedliche Formen der Medienaneignung, z.B. auf dem Hintergrund einer familiennahen Adoleszenz bei Migrantenjugendlichen aus Hauptschulen.[5]

---

4 Siehe den Beitrag von Buckingham in diesem Band.
5 Zur Migrationsproblematik unter Bildungsaspekten siehe vor allem Hamburger et al. (2005).

Zum Bereich „*Medien und Gender*" formulieren Treibel/Maier (2006: 22) als Fazit aus verschiedenen Studien: „Digitale Spaltungen haben sich, bezogen auf das Geschlecht, verringert oder neu justiert. Als weitere Kategorien sind in zukünftigen (medienbezogenen) Studien Ethnie bzw. Migrationshintergrund, gesellschaftliche Kontexte, sozialer Status und Generationszugehörigkeit hinzu zu ziehen". Kaschuba/Stauber betonen bei einer Evaluationsstudie zu einem medienpraktischen Projekt der Landesstiftung Baden-Württemberg (Hrsg., 2005), dass die häufig diskutierte These einer schicht- und bildungsbezogenen Wissenskluft andere Formen der Mediennutzung und -produktion außer Acht lasse und auch zu einer „Reifizierung von Geschlechterstereotypen" beitrage (ebd., 17).

In einem Überblicksbeitrag über „*Die Rolle digital-interaktiver Medien für gesellschaftliche Teilhabe*" wertet Bonfadelli (2005) Befunde aus zahlreichen Studien aus. Sein Fazit verdeutlicht, dass das Problem der digitalen Spaltung im engeren Sinn als fehlender Zugang zum Internet nicht verabsolutiert werden sollte:

> „Die neuen Informations- und Kommunikationstechniken bringen lediglich bekannte Probleme wie Unterprivilegierung und Marginalisierung ans Licht bzw. akzentuieren und verstärken sie. Darum sind die digitalen Klüfte im Ausmaß und in der Qualität des gesellschaftlichen Wissens auch keine nur digitalen, sondern sie sind nach wie vor das Resultat ungleicher Bildungsvoraussetzungen bzw. der gesellschaftlichen Benachteiligung bildungsferner Bevölkerungsschichten" (ebd., 14f.).

Bonfadelli betont, dass darum die elementare Kulturtechnik des Lesens und Schreibens weiterhin zentral und durch Medienkompetenz und digitale Literalität bzw. Internet-Kompetenz zu ergänzen sei (ebd.).

1.3   Zwischenbilanz

Die Auseinandersetzung mit dem Themenfeld „Medien und soziale Benachteiligung" zeigt aus medienpädagogischer Perspektive keine einheitlichen Befunde, sondern verweist auf vielschichtige Problemstellungen. Als Kernpunkte lassen sich zunächst festhalten:

– Bezüglich des *Zugangs* zu digitalen Medien zeichnet sich in den letzten Jahren eine enorme Veralltäglichung insbesondere bei Jugendlichen ab.[6] Dennoch ist nicht zu übersehen, dass im Sozialisationsfeld Schule nach wie vor schulartenspezifische Unterschiede bestehen (schlechtere Ausstattung und Zugänge an Grundschulen und in der Sekundarstufe I).

---

6   Siehe u.a. die JIM-Studie (Medienpädagogischer Forschungsverbund 2005).

- Die Formen und Funktionen der *Medienaneignung* sind unterschiedlich und lassen Bezüge zu sozialen und bildungsbezogenen Kontexten erkennen. Dies betrifft vor allem Unterschiede in der Nutzung von mehr wissens- bzw. mehr unterhaltungsorientierten Angeboten[7] sowie Unterschiede bezüglich vorhandener Lese- und Schreibkompetenzen (auch im Hinblick auf Nutzungsmotivationen und Navigationspraxen im Internet).

- Im Bereich der *schulischen Medienbildung* reicht es nicht aus, Lehrkräfte technisch und methodisch zu qualifizieren. Angesichts einer Kluft in den medialen Habitusformen zwischen vielen Pädagog/innen einerseits und vielen Schüler/innen andererseits gilt es, „nicht nur die Medienkompetenz der Schülerinnen und Schüler und Auszubildenden, sondern auch die medien*pädagogische* Kompetenz der Lehrkräfte zu stärken" (Treibel/Maier 2006: 22), um Blockaden in pädagogischen Prozessen zu verhindern.[8]

- Entgegen medienfixierten Konzepten bewahrheit sich der alte Grundsatz, von den *Lebenswelten* der Kinder und Jugendlichen, ihren sozialen und kommunikativen Kontexten, ihren handlungsleitenden Themen auszugehen. Subjekt- und Lebensweltorientierung bedeutet auch, die vorhandenen Formen der Medienaneignung zu kennen und zu respektieren und die in professionell-pädagogischen Kontexten entwickelten Kompetenzkriterien nicht zu verabsolutieren.

- Die zuletzt genannten Punkte legen die Schlussfolgerung nahe, stärker an *zielgruppenspezifischen* Konzepten der Medienbildung zu arbeiten, um die vorhandenen Potenziale und Ressourcen von Kindern und Jugendlichen aus benachteiligten Milieus besser fördern zu können.

- Im Bereich der medienpädagogischen Forschung mangelt es vor allem an Studien in Hauptschul- und Migrationsmilieus.[9] Dies betrifft sowohl Fragen der

---

7   Buchen/Straub (2006: 3) formulieren hierzu folgende Strukturhypothese: „Das Interesse Jugendlicher, die digitalen Medien zur Wissensakkumulation im schulrelevanten bzw. zweckrationalen Sinn zu nutzen, scheint mit dem im Herkunftsmilieu zur Verfügung gestellten (medialen) Bildungskapital und/oder den Bildungschancen zu korrespondieren, die eine Schule (im Ausnahmefall) für eine aufstiegsorientierte Klientel bereithält".

8   Vgl. in diesem Zusammenhang die Unterscheidung von Medienkompetenz und medienpädagogischer Kompetenz bei Blömeke (2000).

9   Erfreulicherweise startete vor kurzem ein mehrjähriges Forschungsprojekt zum Thema „Bildungsbenachteiligung und multifunktionale Medien", das vom JFF – Institut für Medienpädagogik (München) mit Förderung des Bundesministeriums für Bildung und Forschung (BMBF) von Anfang Juli 2006 bis Ende August 2008 durchgeführt wird. Hauptzielgruppe sind Hauptschüler/innen. Im Migrationsbereich fanden in den letzten Jahren Forschungsprojekte zur Mediennutzung statt (u.a. Moser 2006, Treibel 2006, Niesyto/Holzwarth 2005); mit Ausnahme des EU-Projekts CHICAM mangelt es jedoch nach wie vor an längerfristig angelegten Studien, die systematisch die medienpädagogische Praxis mit Kindern und Jugendlichen aus Migrationskontexten wissenschaftlich begleiten und auswerten.

(prozessbezogenen) Medienaneignung und Mediensozialisation als auch die Untersuchung des vorhandenen Medieneinsatzes und der medienbildnerischer Aktivitäten in den entsprechenden pädagogischen Einrichtungen. An Hochschulen mangelt es an empirischen Studien zur Entwicklung von Medienkompetenzen und medienpädagogischen Kompetenzen im Studienverlauf (Lehramtsstudium; andere pädagogische Studiengänge).

In der Zusammenschau dieser Punkte wird deutlich, dass die Frage „Medien und soziale Benachteiligung" primär kein Medienproblem ist. Medien transportieren einerseits Chancen und Potenziale für mehr selbstgesteuerte Aneignungs- und Bildungsprozesse. In Verbindung mit unterschiedlichen Ressourcen – zu denen wesentlich familiäre und schulische Erfahrungsfelder gehören – können sie aber auch vorhandene Unterschiede im Sinne von Bildungsbenachteiligung verfestigen. Medienbezogene Grundhaltungen und pädagogische Konzepte von Lehrkräften, die sich zu wenig für die Lebens- und Medienwelten der Kinder und Jugendlichen öffnen und keine zielgruppenspezifischen Lernarrangements bieten, sind in diesem Zusammenhang ein benachteiligender Faktor.

In gesellschafts- und medienkritischer Perspektive ist hinzuzufügen, dass sich mit der Veralltäglichung und Globalisierung der Medienkommunikation sowie der Privatisierung und Kommerzialisierung des Rundfunk- und Fernsehbereichs (in Deutschland seit Mitte der 1980er Jahre) Angebotsstrukturen herausgebildet haben, die kommunikationskulturelle Problemlagen befördern. Hierzu gehören z.B. Fragen der Auswahl (Bewältigung der Optionenvielfalt) und der Qualitätsbestimmung von Medien, aber auch Formen der Personalisierung, Emotionalisierung und Polarisierung, die auf (mediale) Aufmerksamkeitserregung abzielen und eine reflexive Verarbeitung von Medienangeboten erschweren. Hinzu kommen sog. entwicklungsbeeinträchtigende und jugendgefährdende Angebote im Internet und in anderen Medien (Pornographie etc.), die deutlich zugenommen haben. Außerschulische und schulische Medienpädagogik können diese Problemlagen nicht beseitigen. Hier sind die Verantwortung und der Gestaltungswille von Medienpolitik und allen gesellschaftlichen Kräften gefragt, die an einer Vielfalt medienkultureller Angebote und einer humanen Gesellschaftsentwicklung interessiert sind. Medienpädagogik kann aber dazu beitragen, dass Kinder und Jugendliche aus sozial und bildungsmäßig benachteiligenden Verhältnissen durch Bildungsprozesse mehr Selbstwirksamkeit erfahren und – in medienkritischer Perspektive – sich mehr „Selbstsorge"-Fähigkeiten (Wunden 2006) aneignen. Diese Aufgabe hat auf dem Hintergrund einer „medialen Aufmerksamkeitserregung" (Niesyto 2004) und damit verbundener kommunikationskultureller Problemlagen an Bedeutung gewonnen und verweist zugleich auf die kritische Reflexion mediensozialisationstheoretischer Annahmen.

2 Mediensozialisation – Kritische Anmerkungen

Die Frageperspektive „Was machen die Menschen mit Medien?" führte in den vergangenen zwanzig Jahren zwar zu wichtigen neuen Einsichten in das alltägliche Medienhandeln von Kindern, Jugendlichen und Erwachsenen. Gleichzeitig rückte jedoch die Frageperspektive „Was machen die Medien mit den Menschen?" immer mehr in den Hintergrund. Ohne in deterministische mediale Wirkungstheorien zurückzufallen scheint es mir notwendig, auch danach zu fragen, was für inhaltliche und ästhetische Orientierungs- und Strukturmuster Medien anbieten, wie diese Strukturmuster den Prozess der Mediensozialisation beeinflussen und wie unter diesen Bedingungen Fähigkeiten zu reflexiver Distanz gegenüber Medienangeboten gebildet werden können. Diese Frage ist für Medienbildung insgesamt wichtig, erhält jedoch in Verbindung mit dem Ressourcenaspekt (vorhandenes soziales und kulturelles Kapital) eine besondere Brisanz.

Ausgangspunkt meiner Überlegungen ist die These, dass jugend- und kulturtheoretisch motivierte Medienrezeptionsstudien in den vergangenen Jahren Aspekte wie personalisierende, emotionalisierende, polarisierende Mediengestaltung und deren Bedeutung für die Mediensozialisation, auch im Hinblick auf schicht-/milieuspezifische Unterschiede, nicht hinreichend berücksichtigten (vgl. beispielsweise Mikos 1994 sowie Müller et al. 2002). Notwendig erscheinen differenzierende Sichtweisen, die sowohl die Perspektive eines aktiven, widerständigen Publikums als auch problematische mediale Inszenierungsstrategien[10] sowie schicht-/milieuspezifische Mediennutzungen berücksichtigen. Der Medienforscher Michael Charlton plädierte in diesem Zusammenhang für eine Forschung, die sich weniger der Frage widmet, „in welchem Ausmaß das Publikum gegenüber Medienangeboten autonom handeln kann"; vielmehr müsse untersucht werden, „wie der Rezipient sich dem Text hingibt bzw. entzieht". Charlton meint damit u.a. Studien zu „Strategien der Rezeptionssteuerung" und zu „reading formations" (Charlton 1997: 29).

Hierzu gehören meines Erachtens auch Untersuchungen über die ungleich vorhandenen kulturellen, sozialen und bildungsmäßigen *Ressourcen* für alltägliches Medienhandeln. Gerade eine gesellschaftskritische, soziologisch motivierte Mediensozialisationsforschung sollte ihren Ausgang von einer Analyse der sich histo-

---

10 Beispiele: Talkshows als Ort der Veröffentlichung und Offenbarung privater, intimer Details, teilweise als entwürdigende „Anbrüll-Shows"; Castingshows, bei denen junge Menschen dem öffentlichen Kurzzeitgedächtnis für Sensationslust und den Verkauf von CDs, Zeitschriften und Merchandising-Artikel wissentlich preisgegeben werden; Boulevardisierung und hochgradige Kommerzialisierung der Sportberichterstattung; mediale Kriegsberichterstattung: „embedded journalism" als neue Form militärischer Hofberichterstattung; jeweils Einsatz filmästhetischer Mittel, die auf Personalisierung, Emotionalisierung, Polarisierung setzen. Ausführlich hierzu: Niesyto (2004).

risch entwickelnden und verändernden gesellschaftlich-medialen Angebotsstruktur nehmen und sozialisationsrelevante Einflüsse herausarbeiten.[11] Um nicht missverstanden zu werden, möchte ich noch einmal betonen: Das Postulat des „autonomen Subjekts" und die damit verbundenen Attribute wie Selbststeuerung, Selbstverortung, Wahlfreiheit, symbolische Kreativität sind im Sinne eines auf Emanzipation orientierten Persönlichkeits- und Gesellschaftsverständnisses als anthropologisch-normative Orientierung wichtig – sie sollten aber nicht mit der empirischen Wirklichkeit verwechselt werden.

Im Hinblick auf die Medienrezeptionsforschung stellte Michael Charlton selbstkritisch fest, dass der von ihm präferierte, sog. strukturanalytische Forschungsansatz zwar insgesamt in der Fachöffentlichkeit positiv aufgenommen wurde. Es habe aber auch einige ernstzunehmende Vorbehalte und kritische Anmerkungen gegeben, z.B. den Hinweis auf die zu geringe Berücksichtigung der sozialen Schicht (Mediennutzer), die mangelnde Differenzierung nach spezifischen sozialen Problemlagen, die Überschätzung der Souveränität der (kindlichen) Rezipienten gegenüber dem Medium (Charlton 1997: 32 f). Charlton schlussfolgert: „Auf der Grundlage von Überlegungen zur Handlungsautonomie im Mediensystem […] müssen weitere Untersuchungen konzipiert werden, die es erlauben, die Durchdringung des Bewusstseins der Subjekte durch Medienerfahrungen, das Ausmaß an Offenheit vs. Geschlossenheit von Texten und die Beliebigkeit vs. Determination von Lesarten auszuloten" (ebd., 33).

2.1   Zur Kritik am Konzept medialer Selbstsozialisation

Gerade die *Überschätzung* der Möglichkeiten zu einem medien-autonomen Handeln scheint mir ein kritischer Punkt bei neueren Medienrezeptions- und Mediensozialisationstheorien zu sein. Dies betrifft insbesondere die Überschätzung der „Distanzierungsmöglichkeiten des Subjekts" (Bonfadelli 2004: 195) sowie die mangelnde Auseinandersetzung mit dominanten Leseweisen auf dem Hintergrund medialer Formatierungsprozesse. Neuere Konzepte zur „Selbstsozialisation mit Medien" klammern diese kritischen Punkte weitgehend aus – akzentuiert werden die *Eigenleistungen* der Individuen im Sozialisationsprozess. Diese Eigenleistungen haben im Laufe der letzten zwei Jahrzehnte zweifelsohne zugenommen. Meine Bedenken gegenüber dem Konzept medialer Selbstsozialisation beziehen sich nicht auf diesen empirisch belegbaren Prozess, sondern auf die begriffliche Fas-

---

11   Vgl. in diesem Zusammenhang auch die Analysen von Krotz (2004) und Paus-Hasebrink (2006).

sung dieses Prozesses sowie auf bestimmte Annahmen, die mit dem Konzept medialer Selbstsozialisation verbunden sind.[12] Eine dieser Annahmen betrifft das Postulat einer starken *Autonomie- und Wahlfähigkeit* von Individuen, die als „Selbstsozialisierer" ihre Mitgliedschaften in verschiedenen soziokulturellen Kontexten „selbst wählen und/oder gestalten" (Müller u.a. 2002: 14). „Wahl" und „Wahlfähigkeit" betonen die Eigenleistung des Individuums im Sinne aktiven, selbstständigen Handelns: „Wählbar sind neben Gegenständen und Symbolen Mitgliedschaften, Beziehungsformen und Werthaltungen, Deutungsmuster und sinngebende Inhalte, deren Vermittlungsinstanzen die Wahlnachbarschaften sind" (Müller/Rhein/Glogner 2004: 240). Konzepte zur medialen Selbstsozialisation (siehe auch Fromme et al. 1998) betonen diese Wahlentscheidungen in engem Zusammenhang mit dem gesellschaftlichen Prozess der Individualisierung, der von den Individuen in erheblichem Masse Eigenleistungen abverlangt. Müller et al. weisen auch darauf hin, dass es eine wichtige Frage ist, „ob und wie individuelle Wahlentscheidungen, die musikalischen und medialen Aktivitäten und Präferenzen zugrunde liegen und sich in Lebensstilmustern niederschlagen, von sozialen Bedingungen wie Geschlecht, Alter, Ethnizität, soziale Schichtzugehörigkeit beeinflusst werden" (Müller et al. 2002: 10). Damit wird generell die Bedeutung *struktureller* Faktoren angesprochen. Mein Eindruck ist jedoch, dass in der Vergangenheit insbesondere die Erhebung und Analyse unterschiedlicher sozialer und lebenslagenbezogener Bedingungen und Ressourcen zu wenig thematisiert wurde und nicht mit einem entsprechenden Gewicht in Forschungsdesigns Eingang fand. Dies betrifft im Übrigen nicht nur Ansätze zur Selbstsozialisation, sondern einen Großteil von Jugend- und Medienstudien. Gerade aus medienpädagogischer Perspektive ist es wichtig, soziale und bildungsbezogene Bedingungen und Ressourcen stärker zu berücksichtigen, um zielgruppenspezifische Konzepte z.B. für eine Medienbildung in Hauptschulmilieus entwickeln zu können.

2.2   Zu Fragen reflexiver Distanz gegenüber Medienangeboten

Strategien der medialen Aufmerksamkeitserregung erschweren Formen der reflexiven Distanz. Aus diversen Studien sind Formen der Über-Identifikation mit Medienfiguren und der dauerhaften Flucht in Medienwelten als problematische Formen der Medienaneignung in Teilen der Jugendkultur bekannt (u.a. Wagner/Thennert 2006). Nicht wenige Jugendliche, die in schwierigen sozialen Verhältnissen

---

12   Zur Kritik am Ansatz der Selbstsozialisation siehe auch Bauer (2002).

leben, gehören zu den entsprechenden „Risikogruppen". Die Fähigkeit zur reflexiven Distanz gegenüber Medienangeboten ist wichtig, um selbstbestimmt und sozial verantwortlich mit Medien umgehen, reale und virtuelle Wirklichkeiten unterscheiden und eine Balance von medialen und nicht-medialen Aktivitäten entwikkeln zu können.

Vor ca. zwanzig Jahren erfolgte in Zusammenhang mit dem Theorem der „parasozialen Interaktion" (Horton/Wohl 1956; Horton/Strauss 1957) zunächst eine Theoriebildung, die das *distanzierte Miterleben* des Zuschauers als „In-lusion" bezeichnete und der „Il-lusion" gegenüberstellte: „Der Zuschauer muß eine teilnehmende, zugleich aber auch distanzierte Doppelhaltung einnehmen" (Charlton/ Neumann 1986: 21). Diese „Über-Perspektivität" umfasst die Fähigkeit, die in den Medien erlebten Handlungsmuster nachzuvollziehen, sich in sie hinein zu versetzen (role-taking) und sie zu den jeweils eigenen Handlungsentwürfen in Beziehung zu setzen und für sich verfügbar zu machen (role-making). Es geht um das Gewinnen *neuer* Perspektiven für eigene Lebenssituationen und soziale Deutungsmuster, um Prozesse des reflexiven Vergleichens und Neu-Interpretierens von Erfahrungsbeständen. Charlton und Neumann betonen, dass reflexive Distanz unverzichtbar die Fähigkeit voraussetzt, sein eigenes Handeln vom Standpunkt des anderen aus zu betrachten.

Hier sind wir nun an einem kritischen Punkt angekommen: Was ist reflexive Distanz unter den Bedingungen medienästhetischer Kommunikations- und Erfahrungswelten? Zweifelsohne reicht es heute nicht mehr aus, allein auf sozial-*kognitive* Akte und Dimensionen bei Prozessen der Rollenübernahme hinzuweisen – sozial-*emotionale* und sozial-*ästhetische* Dimensionen sind mindestens ebenso wichtig. Das Symbolsystem (Wort)Sprache ist eng mit nonverbalen Symbolsystemen verknüpft, die gerade in Mediendarstellungen eine große Bedeutung haben. Symbolisches Probehandeln in Medienräumen ist nicht möglich, ohne Verstehen diskursiver *und* präsentativer Ausdrucks- und Kommunikationsformen; medienästhetische Reflexivität lässt sich nicht auf Verbalisierungsfähigkeit reduzieren. Doch wir haben heute das Problem, dass sich diskursive Sprachkulturen durch eine auf das Hier und Jetzt fixierte mediale Aufmerksamkeitserregung verändert haben; stereotype Handlungsmuster sowie idealisierende Konsum- und Leitbilder dominieren in diversen neuen Medienformaten (vgl. u.a. Hinrichs 2006; Holzwarth 2006). Zu diesen Medienentwicklungen und damit verbundenen Aneignungsformen (Über-Identifikationen, Flucht in Medienwelten etc.) liegen bislang kaum empirische Studien vor. Mit dem Ausklammern medienkritischer Analysen und Studien ist die Gefahr verbunden, sich affirmativ gegenüber problematischen Medienentwicklungen zu verhalten und eine selektive Sicht auf die vorhandenen Medienkompetenzen bei Kindern und Jugendlichen einzunehmen. Im Ergebnis mündet diese Haltung in eine Unterschätzung medienpädagogischer Aufgaben zugunsten der einseitigen Betonung (informeller) medialer Selbstbildungsprozesse. Gerade im Hinblick auf den notwendigen Förderbedarf für Kinder und Jugendliche aus benachteiligenden Verhältnissen ist diese Haltung fatal.

3 Kernpunkte einer Medienbildung mit Kindern und Jugendlichen aus Hauptschul- und Migrationsmilieus

Was folgt aus diesen Überlegungen? Medienbildung ist sehr wohl gefordert, Gegengewichte zu Prozessen gesellschaftlicher Ausgrenzung und Diskriminierung zu setzen – z. B. um Kindern und Jugendlichen aus Hauptschul- und Migrationsmilieus Erfahrungen der Selbstwirksamkeit durch handlungsorientierte Formen der Mediengestaltung zu ermöglichen. Vor allem in dieser praktischen Auseinandersetzung mit Medien gelingt es, Fähigkeiten zur reflexiven Distanz gegenüber medialen Inszenierungen in der Kombination unterschiedlicher Komponenten auszubilden (Aufenanger 2006; Sonnenschein 2006). Dabei kann an Formen „alltäglicher Medienkritik" (Kübler 2006: 33f.) angeknüpft werden. Gleichzeitig sollte Medienbildung darauf achten, nicht in eine Modernisierungsfalle zu tappen, die einseitig kognitive, auf Wissenserwerb orientierte Konzepte favorisiert und die sozial-kommunikativen und sozial-ästhetischen Dimensionen von Kompetenzbildung unterschätzt. Dies bedeutet, dass Medienpädagogen genau hinschauen sollten wie Kinder und Jugendliche aus benachteiligenden Verhältnissen mit traditionellen und neuen Medien umgehen, welche Form des Zugangs, der Aneignung und des Ausdrucks sie bevorzugen und entwickeln. Was wir brauchen, sind *zielgruppenspezifische Konzepte*, die ästhetisch, sozial und kommunikativ auf die jeweiligen Bedürfnisse, Aneignungsformen und Themen hin ausgelegt sind.

3.1 Konzeptionelle Erfahrungswerte

Auf dem Hintergrund vieljähriger Berufspraxis und verschiedener Studien möchte ich folgende Punkte hervorheben:

– *Erfahrungs- und Lebensweltorientierung:* Anknüpfen an den vorhandenen Stärken und an den vorhandenen Themen, die Kinder und Jugendliche haben, die für sie zentral und handlungsleitend sind.

- *Bilder, Musik, Körpersprache stärker integrieren.* Dies ist besonders für Kinder und Jugendliche wichtig, die Schwierigkeiten mit der Wort- und Schriftsprache haben. Aus Studien über Bildungsbenachteiligung die Schlussfolgerung zu ziehen, Kindern und Jugendlichen aus benachteiligenden Verhältnissen verstärkt schriftsprachliche Kompetenzen zu vermitteln, reicht nicht aus. Notwendig ist ein integriertes Konzept, das wort- und schriftsprachliche mit bildhaften und multimedialen Ausdrucks- und Kommunikationsformen in eine Balance bringt. Dieser Grundsatz gilt nicht nur für die Eigenproduktion mit Medien, sondern auch für die Gestaltung von Internet-Portalen, die Kinder und Jugendliche ästhetisch ansprechen sollen.
- *Ästhetische Reflexivität fördern:* Mit der Integration medialer Kompetenzen verbinden sich auch Formen einer anderen Reflexivität. Dies bedeutet z.b. im Bereich audiovisueller und multimedialer Produktion, von den selbst erstellten Aufnahmen auszugehen, diese gemeinsam anzusehen, zu vergleichen, sich gegenseitig Verbesserungshinweise zu geben. Ausgangspunkt und Gegenstand von Reflexionen sind die (audio)visuellen Materialien und die damit verbundenen Ausdrucksintentionen; sinnliche Wahrnehmung und reflexive Verarbeitung sind als Symbolverstehen miteinander verknüpft.
- *Medienästhetisch-kulturelle Kompetenzen sind auch für die Arbeitswelt wichtig:* Jugendliche haben erst einmal das Bedürfnis, für eigene Medienproduktionen Themen aufzugreifen, die sie in ihrer Freizeit beschäftigen. Die dabei erworbenen Kompetenzen sind auch für die Arbeitswelt wichtig: sozial-kommunikative, ästhetische, technische, methodische Kompetenzen. Diese Verknüpfungsmöglichkeiten von „ästhetisch-kulturell" und „arbeitsweltbezogen" sollte man konzeptionell viel stärker im Auge haben – anstatt in Berufsschule und Arbeitswelt einseitig auf technisch-instrumentelle Medienkurse zu setzen.
- *Spielerische und non-lineare Arbeitsweisen fördern:* Heute leben wir in einer Zeit, in der wir mit einer enormen Fülle verschiedenartigster Informationen konfrontiert sind. Es ist notwendig, eigene Kriterien für die Auswahl zu entwickeln und gleichzeitig für unterschiedliche Perspektiven offen zu sein, um eigene Horizonte zu erweitern. In pädagogischen Kontexten hat sich hierfür ein Mix aus spielerischen Arbeitsformen, einem Rahmen und situationsspezifischen Inputs bewährt. „Rahmen" meint, eine gewisse Struktur bieten, aber auch genügend Zeit und Flexibilität, die eine Beweglichkeit im Sinne von Experimentieren ermöglicht. Hierzu gehören auch kleinschrittige Übungsaufgaben und Produktionsmöglichkeiten, die weder unter- noch überfordern.
- *Präsentation und Kommunikation lernen:* Dies sind sog. Schlüsselkompetenzen, die immer wichtiger werden: nicht nur zu produzieren, sondern das selbst

Gestaltete anderen zu zeigen und vorzustellen, Feedbacks zu erhalten, zuzuhören, auf andere einzugehen. Das Präsentieren befähigt, zu dem eigenen Produkt zu stehen, Kritik auszuhalten, auf Kritik einzugehen. Dies ist ein Erfahrungswert aus vielen Projekten: durch das Präsentieren selbst erstellter Medienproduktionen Selbstbewusstsein gewinnen und ermutigt werden, die eigene Arbeit fortzusetzen.

3.2 Medienpädagogische Praxisforschung verstärken

Während es zahlreiche Rezeptionsstudien zur Medienaneignung von Kindern und Jugendlichen (national wie international) gibt, mangelt es an systematischen Studien zur Beobachtung und Analyse medienpädagogischer Praxisaktivitäten. Die skizzierten Erfahrungswerte wurden in interkulturellen Medienprojekten wie „Video-Culture" (Niesyto 2003; Witzke 2004) und „CHICAM – Children in Communication about Migration" (de Block et al. 2004; Maurer 2004; Niesyto/Holzwarth 2004; Holzwarth 2007) gewonnen, die als Praxisforschungsprojekte in Zusammenarbeit mit verschiedenen Projektpartnern in jeweils mehreren Ländern durchgeführt wurden. Eine wichtige methodologische Grundlage war der Forschungsansatz „Eigenproduktionen mit Medien" (Niesyto 2006). Diesem Ansatz liegt die These zugrunde: Wer in der heutigen Mediengesellschaft etwas über die Vorstellungen, die Lebensgefühle, das Welterleben von Kindern und Jugendlichen erfahren möchte, der sollte ihnen die Chance geben, sich – ergänzend zu Wort und Schrift – auch mittels eigener, selbst erstellter Medienprodukte auszudrücken. Die methodischen Erfahrungen mit diesem Forschungsansatz deuten darauf hin, dass das Einbeziehen präsentativ-symbolischer Ausdrucksformen (Bilder, Musik, Körpersprache) gerade für jene Kinder und Jugendliche wichtig ist, die Schwierigkeiten im wort- und schriftsprachlichen Bereich haben. Gleichzeitig fördern präsentativ-symbolische Methoden den Ausdruck von emotional besetzten und tabuisierten Themen.[13] Der Forschungsansatz verknüpft medienethnografische Dimensionen zur Erkundung von Lebens- und Medienwelten mit Dimensionen medienpädagogischer Praxisforschung, die der Beobachtung, Analyse und Weiterentwicklung medienpädagogischer Konzepte dienen.

Björn Maurer entwickelte z.B. für das CHICAM-Projekt Lernumgebungen mit klar strukturierten ästhetischen Problemstellungen, die den Kindern die Möglichkeit gaben, sich auf spielerische und selbstentdeckende Weise ein breites Spek-

---

13 Überblicksbeiträge zu dem Forschungsansatz: Niesyto (2006) und Witzke (2005).

trum mediengestalterischer Kompetenzen anzueignen (Maurer 2004). Als sinnvoll erwies sich z.b. eine Orientierung an Media-models (Genres), die den 10- bis 14-jährigen Kindern bekannt waren: an Clips, kleinen spielfilmartigen Szenen, Animationsfilmen konnten sie vorhandenes, „passives" Medienwissen aktivieren und waren aufnahmebereit für vertiefende Inputs. Das Genre fungierte als ästhetisch strukturierender Rahmen, der mit eigenen Inhalten und Formen „gefüllt" werden konnte. Gefragt waren kurze Produktionen, die in einem überschaubaren Zeitraum entstanden und die Kinder/Jugendliche vom technischen und ästhetischen Aufwand her nicht überforderten. Als problematisch erwiesen sich Arbeitsformen, die ein zu starkes Gewicht auf planerische Elemente legten, z.b. zu ausführliche Storyboards (Überforderungssituationen). Motivationsfördernd war es, wenn die Projektaktivitäten spielerische Formen in der Medienaneignung boten und zugleich nicht-mediale Ausdrucksformen integrierten (z.b. Mitbringen präferierter Musikstücke, Tanzen, körperliches Agieren bei Ballspielen). Zentraler Erfahrungswert: *Vorhandene Stärken* sind zu fördern und von den Betreuer/innen gezielt einzubeziehen, damit die Kinder/Jugendlichen mehr Selbstsicherheit und Selbstwirksamkeit erfahren. Deutlich wurde auch ein *besonderer Betreuungsaufwand:* Kinder/Jugendliche aus Migrationskontexten benötigen in besonderer Weise individuelle Aufmerksamkeit, um auf ihre jeweils spezielle Situation einzugehen, sie zum Mitmachen zu motivieren und ihnen Erfolgserlebnisse zu vermitteln. Es reicht nicht aus, adäquate Media-models zu finden; notwendig sind sowohl Formen der Einzel- und Gruppenbetreuung, um ein Klima der Offenheit und der Integration aller Gruppenmitglieder zu erreichen.

Im EU-Projekt CHICAM konnten die Kinder ihre Produktionen in ein passwortgeschütztes Intranet einstellen und sich mit Unterstützung von Medienpädagogen austauschen. Auf dem Hintergrund dieser Erfahrungen möchte ich auf einzelne Punkte hinweisen, die die Gestaltung und die Kommunikation mit *Intranet-Plattformen* betreffen. Sie unterstreichen die Relevanz der bereits skizzierten Prinzipien (Subjektorientierung; Visualität; Möglichkeiten für kreative Gestaltungsräume):

– Orientierung des Designs an den ästhetischen Bedürfnissen der Kinder/Jugendlichen; Integration von spielerischen Elemente und Animationen; Navigation-Buttons mit ausreichend visuellen Elementen;
– Verknüpfung von Intranetbotschaften mit Einzelbildern des Absenders (Portraitgröße);
– Möglichkeiten zum Versenden von Audio-Botschaften und Tondokumenten;
– Möglichkeit, sich gegenseitig Videoaufgaben oder Fragen zu stellen, die audio-visuell beantwortet werden können.

3.3 Schlussbemerkung

Für eine Medienbildung mit Kindern und Jugendlichen aus Hauptschul- und Migrationsmilieus benötigen wir Pädagog/inn/en, die die über eine große Bandbreite von Medienkompetenzen, von Wissen über den Sozialisationshintergrund sowie über geeignete gruppenpädagogische und methodisch-didaktische Qualifikationen verfügen. Gleichzeitig brauchen wir in allen pädagogischen Berufen eine *medienpädagogische Grundbildung* – von der frühen Bildung bis zur Erwachsenen- und Seniorenbildung, um ein Grundverständnis für Fragen der Mediensozialisation und der Möglichkeiten von Medienbildung zu schaffen. Hierzu gehört auch ein Wissen, wie im Kontext von lokalen und regionalen Netzwerken Personen und Ressourcen gezielt für bestimmte Vorhaben zu aktivieren sind, die man aus eigenen Kräften nicht realisieren kann. Es gibt inzwischen eine Reihe regionaler und bundesweiter Online-Plattformen, verschiedene Modellprojekte[14] und eine Vielzahl medienpädagogischer Literatur. Woran es vor allem fehlt, ist die verbindliche Verankerung medienpädagogischer Inhalte in der Ausbildung von pädagogischen Fachkräften sowie schulnahe Fort- und Weiterbildungsmöglichkeiten.

Nach wie vor sind viele Pädagog/inn/en noch zu sehr in einer Symbolsozialisation befangen, die auf dem Diskursiven, auf dem Wort- und Schriftsprachlichen beruht. Oft haben sie Angst, sich auf bestimmte Gesten, Ausdrücke, körperliche Ausdrucksformen einzulassen, gehen zu thematisch und pädagogisch-funktional vor, anstatt erst einmal soziale Beziehungen[15] herzustellen. Das ist ein Punkt, der gerade für Kinder und Jugendliche aus benachteiligenden Verhältnissen sehr wichtig ist. Ihnen das Gefühl zu geben: sie werden akzeptiert, mit all dem, wie sie sind, einen Raum zu haben, dies auszuleben – und ihnen zugleich Möglichkeiten zu geben, neue Kompetenzen zu erwerben, neue Erfahrungen zu machen auf einer Grundlage, die gegenseitige persönliche Wertschätzung mit sozial-emotionalen, ästhetischen und inhaltlichen Lernprozessen verbindet. Es geht um „Spaß" als Gefühl von Stimmigkeit: lustvolles Sich-Veräußern, Neues an sich zu entdecken, Freude am Gelingen, Befriedigung beim Erstellen eines Produkts. Stefan Welling (2005: 220) formulierte dies in einer Studie über milieuspezifische Orientierungsmuster Jugendlicher so: „Letztlich ist es aber für die Jugendlichen weniger wichtig, was die Jugendarbeiter/innen mit ihnen tun, als wie sie es tun, da nur auf diesem Wege die Beziehungen zu den Pädagog/innen erfahrbar werden".

---

14 Zu nennen ist u.a. das von der Landesanstalt für Medien NRW geförderte Modellprojekt „Förderung der Medienkompetenz sozial benachteiligter Kinder und Jugendlicher" (siehe http://www.lfm-nrw.de/downloads/veranstaltungen/11fachtagung-prog.pdf) (Zugriff: 20.03.2007))

15 Zur Relevanz der Entwicklung sozialer Beziehungen in der Jugendarbeit und in der Jugendmedienarbeit siehe auch Böhnisch et al. (1998) bzw. Bader et al. (2001).

Literatur

Aufenanger, Stefan (2006): Medienkritik. In: Computer + Unterricht 16/06, Heft 64, 6-9.

Bader, Roland/Eckmann, Bernhard/Schindler, Wolfgang (Hrsg.) (2001): Bildung in virtuellen Welten. Praxis und Theorie außerschulischer Arbeit mit Internet und Computer. Frankfurt/M.: Gemeinschaftswerk der Evangelischen Publizistik.

Bauer, Ullrich (2002): Selbst- und/ oder Fremdsozialisation: Zur Theoriedebatte in der Sozialisationsforschung (Schwerpunkt). Eine Entgegnung auf Jürgen Zinnecker. Reply to Jürgen Zinnecker 2/ 118. In: ZSE 22/02, 118-142.

Beck, Ulrich (1986): Risikogesellschaft. Auf dem Weg in eine andere Moderne. Frankfurt/Main: Suhrkamp.

Becker, Rolf/Lauterbach, Wolfgang (Hrsg.) (2004): Bildung als Privileg? Erklärungen und Befunde zu den Ursachen der Bildungsungleichheit. Wiesbaden: VS-Verlag.

Billes-Gerhart, Elke (2006): Leben in zwei Welten? – Die Medienkompetenz von Lehrerinnen und Schülerinnen. In: Treibel, Annette/Maier, Maja S./Kommer, Sven/Welzel, Manuela (Hrsg.): Gender medienkompetent. Medienbildung in einer heterogenen Gesellschaft. Wiesbaden: VS-Verlag, 179-192.

Blömeke, Sigrid (2000): Medienpädagogische Kompetenz. Theoretische und empirische Fundierung eines zentralen Elements der Lehrerausbildung. München: kopaed.

Böhnisch, Lothar/Rudolph, Martin/Wolf, Barbara (Hrsg.) (1998): Jugendarbeit als Lebensort. Jugendpädagogische Orientierungen zwischen Offenheit und Halt. Weinheim und München: Juventa.

Bonfadelli, Heinz (2005): Die Rolle digital-interaktiver Medien für gesellschaftliche Teilhabe. In: medien + erziehung, 49. Jhg., Heft 6/05: 6-16.

Bonfadelli, Heinz (2004): Medienwirkungsforschung I. Grundlagen. Konstanz: UTB.

Bourdieu, Pierre (1970): Zur Soziologie der symbolischen Formen. Frankfurt/Main: Suhrkamp.

Buchen, Sylvia/Straub, Ingo (2006): Die Rekonstruktion der digitalen Handlungspraxis Jugendlicher als Theoriegrundlage für eine geschlechterreflexive schulische Medienbildung. In: Onlinezeitschrift MedienPädagogik, Nr. 12/06; URL: http://www.medienpaed.com/ (Zugriff: 05.01.2007).

Charlton, Michael (1997): Rezeptionsforschung als Aufgabe einer interdisziplinären Medienwissenschaft. In: Charlton, Michael/Schneider, Sylvia (Hrsg.): Rezeptionsforschung. Opladen: Westdeutscher Verlag, 16-39.

Charlton, Michael/Neumann, Klaus (1986): Medienkonsum und Lebensbewältigung in der Familie. Methode und Ergebnisse der strukturanalytischen Rezeptionsforschung – mit fünf Falldarstellungen. München/Weinheim: Psychologie Verlags Union.

de Block, Liesbeth/Buckingham, David/Holzwarth, Peter/Niesyto, Horst (2004): Visions Across Cultures: Migrant Children Using Audio-Visual Images to Communicate. Children in Communication about Migration (CHICAM). Deliverables 14 und 15, August 2004. http://www.chicam.net/reports/download/visions_across_cultures.pdf

Fromme, Johannes/Kommer, Sven/Mansel, Jürgen (Hrsg.) (1998): Selbstsozialisation, Kinderkultur und Mediennutzung. Opladen: Leske + Budrich.

Hamburger, Franz/Badawia, Tarek et al. (Hrsg.) (2005): Migration und Bildung. Über das Verhältnis von Anerkennung und Zumutung in der Einwanderungsgesellschaft. Wiesbaden: VS-Verlag.

Hinrichs, Boy (2006): TV-Formate zwischen Standardisierung und Diversifizierung. In: Niesyto, Horst/Rath, Matthias/Sowa, Hubert (Hrsg.): Medienkritik heute. Grundlagen, Beispiele und Praxisfelder. München: kopaed, 197-210.

Hoffmann, Bernward (2006): Medienkompetenz sozial benachteiligter Kinder. In: tv diskurs, 10. Jhg., Nr. 4/06, 14-17.

Holzwarth, Peter (2007): Qualitative Migrationsforschung im Kontext interkultureller Medienarbeit. München: kopaed (in Vorbereitung).

Holzwarth, Peter (2006): „Optik ist das Hauptkriterium sagt Dir Dein Medium" – Medienbild, Körperbild, Selbst- und Fremdwahrnehmung. In: Niesyto, Horst/Rath, Matthias/Sowa, Hubert (Hrsg.): Medienkritik heute. Grundlagen, Beispiele und Praxisfelder. München: kopaed, 211-222.

Horton, Donald/Strauss, Anselm (1957): Interaction in Audience-Participation Shows. In: American Journal of Sociology 62:6, 579-587.

Horton, Donald/Wohl, R. Richard (1956): Mass Communication and Para-Social Interaction. In: Psychiatrie 19:3, 215-229.

Iske, Stefan/Klein, Alexandra/Kutscher, Nadia (2004): Digitale Ungleichheit und formaler Bildungshintergrund – Ergebnisse einer empirischen Untersuchung über Nutzungsdifferenzen von Jugendlichen im Internet. URL: http://www.kib-bielefeld.de/externelinks2005/digitaleungleichheit.pdf (Zugriff: 05.01.2007).

Kommer, Sven (2006): Zum medialen Habitus von Lehramtsstudierenden. Oder: Warum der Medieneinsatz in der Schule eine so ‚schwere Geburt' ist. In: Treibel, Annette/Maier, Maja S./Kommer, Sven/Welzel, Manuela (Hrsg.): Gender medienkompetent. Medienbildung in einer heterogenen Gesellschaft. Wiesbaden: VS-Verlag, 165-177.

Krotz, Friedrich (2004): Identität, Beziehungen und die digitalen Medien. In: medien + erziehung, Heft 6/04, 32-45.

Kübler, Hans-Dieter (2006): Zurück zum ‚kritischen Rezipienten'? Aufgaben und Grenzen pädagogischer Medienkritik. In: Niesyto, Horst/Rath, Matthias/Sowa, Hubert (Hrsg.): Medienkritik heute. Grundlagen, Beispiele und Praxisfelder. München: kopaed, 17-52.

Landesstiftung Baden-Württemberg (Hrsg.): Jugend und verantwortungsvolle Mediennutzung – Medien und Persönlichkeitsentwicklung. Stuttgart: Schriftenreihe der Landesstiftung Baden-Württemberg, Heft 10.

Maurer, Björn (2006): Subjektorientierte Filmbildung an Hauptschulen. In: Niesyto, Horst (Hrsg.): film kreativ. Aktuelle Beiträge zur Filmbildung. München: kopaed, 21-44.

Maurer, Björn (2004): Medienarbeit mit Kindern aus Migrationskontexten. Grundlagen und Praxisbausteine. München: kopaed.

Medienpädagogischer Forschungsverbund Südwest (Hrsg.) (2005): JIM-Studie 2005 Jugend, Information (Multi-) Media. Stuttgart: Landesanstalt für Kommunikation.

Mikos, Lothar (1994): Fernsehen im Erleben der Zuschauer. Vom lustvollen Umgang mit einem populären Medium. Berlin/ München: Quintessenz.

Moser, Heinz (2006): Medien und die Konstruktion von Identität und Differenz. In: Treibel, Annette/Maier, Maja S./Kommer, Sven/Welzel, Manuela (Hrsg.): Gender medienkompetent. Medienbildung in einer heterogenen Gesellschaft. Wiesbaden: VS-Verlag, 53-74.

Müller, Renate/Glogner, Patrick/Rhein, Stefanie/Heim, Jens (Hrsg.) (2002): Wozu Jugendliche Musik und Medien gebrauchen. Jugendliche Identität und musikalische und mediale Geschmacksbildung. Weinheim und München: Juventa.

Müller, Renate/Rhein, Stefanie/Glogner, Patrick (2004): Das Konzept musikalischer und medialer Selbstsozialisation – widersprüchlich, trivial, überflüssig? In: Hoffmann, Dagmar/Merkens, Hans (Hrsg.): Jugendsoziologische Sozialisationstheorie. Impulse für die Jugendforschung. Weinheim und München: Juventa, 237-252.

Niesyto, Horst/Holzwarth, Peter (2005): Qualitative Forschung auf der Basis von Eigenproduktionen mit Medien – Erfahrungswerte aus dem EU-Forschungsprojekt CHICAM – Children In Communication about Migration. In: Bachmair, Ben/Diepold, Peter/de Witt, Claudia (Hrsg.): Jahrbuch Medienpädagogik (Band 5). Evaluation und Analyse. Wiesbaden: VS-Verlag, 163-189.

Niesyto, Horst (2006): Medienpädagogische Forschung auf der Grundlage handlungsorientierter Medienarbeit. In: medien + erziehung, 50. Jhg., Heft 5 /06, 29-37.

Niesyto, Horst (2004): Aufmerksamkeitserregung. Kritische Anmerkungen zum kulturellen Kapitalismus unserer Zeit und den Aufgaben einer emanzipatorischen Medienbildung. In: Pirner, Manfred L./Breuer, Thomas (Hrsg.): Medien – Bildung – Religion. Zum Verhältnis von Medienpädagogik und Religionspädagogik in Theorie, Empirie und Praxis. München: kopaed, 52-72.

Niesyto, Horst (Hrsg.) (2003): VideoCulture. Video und interkulturelle Kommunikation. Grundlagen, Methoden und Ergebnisse eines internationalen Forschungsprojekts. München: kopaed.

Niesyto, Horst (2000): Medienpädagogik und soziokulturelle Unterschiede. Eine Studie zur Förderung der aktiven Medienarbeit mit Kindern und Jugendlichen aus bildungsmäßig und sozial benachteiligten Verhältnissen. Baden-Baden / Ludwigsburg: Medienpädagogischer Forschungsverbund Südwest.

Niesyto, Horst (1991): Erfahrungsproduktion mit Medien. Selbstbilder, Darstellungsformen, Gruppenprozesse. Weinheim und München: Juventa.

Otto, Hans-Uwe/Kutscher, Nadia (2004): Informelle Bildung online. Perspektiven für Bildung, Jugendarbeit und Medienpädagogik. Weinheim/München: Juventa.

Paus-Hasebrink, Ingrid (2006): Medienpädagogische Forschung braucht gesellschaftskritischen Handlungsbezug. Besondere Verantwortung gebührt sozial benachteiligten Kindern und Jugendlichen. In: medien + erziehung, 50. Jhg., Heft 5/06, 22-28.

PISA-Konsortium Deutschland (Hrsg.) (2004): PISA 2003. Der Bildungsstand der Jugendlichen in Deutschland – Ergebnisse des zweiten internationalen Vergleichs. Münster: Waxmann.

Rehberg, Karl-Siegbert (Hrsg.) (2006): Soziale Ungleichheit, Kulturelle Unterschiede, Verhandlungen des 32. Kongresses der Deutschen Gesellschaft für Soziologie in München 2004, 2 Bände mit CD-ROM, Frankfurt / New York, Campus.

Röll, Franz-Josef (1998): Mythen und Symbole in populären Medien. Der wahrnehmungsorientierte Ansatz in der Medienpädagogik. Frankfurt/M.: Gemeinschaftswerk der Evangelischen Publizistik.

Rüsel, Manfred (2006): Filmarbeit in sozialen Brennpunkten. In: Niesyto, Horst (Hrsg.): film kreativ. Aktuelle Beiträge zur Filmbildung. München: kopaed, 45-55.

Schelhowe, Heidi (2006): Medienpädagogik und Informatik: Zur Notwendigkeit einer Neubestimmung der Rolle digitaler Medien in Bildungsprozessen. In: Onlinezeitschrift MedienPädagogik, Ausgabe 12 (2006), URL: http://www.medienpaed.com/ (Zugriff: 05.01.2007).

Schwinn, Thomas (2006): Ungleichheitsstrukturen versus Vielfalt der Lebensführungen. In: Rehberg, Karl-Siegbert (Hrsg.): Soziale Ungleichheit, Kulturelle Unterschiede, Verhandlungen des 32. Kongresses der Deutschen Gesellschaft für Soziologie in München 2004, Band 2, Frankfurt / New York, Campus: 1283-1297.

Schwinn, Thomas (2004): Differenzierung und soziale Ungleichheit. Die zwei Soziologien und ihre Verknüpfung. Frankfurt/Main: Verlag Humanities.

Sonnenschein, Sabine (2006): Methoden für „Kritische Zeiten". Förderung der Medienkritikfähigkeit – ein Streifzug durch die medienpädagogische Praxis. In: Niesyto, Horst/Rath, Matthias/Sowa, Hubert (Hrsg.): Medienkritik heute. Grundlagen, Beispiele und Praxisfelder. München: kopaed, 275-283.

Süss, Daniel (2004): Mediensozialisation von Heranwachsenden. Dimensionen – Konstanten – Wandel. Wiesbaden: VS-Verlag.

Treibel, Annette/Maier, Maja S. (2006): Gender medienkompetent? Eine Einleitung. In: Treibel, Annette/Maier, Maja S./Kommer, Sven/Welzel, Manuela (Hrsg.): Gender medienkompetent. Medienbildung in einer heterogenen Gesellschaft. Wiesbaden: VS-Verlag, 11-23.

Tulodziecki, Gerhard (2006): Schulische Medienpädagogik – von den 1950er Jahren bis heute. In: medien + erziehung, 50. Jahrgang, Nr. 5, Oktober 2006, S. 49-56.

Tulodziecki, Gerhard (1997): Medien in Bildung und Erziehung. Grundlagen und Beispiele einer handlungs- und entwicklungsorientierten Medienpädagogik. Bad Heilbrunn: Klinkhardt.

Wagner, Ulrike/Thennert, Helga (Hrsg.) (2006): Neue Wege durch die konvergente Medienwelt. BLM-Schriftenreihe, Bd. 85. München: Fischer-Verlag.

Welling, Stefan (2005): Medienpädagogisches ‚Brötchenbacken' – ein integriertes Modell medienpädagogischer Praxisentwicklung als Grundlage professioneller Qualifizierung. URL: http://www.josefstal.de/mac/days/2004/buch/stefan_welling.pdf (Zugriff: 05.01.2007).

Witzke, Margit (2005): Jugendforschung mit Video-Eigenproduktionen. In: Mikos, Lothar/Wegener, Claudia (Hrsg.): Qualitative Medienforschung. Ein Handbuch. Konstanz: UVK, 323-332.

Witzke, Margrit (2004): Identität, Selbstausdruck und Jugendkultur. Eigenproduzierte Videos Jugendlicher im Vergleich mit ihren Selbstaussagen. Ein Beitrag zur Jugend(kultur)forschung. München: kopaed.

Wunden, Wolfgang (2006): Selbstsorge als Quelle kritischer Kompetenz. In: Niesyto, Horst/Rath, Matthias/Sowa, Hubert (Hrsg.): Medienkritik heute. Grundlagen, Beispiele und Praxisfelder. München: kopaed, 87-99.

New Perspectives for Media Education /
Neue Perspektiven für Medienbildung

David Buckingham

Digital Culture, Media Education and the Place of Schooling

It is now more than a quarter of a century since the first microcomputers began arriving in British schools. I can personally recall the appearance of one such large black metal box – a Research Machines 380Z – in the North London comprehensive school where I was working in the late 1970s; and I can also remember the computer programme that was demonstrated to the English Department – a simple but genuinely thought-provoking package called *Developing Tray*, a kind of 'hangman' game in which a poem gradually emerged like a photographic image in a developing tray. I can also recall, perhaps a couple of years later, being involved in a research project called 'Telesoftware', where educational software was (amazingly to us at the time) sent over the telephone line and recorded onto little cassette tapes. Actually, very few of the other teachers were interested in the software that was being delivered; but the students in my Media Studies class were quick to commandeer the equipment to make animated title sequences for their scratch-edited video productions.

Around the same time, the American technology guru Seymour Papert was telling us that computers would fundamentally transform education – and ultimately make the school itself redundant. 'Computers,' he wrote in a book published in 1980, 'will gradually return to the individual the power to determine the patterns of education. Education will become more of a private act' (Papert, 1980: 37). And four years later, he told readers even more bluntly, 'There won't be schools in the future. The computer will blow up the school' (Papert, 1984: 38). He was not alone. Steve Jobs, the founder of Apple Computers, then pitching relentlessly to capture the education market in the US, was another passionate advocate of the revolutionary potential of educational computing; and he was later joined by an enthusiastic cohort of visionary marketers, such as Bill Gates of Microsoft, who were keen to use schools as a springboard into the much more valuable home market. Indeed, ten years earlier, the radical theorist Ivan Illich was creating a vision of a 'deschooled society', in which computers would permit the creation of informal, 'convivial' networks of learners, and schools and teachers would simply wither away (Illich, 1971).

Such predictions about the transformative potential of technology have a very long history, not just in education; and in retrospect, it is easy to show that they have largely failed to come true. The wholesale revolution Papert and others were predicting patently has not taken place: for better or worse, the school as an institution is still very much with us, and most of the teaching and learning that happens there has remained completely untouched by the influence of technology. And yet, over the same period, electronic technology has become an increasingly significant dimension of most young people's lives. Digital media – the internet, mobile phones, computer games, interactive television – are now an indispensable aspect of children's and young people's leisure-time experiences. Indeed, young people's relationship with digital technology is now no longer primarily formed in the context of the school – as it was during the 1980s, and even into the 1990s – but in the domain of popular culture.

In this chapter, I seek to address some of the challenges that are posed for schools by young people's emerging digital cultures. I question the idea that the school is necessarily an outdated institution, and that its demise is either imminent or something to be eagerly anticipated. I also question the rather loosely celebratory account of young people's relationships with digital media that often circulates among enthusiasts for technology – the idea that this technology is somehow inevitably liberating or empowering young people, or indeed that it automatically promotes more spontaneous and 'informal' styles of learning. Yet at the same time, I also challenge the idea that technology merely offers a more efficient way for schools to achieve their traditional mission – or, in terms that are axiomatic among educational policy-makers, to 'raise standards'. Instead, I argue that schools can play a more proactive role, by offering both critical perspectives and participatory opportunities in relation to new media, and by attempting to redress some of the forms of inequality that are explored by other contributors to this book. Yet while seeking to avoid the perils of utopianism and a narrow instrumentalism, I argue that young people's participation in contemporary 'cyberworlds' does raise some fundamental questions about the future of the school as an institution; although, as I shall indicate, we may need some relatively traditional answers to those questions.

Why no technological revolution?

'I believe that the motion picture is destined to revolutionize our educational system, and that in a few years it will supplant largely, if not entirely, the use of textbooks. The education of the future will be conducted through the medium of the motion picture, a visualized education, where it should be possible to obtain one hundred percent efficiency.' Thus spoke the American inventor Thomas Edison in 1922, extolling in grandiose but strangely familiar terms the educational potential of the new media technology of his time.

The American educational historian Larry Cuban (1986) has written a valuable history of these visions of technological utopia, and of the ways in which they have largely failed to materialise. Edison was by no means the only advocate of the revolutionary potential of the cinema; and, at around the same time, many similar claims were being made about the medium of radio. Thirty years on, the same kind of rhetoric was arising around the new medium of television – and, as we entered the 1960s, hopes were again fixed on a new generation of 'teaching machines' in the form of programmed learning laboratories. Cuban's history traces how the same kinds of educational claims recurred with each new medium; and how, in each case, those claims were largely refuted by subsequent developments. Educational reformers and technology marketers (often singing from the same hymn sheet) repeatedly claimed that new media would bring fresh new forms of learning into the classroom, making old media such as books, and in many cases also teachers, redundant. And as Cuban shows, the large majority of teachers ignored these apparently revolutionary devices: after extensive investment and (in some cases) a period of initial fascination, the projectors and the television monitors were generally consigned to the classroom cupboard or left to gather dust.

Is there any reason to believe that the situation with regard to contemporary information and communication technologies will be any different? The debate about ICTs in education has consistently been dominated by the technology boosters – as has much of the research. But in recent years, some more critical research has begun to emerge that paints a rather different picture. Larry Cuban's own study, pithily entitled *Oversold and Underused: Computers in the Classroom* (2001) shows how this technology has remained marginal to the practice of most teachers – even enthusiastic and competent teachers in extremely well-equipped, affluent schools such as (in his research) those of Silicon Valley, California. Several other studies in the US and the UK are now beginning to tell a similar story (for a comprehensive review, see Buckingham, in press): they show that most teachers remain sceptical about the educational benefits of computer technology, and that investment in technology does not necessarily result in new or creative forms of learning, or even in improvements in test results. In the area of literacy, for example, a definitive recent review conducted at my own university concluded that there was no evidence that non-ICT methods of teaching and non-ICT resources were inferior to the use of ICT; and it urged policy-makers to refrain from any further investment in the area until more persuasive findings were available (EPPI Centre, 2004). Likewise, a recent report for the OECD found that the level of day-to-day use of computers in schools was 'disappointing', with only a minority of teachers using even standard computer applications (OECD, 2004); while a recent UK government inspection report found that while most teachers were keen to use ICT for routine administration and management, and for preparing teaching materials, very few were using it to support students' learning in the classroom (Ofsted, 2004).

There are many possible explanations for this situation. Part of the problem clearly lies in the way investment has been allocated: the bulk of the funding has been spent on hardware, significantly less on software and even less on training teachers. There are undoubtedly some very valuable software tools available, but truly high-quality educational packages remain in short supply, and there are few genuinely independent evaluations of the material available: not least for economic and technological reasons, the education market remains dominated by 'drill-and-skill' packages which are very far from the creative, student-centred software envisaged by the ICT pioneers. The technology itself has also often failed to deliver: incompatible formats, equipment crashes, poorly-written software, the need to constantly purchase the latest upgrades – these are not merely temporary technical difficulties, but phenomena that are endemic to an industry whose ability to generate profit is fundamentally premised on planned obsolescence. Furthermore, the rapidly changing nature of the technology has resulted in some rushed and ill-advised decisions on the part of policy-makers keen not to be 'left behind' by what appear to be the latest educational advances.

Even so, advocates of technology have generally been far too ready to blame teachers, arguing that they are simply too old-fashioned or lazy to adapt, or alternatively too threatened by such an apparently fundamental challenge to their authority. Larry Cuban's research recognises that teachers have been inclined to resist the implementation of technology; but he argues that this has been characteristic of a whole range of attempts at educational reform that go well beyond technology (see also Tyack and Cuban, 1995). The problem, he argues, is not that teachers are hopelessly inflexible, but that the large majority of educational reforms – including those that are driven by technology – are implemented without the active involvement of teachers themselves. Lasting educational reform, he suggests, must involve teachers as leading agents, not simply as consumers or as deliverers of plans derived elsewhere. While there are certainly many exceptions to this argument, it does seem to hold true in the case of technology.

Nevertheless, the drive to insert ICT in education has continued to accelerate. As Neil Selwyn (1999, 2003) has shown, the move has been informed, on the one hand, by governments' largely uncritical acceptance of nebulous rhetorics of the 'information society'. Much of the policy discourse is characterised by a form of technological determinism – the notion that digital technology will automatically produce certain kinds of effects (for example, in relation to 'learning styles' or particular forms of cognition) irrespective of the social contexts in which it is used, or indeed the social actors who use it.

Yet the apparently unstoppable advance of ICT in education has also been driven by commercial industry, and by governments' sometimes highly interventionist efforts to support it (see Scanlon and Buckingham, 2003; Selwyn, 2005). To state the obvious, computers are very big business. Amid a volatile and rapidly changing economy, education has provided a relatively stable market for corporations eager to sustain their profit margins; and it has also been widely seen as a springboard into the lucrative domestic market. As education spending has moved to a free-market model, it may be that teachers have become more susceptible to the appeals of educational hucksters and profiteers. At the same time, as Bettina Fabos (2004) has amply demonstrated, the internet has itself become increasingly commercialised – albeit often in ways that are invisible to many of its users.

In many respects, then, the story of ICT in education could be seen as one of another failed technological revolution. Yet in questioning the claims that are typically made here, it is not my intention simply to reinforce the arguments of those who would seek to abandon technology in favour of a return to 'basics' or more 'natural' forms of learning – whatever they may be (see, for example, Cordes and Miller, 2000). Ultimately, one of the major problems with the debate about technology and education – and one of the symptoms of its immaturity – is that it has been far too readily polarised as a debate between the enthusiasts and the resisters. Those who question or challenge the uses of ICT in education are all too easily condemned as prehistoric 'technophobes' or as 'Luddites', irrationally resisting 'progress'; while those who profess the benefits of technology are perhaps too easily stereotyped as naïve and unrealistic in their aspirations. In the process, fundamental questions about what teachers and students might want to use technology for, and about what we need to know about technology, tend to be marginalised.

Digital childhoods?

If schools have remained relatively unaffected by the advent of digital technology, the same cannot be said of children's lives outside school. On the contrary, contemporary childhoods are now permeated, even in some respects defined, by the modern media – by television, video, computer games, the internet, mobile phones and popular music, and by the enormous range of media-related commodities that make up contemporary consumer culture (see Buckingham, 2000). In fact, this has long been the case. As early as the 1960s, it was apparent that children were spending more time watching television than they were spending in school.

Even so, the advent of digital technology has produced, and been accompanied by, some significant changes in children's media experiences. These do not need to be rehearsed in any detail here, but they would include: the proliferation of media outlets; the individualisation of access to media; the advent of so-called interactive media; the increasing potential for using media for communication and participation; the steady commercialisation of media; and the increasingly (although perhaps superficially) subversive appeals of much of this new media culture. As many authors have noted, these changes have had significant – but quite ambiguous – implications in terms of our conceptions of childhood. Some have argued that the modern media are effectively destroying childhood – or at least blurring the boundaries between childhood, youth and adulthood – and that traditional moral values need to be reasserted (e.g. Postman, 1983). On the other hand, advocates of the new 'digital generation' see technology as a force of liberation for children – a means for them to reach past the constraining influence of their elders, and to create new, autonomous forms of communication and community (e.g. Tapscott, 1998).

In my view, there are good reasons to be wary of the rhetoric of the 'digital generation' (Buckingham, 2006). Like many of the arguments about ICT in education, they are characterised by a form of technological determinism – by the notion that technology will bring about social or psychological changes irrespective of how, and by whom, it is used. The notion of the 'digital generation' also essentialises young people, and can lead us to ignore inequalities and differences between them. Most enthusiasts for technology appear to believe that the so-called 'digital divide' is a temporary phenomenon, and that the technology poor will eventually catch up as the equipment falls in price. However, this is to assume that the 'early adopters' of such technology will stay where they are; and, more broadly, that the market is a neutral mechanism, that functions simply by giving individuals what they need.

Furthermore, this generational rhetoric also leads us to ignore what one can only call the *banality* of much new media use. Recent studies suggest that most children's everyday uses of new technology are characterised not by spectacular manifestations of innovation and creativity, but by relatively mundane forms of communication and information retrieval (e.g. Facer et al., 2003; Holloway and Valentine, 2003; Livingstone and Bober, 2005). Furthermore, many young people

– like many adults – also find technology frustrating; and many, for various reasons, positively refuse to engage with it (Facer and Furlong, 2001). One could even argue that for most young people, technology *per se* is a relatively marginal concern. Very few are interested in technology in its own right, or believe it has magical powers: they are simply concerned about what they can use it for.

Yet despite the limitations of these arguments, it remains the case that most young people's experiences with technology are now taking place outside school, in the context of what has been termed 'techno-popular culture'. And the contrast between what happens there and what happens in the classroom is often very striking. For example, children's use of the internet outside school is likely to involve a wide range of activities. They are chatting in chat-rooms and exchanging instant messages with friends. They are seeking out information about hobbies, sports and leisure interests. They are playing games, sometimes with others in distant parts of the world. They are shopping – or at least window-shopping – and downloading pop music and Hollywood movies. Increasing numbers of them are posting up their own images and music on social networking sites like *My Space*. And, perhaps above all, they are visiting sites related to their other media enthusiasms – soap operas, computer games, reality TV shows and pop celebrities. What they are not doing to any significant degree is engaging in the purposeful pursuit of education.

Meanwhile, what are young people doing on the internet in school? In most cases, very little. Few schools offer extended or unrestricted access for students; and many employ filtering systems that turn web surfing into an obstacle course. Most formal ICT classes cover just the rudiments of information retrieval, alongside word-processing and simple spreadsheets. Some teachers offer web-based homework assignments, but these are often restricted to visiting prescribed sites. Of course, there are some good reasons for these limitations. But it is not surprising that many children are bored and frustrated by their use of ICT in schools (Levin and Arafeh, 2002; Selwyn, 2006). Compared with the complex multi-media experiences some children have outside school, much classroom work is bound to appear unexciting. Children who use the internet at home are likely to be developing a strong sense of their own autonomy and authority as users of technology, yet this is precisely what is so often denied to them in school.

This new 'digital divide' could be seen as symptomatic of a much broader phenomenon – a widening gulf between children's worlds outside school and the emphases of many education systems. The classrooms of today would be easily recognisable to the pioneers of public education of the mid-nineteenth century: the ways in which teaching and learning are organised, the kinds of skills and knowledge that are valued in assessment, and even a good deal of the actual curriculum content, have changed only superficially since that time. Indeed, some have argued that schooling is now heading determinedly backwards, retreating from the uncertainty of contemporary social change towards the apparently comforting stability of a new 'educational fundamentalism', in which traditional relationships of authority between adults and children can be restored (Kenway and Bullen, 2000).

This is not to posit an absolute opposition between 'school culture' and 'children's culture'. The school is inevitably a site for negotiation (and often for struggle) between competing conceptions of knowledge and cultural value. Nevertheless, there is now an extraordinary contrast between the high levels of activity and enthusiasm that characterise children's consumer cultures and the passivity that increasingly suffuses their schooling. Of course, teachers have perennially complained about children's weakening 'attention span'; although in fact the levels of intense concentration and energy that characterise children's playground engagements with phenomena like Pokémon are quite at odds with the deadening influence of mechanical testing that currently prevails in many classrooms (Buckingham and Sefton-Green, 2003). Children are now immersed in a consumer culture that positions them as active and autonomous; yet in school, a great deal of their learning is passive and teacher-directed. Indeed, as Jane Kenway and Elizabeth Bullen (2000) point out, the 'knowledge politics' of children's consumer culture often explicitly oppose those of formal schooling, presenting teachers as dull and earnest, worthy not of emulation but of well-justified rebellion and rejection. Like a Rabelaisian 'carnival', children's media culture has increasingly become an arena in which authoritarian values of seriousness and conformity are subverted and undermined. In this context, it is hardly surprising if children come to perceive schooling as marginal to their identities and concerns – or at best, as a kind of functional chore.

Making connections?

On one level, schools have a great deal to learn from children's popular culture. Young people's everyday uses of computer games or the internet involve a whole range of informal learning processes, in which there is often a highly democratic relationship between 'teachers' and 'learners'. Children learn to use these media largely through trial and error – through exploration, experimentation and play; and collaboration with others – both in face-to-face and virtual forms – is an essential element of the process. Playing some types of computer games, for example, involves an extensive series of cognitive activities: remembering, hypothesis testing, predicting and strategic planning. While game players are often deeply immersed in the virtual world of the game, dialogue and exchange with others is crucial. And game playing is also a 'multi-literate' activity: it often involves interpreting complex three-dimensional visual environments, reading both on-screen and off-screen texts (such as games magazines and websites) and processing auditory information. In the world of computer games, success ultimately derives from the disciplined and committed acquisition of skills and knowledge (Carr et al., 2006).

Likewise, online chat and instant messaging require very specific skills in language and interpersonal communication (Davies, 2006; Tingstad, 2003). Young people have to learn to 'read' subtle nuances, often on the basis of minimal cues. They have to learn the rules and etiquette of online communication, and to shift quickly between genres or language registers. Provided they are sensible about divulging personal information, chat rooms provide young people with a safe arena for rehearsing and exploring aspects of identity and personal relationships that may not be available elsewhere. Again, much of this learning is carried out without explicit teaching: it involves active exploration, 'learning by doing', apprenticeship rather than direct instruction. Above all, it is profoundly social: it is not something that can be neatly divided into a set of psychological types (or 'multiple intelligences'), but a matter of participation in 'communities of practice'.

Nevertheless, these arguments can be overstated. The attempt to vindicate the educational value of popular culture has often tipped over into uncritical celebration. James Gee's recent book *What Video Games Have To Teach Us About Learning and Literacy* (2003) is a symptomatic case in point. Gee argues, quite correctly, that computer games involve a wide range of learning processes; and from his account of his own experiences of game-playing, he derives a cogent set of learning principles that provides some important challenges for educators. However, he is so keen to use computer games as a stick with which to beat the formal education system that he ignores many of the limitations of gaming, and indeed much of the value and necessity of formal schooling. He establishes a hierarchy of value, whereby 'good' games are those that follow his principles, while games that do not are barely considered. In fact, academic work on game players suggests that play frequently involves a considerable amount of pointless frustration and wasted time (e.g. Oliver and Pelletier, 2006); and research on online gaming shows that there is often a great deal of 'formality' – and indeed a considerable amount of power-playing – in such allegedly supportive communities (Carr et al., 2006).

Like many 'reader-oriented' accounts of popular culture, this kind of analysis celebrates the 'activity' of the reader (or in this case, the player), but it tends to ignore the ways in which activity is intimately tied up with the act of consumption.

Furthermore, it often tends to conflate activity with *agency* – that is, with power and control. Indeed, it could be argued that a key imperative in the modern media is precisely to create the *illusion* of control, the sense that we the audience are really in charge – a tendency of which the supremely 'interactive' phenomenon of so-called reality TV offers many examples. Games may well involve 'active learning', but it would be simplistic to assume that 'activity' in itself makes them a valid model for learning in general. Likewise, an easy opposition between 'formal' and 'informal' learning tends to obfuscate the issue – not least because schools may provide many more opportunities for 'informal learning' than critics like Gee are prepared to allow (see Sefton-Green, 2003).

There is a great deal more that might be said here about the attempts of educators to co-opt young people's out-of-school culture. At present in the UK, there is considerable interest in the potential of using computer games in classrooms – particularly as a means of re-engaging disaffected learners (who, in contemporary debates, seem to be almost invariably identified as boys). Over the past few years, the media, ICT and publishing industries have become increasingly involved in the education market. There is an ever more competitive market for broadly 'educational' toys, software, books and magazines targeted both at homes and at schools; and we are now seeing the emergence of a significant new market in interactive e-learning, led by well-established television companies. This is a market that has also been primed by very large amounts of government money.

What typically results here is a form of 'edutainment', a hybrid mix of education and entertainment that relies heavily on visual material, on narrative or game-like formats, and on more informal, less didactic styles of address (see Buckingham and Scanlon, 2003, 2004). Yet despite its appeal to parents, this is material that most young people find distinctly lacking in appeal. When compared with the majority of computer games and entertainment websites, most educational materials on the web and on CD-ROM are distinctly limited. They are visually impoverished, lacking in interactivity and thin on engaging content. This is partly a matter of funding: when one compares the production budget of an average Playstation game with that of an educational game, it is not hard to understand why educational games are so lacking in engagement. However, it also reflects a failure of imagination – even a failure to take the pleasures of entertainment seriously. For example, our research on educational games has found that the learning content in such games is often detached from the game-play: the game-play generally functions merely as a kind of reward for getting the test questions right, or as a window dressing for something that is implicitly defined as fundamentally tedious (Scanlon et al., 2005). In other words, the game serves as a kind of sugar for the pill; and in our research, we found that children quickly developed the ability to take the sugar while leaving the pill behind.

Ultimately, if we are seeking to re-engage disaffected learners, the answer is not to adorn teaching materials with computerised bells and whistles – to 'jazz up' the curriculum with a superficial gloss of kid-friendly digital culture. Nor is it to adopt digital technology in the service of narrowly instrumental forms of learning, in an attempt to make them more palatable. Dressing up tests or multiplication tables with a veneer of 'fun' is a strategy that most children will quickly see through. What is required is a much more thoroughgoing, and more critical, engagement with children's digital cultures.

Towards digital literacy

The notion of 'digital literacy' is not new. Indeed, arguments for 'computer literacy' date back at least to the 1980s. Yet as Goodson and Mangan (1996) have pointed out, the term 'computer literacy' is often poorly defined and delineated, both in terms of its overall aims and in terms of what it actually entails. As they suggest, rationales for computer literacy are often based on dubious assertions about the vocational relevance of computer skills, or about the inherent value of learning with computers, which have been widely challenged. In contemporary usage, digital (or computer) literacy often appears to amount to a minimal set of skills that will enable the user to operate effectively with software tools, or in performing basic information retrieval tasks. This is essentially a *functional* definition: it specifies the basic skills that are required to undertake particular operations, but it does not go very far beyond this.

For example, the British government has attempted to define and measure the ICT skills of the population alongside traditional literacy and numeracy as part of its *Skills for Life* survey (Williams et al., 2003). This survey defines these skills at two levels. Level 1 includes an understanding of common ICT terminology; the ability to use basic features of software tools such as word-processors and spreadsheets; and the ability to save data, copy and paste, manage files, and standardise formats within documents. Level 2 includes the use of search engines and databases, and the ability to make more advanced use of software tools. In the 2003 survey, over half of the sample of adults was found to be at 'entry level or below' (that is, not yet at Level 1) in terms of practical skills. Other research suggests that adults' ability to use search engines for basic information retrieval, for example, is distinctly limited (Livingstone et al., 2005: 23-24).

Another context in which the notion of digital literacy has arisen in recent years is in relation to online safety. For example, the European Commission's 'Safer Internet Action Plan' has emphasised the importance of internet literacy as a means for children to protect themselves against harmful content. Alongside the range of hotlines, filters and 'awareness nodes', it has funded several educational projects designed to alert children to the dangers of online paedophiles and pornography – although in fact it is notable that many of these projects have adopted a significantly broader conception of internet literacy, that goes well beyond the narrow concern with safety. The 'Educaunet' materials, for example, provide guidance on evaluating online sources and assessing one's own information needs, as well as recognising the necessity and the pleasure of risk for young people (see www.educaunet.org).

Even so, most discussions of digital literacy remain primarily preoccupied with *information* – and therefore tend to neglect some of the broader cultural uses of the internet (not least by young people). To a large extent, the concern here is with promoting more efficient uses of the medium – for example, via the development of advanced search skills (or so-called 'power searching') that will make it easier to locate relevant resources amid the proliferation of online material. Popular guides to digital literacy have begun to address the need to evaluate online content (e.g. Gilster, 1997; Warlick, 2005); yet these formulations still tend to focus on technical 'know-how' that is relatively easy to acquire, and on skills that are likely to become obsolete fairly rapidly. Much of the discussion appears to assume that information can be assessed simply in terms of its factual accuracy. From this perspective, a digitally literate individual is one who can search efficiently, who compares a range of sources, and sorts authoritative from non-authoritative, and relevant from irrelevant, documents (Livingstone et al., 2005: 31). There is little recognition here of the symbolic or persuasive aspects of digital media, of the emotional dimensions of our uses and interpretations of these media, or indeed of aspects of digital media that exceed mere 'information'.

Bettina Fabos (2004) provides a useful review of such attempts to promote more critical evaluation of online content. In practice, she argues, evaluation 'checklists' are often less than effective. Students may feel inadequate assessing sites when they are unfamiliar with the topics they cover; and they largely fail to apply these criteria, instead emphasising speedy access to information and appealing visual design. More to the point, however, such 'web evaluation' approaches appear to presume that objective truth will eventually be achieved through a process of diligent evaluation and comparison of sources. They imply that sites can be easily divided into those that are reliable, trustworthy and factual, and those that are biased and should be avoided. In practice, such approaches often discriminate against low-budget sites produced by individuals, and in favour of those whose high-end design features and institutional origins lend them an air of credibility. The alternative, as Fabos suggests, is to recognise that 'bias' is unavoidable, and that information is inevitably 'couched in ideology'. Rather than seeking to determine the 'true facts', students need to understand 'how political, economic, and social context shapes all texts, how all texts can be adapted for different social purposes, and how no text is neutral or necessarily of "higher quality" than another' (Fabos, 2004: 95).

As this implies, 'digital literacy' is much more than a functional matter of learning how to use a computer and a keyboard, or how to do online searches. Of course, it needs to begin with some of the 'basics'. In relation to the internet, for example, children need to learn how to locate and select material – how to use browsers, hyperlinks and search engines, and so on. But to stop there is to confine digital literacy to a form of instrumental or functional literacy. The skills that children need in relation to digital media are not confined to those of information retrieval. As with print, they also need to be able to evaluate and use information critically if they are to transform it into knowledge. This means asking questions about the sources of that information, the interests of its producers, and the ways in which it represents the world; and understanding how these technological developments are related to broader social, political and economic forces.

This more *critical* notion of literacy has been developed over many years among media educators; and in this respect, I would argue that we need to extend approaches developed by media educators to encompass digital media. There are four broad conceptual aspects that are generally regarded as essential components of media literacy (see Buckingham, 2003). While digital media clearly raise new questions, and require new methods of investigation, this basic conceptual framework continues to provide a useful means of mapping the field:

Representation. Like all media, digital media represent the world, rather than simply reflect it. They offer particular interpretations and selections of reality, which inevitably embody implicit values and ideologies. Informed users of media need to be able to evaluate the material they encounter, for example by assessing the motivations of those who created it and by comparing it with other sources, including their own direct experience. In the case of information texts, this means addressing questions about authority, reliability and bias; and it also necessarily invokes broader questions about whose voices are heard and whose viewpoints are represented, and whose are not.

Language. A truly literate individual is able not only to use language, but also to understand how it works. This is partly a matter of understanding the 'grammar' of particular forms of communication; but it also involves an awareness of the broader codes and conventions of particular genres. This means acquiring analytical skills, and a meta-language for describing how language functions. Digital literacy must therefore involve a systematic awareness of how digital media are constructed, and of the unique 'rhetorics' of interactive communication: in the case of the web, for example, this would include understanding how sites are designed and structured, and the rhetorical functions of links between sites (cf. Burbules and Callister, 2000: 85-90).

Production. Literacy also involves understanding who is communicating to whom, and why. In the context of digital media, young people need to be aware of the growing importance of commercial influences – particularly as these are often invisible to the user. There is a 'safety' aspect to this: children need to know when they are being targeted by commercial appeals, and how the information they provide can be used by commercial corporations. But digital literacy also involves a broader awareness of the global role of advertising, promotion and sponsorship, and how they influence the nature of the information that is available in the first place. Of course, this awareness should also extend to non-commercial sources and interest groups, who are increasingly using the web as a means of persuasion and influence.

Audience. Finally, literacy also involves an awareness of one's own position as an audience (reader or user). This means understanding how media are targeted at audiences, and how different audiences use and respond to them. In the case of the internet, this entails an awareness of the ways in which users gain access to sites, how they are addressed and guided (or encouraged to navigate), and how information is gathered about them. It also means recognising the very diverse ways in which the medium is utilised, for example by different social groups, and reflecting on how it is used in everyday life – and indeed how it might be used differently. (In some respects, of course, the term 'audience' (which is easily applied to 'older' media) fails to do justice to the interactivity of the internet – although substitute terms are no more satisfactory (Livingstone, 2004)).

This basic framework is not only applicable to 'information' media (if indeed the web can any longer be seen as merely a source of 'information'). In principle, it can also be applied to other aspects of digital media, including 'fictional' media such as computer and video games: further illustrations of this can be found in Buckingham (in press).

'Writing' digital media

Finally, it is important to emphasise that media literacy involves 'writing' the media as well as 'reading' them; and here again, digital technology presents some important new challenges and possibilities. The growing accessibility of this technology means that quite young children can easily produce multimedia texts, and even interactive hypermedia – and increasing numbers of children have access to such technology in their homes. As with older media (Lorac and Weiss, 1981), teachers are increasingly using multimedia authoring packages as a means of assisting subject learning in a range of curriculum areas. Here, students produce their own multimedia texts in the form of websites or CD-ROMs, often combining written text, visual images, simple animation, audio and video material. Vivi Lachs (2000), for example, describes a range of production activities undertaken with primary school students in learning about science, geography or history. These projects generally involve children 're-presenting' their learning for an audience of younger children in the form of multimedia teaching materials or websites. One of the most challenging aspects of this work is precisely the interactivity: the students have to think hard about how different users might interpret and use what they produce, and how they will navigate their way around. Yet although the children's productions frequently draw on elements of popular culture (such as computer games), the content of the productions is primarily factual and informational.

Other potential uses of digital media have emerged from arts education. These projects often involve the participation of 'digital artists' external to the school, and their primary emphasis is on the use of the media for self-expression and creative exploration. Thus, students may experiment with the possibilities of different art forms, and the ways in which they can be combined and manipulated using the computer, in exploring themes such as 'identity' and 'memory'. The implicit model here is that of the avant-garde multimedia art work, although (here again) students tend to 'import' elements of popular culture. This work can also involve an element of critical reflection, particularly where it involves communication with a wider audience. Rebecca Sinker (1999), for example, describes an online multimedia project which set out to develop links between an infant school and its community. The project was intended to mark the school's centenary, and to offer the children opportunities 'to investigate their own families, community, histories and experiences, exploring changes and celebrating diversity'. Using multimedia authoring software, the project brought together photography, video, drawing, storytelling, digital imaging, sound and text. Perhaps most significantly, the results of the project (in the form of a website) were available to a much wider audience than would normally have been the case with children's work.

These approaches are certainly interesting and productive; but there are two factors that distinguish them from the use of digital production in the context of media education. Firstly, media education is generally characterised by an explicit focus on popular culture – or at least on engaging with students' everyday experiences of digital media, rather than attempting to impose an alien 'artistic' or 'educational' practice. In the case of the internet, this means recognising that most young people's uses of the medium are not primarily 'educational', at least in the narrow sense. Teachers need to recognise that young people's uses of the internet are intimately connected with their other media enthusiasms – and that this is bound to be reflected in the texts they produce.

Secondly, there is the element of theoretical reflection – the dynamic relationship between making and critical understanding that is crucial to the development of 'critical literacy'. In the context of media education, the aim is not primarily to develop technical skills, or to promote 'self-expression', but to encourage a more systematic understanding of how the media work, and hence to promote more reflective ways of using them. In this latter respect, media education directly challenges the instrumental use of technology as a transparent or neutral 'teaching aid'. In fact, these digital tools can enable students to *conceptualise* the activity of production in much more powerful ways than was possible with analogue media. For example, when it comes to video production, digital technology can make overt and visible some key aspects of the production process that often remain 'locked away' when using analogue technologies. This is particularly apparent at the point of editing, where complex questions about the selection, manipulation and combination of images (and, in the case of video, of sounds) can be addressed in a much more accessible way. In the process, the boundaries between critical analysis and practical production – or between 'theory' and 'practice' – are becoming increasingly blurred (see Burn and Durran, 2006).

Ultimately, however, my argument here is much broader than simply a call for media education. The metaphor of literacy – while not without its problems – provides one means of imagining a more coherent, and ambitious, approach. The increasing convergence of contemporary media means that we need to be addressing the skills and competencies – the multiple literacies – that are required by the whole range of contemporary forms of communication. Rather than simply adding media or digital literacy to the curriculum menu, or hiving off information and communication technology into a separate school subject, we need a much broader reconceptualisation of what we mean by literacy in a world that is increasingly dominated by electronic media. This is not by any means to suggest that verbal literacy is no longer relevant, or that books should be discarded. However, it is to imply that the curriculum can no longer be confined to a narrow conception of literacy that is defined solely in terms of print.

Conclusion: the place of the school

The idea that technology in itself would radically transform education – and even result in the demise of the school – has proven to be an illusion. The school is likely to remain, not least because it serves social (and indeed economic) functions that are not confined to its role in respect of learning: historically, it has always operated partly as an agency of child-minding. Yet the school cannot afford to ignore the ever-increasing role that digital media have come to play in most young people's lives. As I have argued, we are witnessing a widening gap between the culture of the school and the culture of children's lives outside school. Bridging this gap will require more than superficial attempts to combine education and entertainment, or a celebratory account of the educational potential of new media. The expanded conception of media literacy I have outlined above provides what I see as a much more critical and productive approach.

However, the advent of digital media presents even broader challenges for the school as an institution. One key issue raised by other contributors to this book concerns its role in addressing the inequalities in access to technology that obtain in the wider society. 'Access' in this sense is about more than the availability of equipment, or simply a matter of technical skills: on the contrary, it is also a question of cultural capital – of the ability to use cultural forms of expression and communication. At least in principle, the school could play a vital role in widening access – perhaps in partnership with other 'intermediate' institutions such as libraries and community technology centres. Yet far from narrowing inequalities, there is some evidence that schools may actually widen them. Young people who already enjoy a high degree of access outside school are more likely to engage in technology-based activities in school, and to get more from them, than those who do not (Selwyn, 1998). There is a danger here of what Attewell and Battle (1999) call a 'Sesame Street effect': that is, an intervention designed to enable poorer children to 'catch up' educationally with their more affluent counterparts may end up widening existing inequalities based on social class, ethnicity and gender, since it is boys, middle-class children and whites (who enjoy greater access outside school) who are likely to benefit most from it. Pessimists would see this as merely another instance of the function of schooling as a means of social reproduction – or at least as further evidence that, in the words of Basil Bernstein (1970), 'education cannot compensate for society'. This is likely to remain the case unless specific targeted efforts are made to address the needs of those who are technologically and culturally excluded.

More broadly, one could argue that the commercially-driven incursion of technology into so many spheres of public and private life requires a new focus on the role of the school as a public sphere institution. In much the same way as Habermas's (1962) eighteenth century public sphere, the school should provide a forum for open public communication and critical debate, that is equally accessible to all. It should stand between the citizen (in this case, the student) and the operations of both the market and the state. And, like the university, it should be staffed by professionals, who have the power to make their own decisions about how the business of education should be carried out. If this seems bland and uncontroversial, it is worth reminding ourselves of the inequalities of access and provision that increasingly characterise public education; of the growing importance of commercial companies in the management of schools; and of the governmental view of teaching as a matter of 'delivering' an externally-defined curriculum.

While reasserting the public functions of the school, we also need to develop its connections with other public sphere institutions – and perhaps to imagine new ones. Bridging the divide between the school and students' lives outside school can be facilitated by 'intermediate' social institutions such as libraries, adult education centres, community arts projects and even museums. School buildings constitute a valuable community resource, that could be open for a wider range of activities well beyond the school day. In this respect, schools can certainly learn from the more informal, accessible institutions that have developed around new technologies. Cybercafes, for example, have been seen as important 'liminal spaces' located at the junctions between home, school and street, online and offline spaces, and work and play (Beavis et al., 2005). Likewise, Chris Bigum (2002) provides an interesting case study of the ways in which schools can use technology (and specifically creative media technology) as a means of developing a stronger engagement with community needs and interests. In the process, the community also becomes an audience for students' creative productions. Of course, the internet itself can be seen as a public space of this kind, although it is one that is increasingly being overtaken by the imperatives of business – and, in the case of schools, is largely used as a form of public relations. The need to sustain participatory, non-commercial spaces on the internet – by which I do not mean officially sanctioned and controlled spaces – is now a significant issue for public policy.

Obviously, the school is not about to disappear. Yet in an environment that is increasingly dominated by the proliferation of electronic media and the demands and imperatives of consumer culture, it urgently needs to assume a much more proactive role. Technology can perhaps contribute to this, although it will not bring it about of its own accord. Ultimately, we need to stop thinking about such issues merely in terms of technology, and start thinking afresh about learning, communication and culture.

References

Attewell, P. and Battle, J. (1999) 'Home computers and school performance', *The Information Society* 15(1): 1-10

Beavis, C., Nixon, H. and Atkinson, S. (2005) 'LAN cafés: cafés, places of gathering or sites of informal teaching and learning?' *Education, Communication and Information* 5(1): 41-60

Bernstein, B. (1970) 'Education cannot compensate for society', in B.R. Cosin, R. Dale, G.M. Esland and D.F. Swift (eds.) *School and Society* Milton Keynes: Open University Press, pp. 61-7

Bigum, C. (2002) 'Design sensibilities, schools, and the new computing and communication technologies' in I. Snyder (ed.) *Silicon Literacies: Communication, Innovation and Education in the Electronic Age* London: Routledge, pp. 130-140

Buckingham, D. (2000) *After the Death of Childhood: Growing Up in the Age of Electronic Media* Cambridge: Polity

Buckingham, D. (2003) *Media Education: Literacy, Learning and Contemporary Culture* Cambridge: Polity

Buckingham, D. (2006) 'Is there a digital generation?' in D. Buckingham and R. Willett (eds.) *Digital Generations: Children, Young People and New Media* Mahwah, NJ: Erlbaum, pp. 1-13

Buckingham, D. (in press) *Beyond Technology: Learning in the Age of Digital Culture* Cambridge: Polity

Buckingham, D. and Scanlon, M. (2003) *Education, Entertainment and Learning in the Home* Buckingham: Open University Press

Buckingham, D. and Scanlon, M. (2004) 'Connecting the family? 'Edutainment' websites and learning in the home', *Education, Communication and Information* 4(2/3): 271-291

Buckingham, D. and Sefton-Green, J. (2003) 'Gotta catch 'em all: structure, agency and pedagogy in children's media culture', *Media, Culture and Society* 25(3): 379-399

Burbules, N.C. and Callister, T.A. (2000) *Watch IT: The Risks and Pormises of Information Technologies for Education* Boulder, CO: Westview

Burn, A. and Durran, J. (2006) 'Digital Anatomies: analysis as production in media education' in D. Buckingham and R. Willett (eds.) *Digital Generations: Children, Young People and New Media* Mahwah, NJ: Erlbaum, pp. 273-293

Carr, D., Buckingham, D., Burn, A. and Schott, G. (2006) *Computer Games: Text, Narrative and Play* Cambridge: Polity

Cordes, C. and Miller, E. (2000) *Fool's Gold: A Critical Look at Computers in Childhood* Alliance for Childhood www.allianceforchildhood.net

Cuban, L. (1986) *Teachers and Machines: The Classroom Use of Technology Since 1920* New York: Teachers College Press

Cuban, L. (2001) *Oversold and Underused: Computers in the Classroom* New York: Teachers College Press

Davies, J. (2006) '"Hello newbie! ●**big welcome hugs** hope u like it here as much as i do!●"
An exploration of teenagers' informal on-line learning', in D. Buckingham and R. Willett (eds.)
Digital Generations: Children, Young People and New Media Mahwah, NJ: Erlbaum

EPPI Centre (2004) *A Systematic Review and Meta-Analysis of the Effectiveness of ICT on Literacy
Learning in English, 5 and 16* London: Institute of Education, EPPI Centre

Fabos, B. (2004) *Wrong Turn on the Information Superhighway: Education and the Commercializa-
tion of the Internet* New York: Teachers College Press

Facer, K., Furlong, J., Furlong, R. and Sutherland, R. (2003) *Screenplay: Children and Computing in
the Home* London: Routledge

Facer, K. and Furlong, R. (2001) 'Beyond the myth of the "cyberkid": young people at the margins of
the information revolution', *Journal of Youth Studies* 4(4): 451-469

Gee, J.P. (2003) *What Video Games Have To Teach Us About Learning and Literacy* Basingstoke,
Hants: Palgrave Macmillan

Gilster, P. (1997) *Digital Literacy* New York: Wiley

Goodson, I. and Mangan, J.M. (1996) 'Computer literacy as ideology', *British Journal of Sociology
of Education* 17(1): 65-79

Habermas, J. (1962/1989) *The Structural Transformation of the Public Sphere* Cambridge, MA: MIT
Press

Holloway, S. and Valentine, G. (2003) *Cyberkids: Children in the Information Age* London: Routledge

Illich, I. (1971) *Deschooling Society* Harmondsworth: Penguin

Kenway, J. and Bullen, E. (2001) *Consuming Children: Education – Entertainment – Advertising*
Buckingham: Open University Press

Lachs, V. (2000) *Making Multimedia in the Classroom: A Practical Guide* London: Routledge

Levin, D. and Arafeh, S. (2002) 'The digital disconnect: the widening gap between internet-savvy
students and their schools', Washington, DC: Pew Internet and American Life Project

Livingstone, S. (2004) 'The challenge of changing audiences: or, what is the audience researcher to do
in the age of the internet?' *European Journal of Communication*, 19(1): 75-86

Livingstone, S. and Bober, M. (2004) *UK Children Go Online: Surveying the Experiences of Young
People and their Parents.* London: London School of Economics and Political Science

Livingstone, S., van Couvering, E. and Thumim, N. (2005) *Adult Media Literacy: A Review of the
Research Literature* London: Ofcom

Lorac, C. and Weiss, M. (1981) *Communication and Social Skills* Exeter: Wheaton.

Ofsted (2004) *ICT in Schools: The Impact of Government Initiatives Five Years On* London: OF-
STED

Oliver, M. and Pelletier, C. (2006) 'Activity theory and learning from digital games: implications for
game design', in D. Buckingham and R. Willett (eds.) *Digital Generations: Children, Young People
and New Media* Mahwah, NJ: Erlbaum

Organisation for Economic Co-operation and Development (OECD) (2004) *Completing the Foundation for Lifelong Learning* Innsbruck: Studien Verlag

Papert, S. (1980) *Mindstorms: Children, Computers and Powerful Ideas* New York: Basic Books

Papert, S. (1984) 'Trying to predict the future', *Popular Computing* October

Postman, N. (1983) *The Disappearance of Childhood* London, W.H. Allen

Scanlon, M. and Buckingham, D. (2003) 'Debating the digital curriculum: intersections of the public
and the private in educational and cultural policy', *London Review of Education* 1(3): 191-205

Scanlon, M., Buckingham, D. and Burn, A. (2005) 'Motivating maths? Digital games and mathema-
tical learning', *Technology, Pedagogy and Education* 14(1): 127-139

Sefton-Green, J. (2003) "Informal learning: substance or style?' *Teaching Education* 14(1): 37-51

Selwyn, N. (1998) 'The effect of using a home computer on students' educational use of IT', *Computers and Education* 31: 211-227

Selwyn, N. (1999) 'Gilding the grid: the marketing of the National Grid for Learning', *British Journal of Sociology of Education* 20(1): 59-72

Selwyn, N. (2003) '"Doing IT for the kids": re-examining children, computers and the "information society"', *Media, Culture and Society* 25: 351-378

Selwyn, N. (2005) 'Online/of-course: exploring the political and social construction of digital learning', paper presented at the Centre for the Study of Children Youth and Media, Institute of Education, University of London, 7th June

Selwyn, N. (2006) 'Exploring the "digital disconnect" between net-savvy students and their schools', *Learning, Media and Technology* 31(1): 5-18

Sinker, R. (1999) 'The Rosendale Odyssey: multimedia memoirs and digital journeys', in Sefton-Green, J. (ed.) *Young People, Creativity and New Technologies* London: Routledge

Tapscott, D. (1998) *Growing Up Digital: The Rise of the Net Generation* New York: McGraw Hill

Tingstad, V. (2003) *Children's Chat on the Net: A Study of Social Encounters in Two Norwegian Chat Rooms* PhD thesis, NTNU Trondheim

Tyack, D. and Cuban, L. (1995) *Tinkering Toward Utopia: A Century of Public School Reform* Cambridge, MA: Harvard University Press

Warlick, D. (2005) *Raw Materials for the Mind: A Teacher's Guide to Digital Literacy* Fourth edition, Raleigh, NC: The Landmark Project

Williams, J., Clemens, S., Oleinikova, K. and Tarvin, K. (2003) *The Skills for Life Survey: A National Needs and Impact Survey of Literacy, Numeracy and ICT Skills* London: Department for Education and Skills

Franz Josef Röll

Ästhetik in der zielgruppenorientierten Medienbildung

Kennzeichnende Begriffe der aktuellen gesellschaftlichen Entwicklung sind Individualisierung, Pluralisierung, Flexibilisierung und Globalisierung. Parallel dazu verläuft eine „Modernisierung" unserer Gesellschaft von einer Industriegesellschaft hin zu einer Informations- bzw. Wissensgesellschaft (Röll 2003). Die traditionalen Strukturen mit ihren normvermittelnden Werten werden zunehmend brüchig. Auf drei Ebenen vollzieht sich ein Modernisierungsprozess, den Beck (1986) als Risikogesellschaft beschreibt. Die Individuen werden aus historisch vorgegebenen Sozialformen- und Bindungen und traditionellen Versorgungszusammenhängen herausgelöst. Frühere Verortungen in Klasse, Schicht, Familie lösen sich zunehmend auf. Dies bezeichnet Beck mit *Freisetzungsdimension* (ebd., S. 206). Da das Handlungswissen, der Glaube und die leitenden Normen keine bindende Orientierung mehr liefern, führt dies zur *Entzauberungsdimension. Reintegrationsdimensionen* werden daher nötig, um eine neue Art der sozialen Einbindung zu ermöglichen. Die weit reichenden Möglichkeiten der selbst bestimmten und eigenständigen Lebensführung stellen allerdings große Herausforderungen an die Individuen.

Im Gegensatz zu früher setzt die aktuelle Lebenssituation keine Grenzen mehr, sondern löst Prozesse aus. Die Subjekte handeln aus diesem Grunde eher durch Wählen als durch Einwirken (traditionale Vorgaben). Eine Begleiterscheinung dieser Situation ist Unsicherheit. „Unsicherheit erzeugt ein ästhetisches Anlehnungsbedürfnis, das sich in Mentalitäten, Gruppenbildungen, typischen Handlungsstrategien und neuen Formen der Öffentlichkeit niederschlägt" (Schulze 1993., S. 62). Täglich besteht die Notwendigkeit von freien Wahlen (Essen, Kleidung, Unterhaltung, Kontakte, Information etc.). Die Alltagssituation zwingt uns ständig, Unterscheidungen nach ästhetischen Kriterien vorzunehmen.

Die *Ästhetisierung* des Alltagslebens zählt somit zu den Suchbewegungen, eine Antwort zu finden auf die durch die Modernisierung der Gesellschaft ausgelösten Prozesse. Besonders Beziehungsmuster und Gruppenbildungen sind dem Einfluss dieser Basismotivation unterworfen. Ohne kollektive Muster sind viele überfordert, so zu leben, wie sie wollen. Soziale Milieus bilden sich als Lebensstilgemeinschaften, die sich über ein System von Zeichen im Raum der sozialen Beziehungen orientieren. „Es entwickelt sich ein Geflecht von Gemeinsamkeiten: alltagsästhetische Schemata, soziale Milieus, typische Existenzformen, existentielle Anschauungsweisen, Rationalitätstypen, Zeichenkosmen, Szenen" (ebd., S. 35). Darüber hinaus dienen sie auch der Abgrenzung, der Distinktion. Distanzierungen und Zuordnungen zu den Milieus laufen über flüchtige Eindrücke wahrnehmbarer alltagsästhetischer Signale. Nur ganz wenige evidente und signifikante Zeichen genügen, um in der Alltagsinteraktion zu komplexen Einschätzungen zu gelangen, die weit über das Sichtbare hinausgehen.

Sowohl zur Distinktion gegenüber anderen, als auch zur Assimilation an Gleichgesinnte bedarf es der Kenntnis ungeschriebener Regeln. Stilvorgaben, Einstellungsmuster und das Verhalten werden zu ästhetischen Ausdrucksformen, die in den Feinheiten nur den Eingeweihten vertraut sind. Ästhetische Ausdrucksformen werden zum Instrument, mit dessen Hilfe die innere und äußere Lebenswelt gedeutet, Erfahrungen organisiert, verarbeitet, gegliedert und geformt werden. Da ästhetisches Denken von Wahrnehmungen ausgeht, wird Wahrnehmungsschulung zu einer Schlüsselqualifikation.

Die Medienbildung steht vor der Herausforderung, bezogen auf die jeweiligen ästhetischen Wahrnehmungsdispositionen ihre Angebote zu entwickeln. Bereits bei der Kontaktaufnahme (Öffentlichkeitsarbeit) bedarf es der Notwendigkeit, die *Aufmerksamkeit* auf die Intentionen unterschiedlicher Zielgruppen zu richten. Bei den jeweiligen Bildungsmaßnahmen, die im Kontext mit Medienbildung stehen, ist es angemessen, auf die unterschiedlichen Sicht- und Wahrnehmungsweisen einzugehen und produktiv mit ihnen zu arbeiten, um den jeweiligen Zielgruppen die Gelegenheit zu geben, ausgehend von ihren spezifischen ästhetischen Ausdrucksformen Inhalte und Aufgaben zu bearbeiten.

Zielgruppenorientierte Medienbildung unter Beachtung ästhetischer Gesichtspunkte beinhaltet somit mindestens zwei Dimensionen: die konzeptionelle Perspektive der Bildungsanbieter (Institutionen) und die didaktische Perspektive, mit der sich die Lehrenden bzw. (Medien-)Pädagogen auseinandersetzen müssen. Bevor dies erläutert wird, bedarf es der Klärung, was in diesem Text unter „Ästhetischer Bildung" verstanden wird.

Ästhetische Bildung und ästhetische Erfahrung

Der Begriff Ästhetik ist von dem griechischen Wort *aisthesis* abgeleitet. Ursprünglich bedeutete er Gefühl, Geschmack, Wahrnehmung, Sinnlichkeit und Erkenntnis. Auf diesen weiten Begriff von Ästhetik beziehen sich diejenigen, die Ästhetik als die Lehre von der „sinnlichen Wahrnehmung" ansehen. Ästhetisch ist dem gemäß alles, was unsere Sinne anregt und in uns Gefühle und Empfindungen hervorruft. Ästhetik bezeichnet das Feld der Weltbezüge des Menschen, die zwischen seiner subjektiven Wahrnehmung und den Eigenschaften der Außenwelt stehen. Ästhetik wird verstanden als Schulung der Wahrnehmungs- und Ausdrucksfähigkeit, der reflexiven Urteilsfähigkeit, der Stärkung der Erlebnisfähigkeit, dem Erleben von Körpererfahrungen (Theater, Tanz), der Persönlichkeitsentfaltung sowie der produktiven (künstlerischen) Kreativität. In diesem Verständniskontext kann die Ästhetik als eine Schlüsselkompetenz bei der Medienbildung angesehen werden. In dem hier verstandenen Sinne dient die Ästhetik dazu, die Funktion und Struktur von Welt besser zu verstehen, sich selbst im Verhältnis zur Welt zu verorten und zum besseren Verständnis der Weltsicht anderer beizutragen.

Die ästhetische Erfahrung bildet den Kern der ästhetischen Bildung. Sowohl bei der Wahrnehmung ästhetischer Objekte und Phänomene als auch durch produktive Gestaltung lassen sich ästhetische Erfahrungen machen. Ästhetische Erfahrungen bedürfen keiner spezifischen Lernumgebung, sie können in der Lebenswelt gemacht werden.

Wichtige Strukturelemente ästhetischer Erfahrung sind Überraschung und Genuss – nicht der sinnliche Wahrnehmungsprozess an sich, sondern die Erfahrung der Diskontinuität und Differenz zu bisher Erlebtem löst die ästhetische Erfahrung aus. Das mit Hilfe der Sinne gewahr werdende Unerwartete, die Aufnahme überraschender Eindrücke führt mit dem ästhetischen Reiz zu Korrekturen bisheriger Annahmen von Wirklichkeit (Duncker 1999, S. 11). Die genussvolle Identifikation, die von der Einsicht einer spielerischen Distanz zur Wirklichkeit bis hin zur Erkenntnis des Neuen reicht, führt dazu „Neues" lustvoll zu erleben und begünstigt dadurch „den Genuß erfüllter Gegenwart" (ebd., S. 15). Die ästhetische Erfahrung kann aber auch zu einem so genannten „Aha-Erlebnis" führen, der inneren Erkenntnis grundlegender Zusammenhänge. Ebenso ist es möglich das „Flow-Erlebnis" (Csikszentmihalyi 1985) zu spüren. Dies tritt dann ein, wenn Handlung und Bewusstsein verschmelzen und der Verlust des Zeitgefühls und Selbstvergessenheit eintritt.

Kennzeichnend für die ästhetische Erfahrung ist die Vermischung von Kulturaneignung und Kulturproduktion. Vornehmlich aktualisieren sich ästhetische Erfahrungen in (be-)greifbaren, manifesten Darstellungen oder ästhetischen Ausdrucksformen (Objekte, Filme, Fotografien, Websites). Diese Ausdrucksformen stehen im Kontext soziokultureller Aneignungsformen. Jugendliche machen andere ästhetische Erfahrungen als Erwachsene und favorisieren daher auch einen anderen ästhetischen Stil. Auch innerhalb der Zielgruppe Jugendlicher ist es sinnvoll und notwendig zu differenzieren.

Chancen und Potentiale für die Medienbildung

Nach jedem gelungenen ästhetischen Entwurf entsteht das Bedürfnis nach Erweiterung. Daher ist die die ästhetische Bildung prädestiniert, ganz unterschiedliche Bildungsprozesse auszulösen. Beispielhaft sollen hier drei Handlungsfelder hervorgehoben werden.

Ästhetische Bildung als Analyse- und Erkenntnisinstrument

In allen Bereich des sozialen Lebens kommt es zur Indienstnahme der Ästhetik durch Durchsetzung partikularer Interessen. Religion und Politik und neuerdings die Medienindustrie verstehen es, Bilder als Vehikel für ihre Botschaften zu instrumentalisieren. Ästhetischen Botschaften kommt daher schon immer eine zentrale Bedeutung im Rahmen der Meinungsbildung zu. Im Hintergrund steht dabei immer die Vorstellung, dass sich in dem Bezeichneten die Natur des Offenbarten spiegelt. Zeichensetzung ist demnach nie beliebig, sondern immer ontologisch. Es wurde bzw. wird vermutet, dass das Subjekt dem Bild (-objekt) einen Komplex von Bedeutungen zuordnet.

In einer immer stärker ästhetisch geprägten Kultur (Welsch 1993) wird ästhetische Bildung, d.h. auch die Kompetenz, die symbolischen Botschaften mittels ästhetischer Instrumentarien zu decodieren, zu einer allseitigen Bildung für alle Kinder und Jugendliche. Die Kenntnis ästhetischer Formensprache und deren Ausdrucks- und Wirkungsmöglichkeiten befähigt nicht nur zur komplexeren Wahrnehmungsfähigkeit der Entzifferung von Zeichensystemen, sondern auch zur kommunikativen Kompetenz, einer wesentlichen Ausgangsbedingung für eine emanzipatorische und aufklärerische Erziehung.

Ästhetische Bildung als Analyse- und Erkenntnisinstrument, das Erkennen von deren Ausdrucksfunktionen und das Beurteilen ihres Symbolcharakters erhält eine Schlüsselfunktion bei der Interpretation und Identifikation des aktuellen Verständnisses von sozialer und politischer Wirklichkeit. Sie ist in der Lage, neben ihrer Relevanz der Decodierung subjektiver Weltbilder und der Befähigung zur bildhaften Kommunikation zu sensibilisieren für wahrnehmbare Veränderungen der Gesellschaft.

Ästhetische Bildung als Instrument der Selbsterkenntnis

Die Thematisierung von Sinnfragen wird besonders durch den ästhetischen Produktionsprozess ausgelöst. Dies gelingt alleine schon deswegen, weil das menschliche Wahrnehmungsverhalten nie von Nutzlosigkeit geprägt und die ästhetische Erfahrung einer Grundform menschlicher Erfahrung entspricht und immer interessegeleitet ist (Dewey 1980, S. 11). Dem ästhetischen Lernprozess kommt die Funktion zu, bisherige Welt-Deutungen zu überprüfen, andere Aneignungen von Wirklichkeit kennen zu lernen und probehaft auszuleben. Ästhetische Bildung und Handeln geht somit über die Nachahmung, die bloße Spiegelung hinaus, sie hat die Kraft des Hervorbringens. Ästhetische Erfahrungen haben das Potenzial, Vorstellungen und Überzeugungen zu transformieren. Diskontinuität und Differenz zu bisher Erlebtem kann durch ästhetische Erfahrung ausgelöst werden. Der ästhetische Umgang mit Medien wird zum Katalysator einer Auseinandersetzung mit der Lebenswelt, den subjektiven Welt-Deutungen und den jeweils benutzten Medien. Das Ästhetische wird, wie Zacharias (2001, S. 105) hervorhebt, zum *interface* bzw. zur Schnittstelle zwischen Subjekt und Welt, Mensch und Natur und Individuum und Gesellschaft.

Der ästhetisch organisierte Bildungsprozess stellt Bezüge her zu Hypothesen, Fiktionen und Ereignissen, die noch nicht existieren. Ästhetische Ausdrucksformen sind Momentaufnahmen; sie fixieren nicht, sie geben eher Anstöße und repräsentieren innere Befindlichkeiten. Damit verbunden sind die Erschließung neuer Felder und Formen der Erfahrung und die utopische Korrektur am Bestand der bisherigen Welterfahrung. In anschaulicher Weise eröffnet die ästhetische Erfahrung dem Menschen einen Verhaltensspielraum zu seiner bisherigen Lebenserfahrung.

In der ästhetischen Erfahrung ist eine selbstzweckhafte Reflexion zur lebensweltlichen Existenz möglich. Wer sich selbst als veränderbar und nicht statisch erfährt, erlebt auch die soziale Umgebung als veränderbaren Raum. Wer gelernt hat, mit ästhetischen Mitteln in „Lebensräume" einzugreifen, hat gute Chancen, diese Erfahrungen auf den Lebensalltag zu übertragen. Beabsichtigt ist dabei, über die Deskription des Vorhandenen hinauszukommen und sowohl sich selbst als auch die Strukturen der Lebenswelt besser verstehen zu lernen. Die aktuelle Lebenserfahrung soll unter einem neuen Gesichtspunkt, mit einem anderen Standpunkt rekonstruiert, die Stabilität des Selbst gestärkt und die sinnliche Kraft gemeinschaftlichen Lernens und Lebens gespürt werden. Leben wird unter diesen Prämissen als Entwurf, als Projekt(ion) verstanden. Die selbst geschaffenen Medienprodukte repräsentieren das Ergebnis der Bearbeitung von Phänomenen der Lebensweltwahrnehmung. Es handelt sich um eine Auseinandersetzung mit dem vergangenen, dem gegenwärtigen oder dem Entwurf für ein zukünftiges mögliches Sein.

Insbesondere gelingt es mittels ästhetischer Lernprozesse, das Fremde nicht als exogen zu deuten. Ästhetisches Lernen führt auf sinnlicher und sinnenorientierter Ebene zum bewussten Erlebnis der perspektivischen Wahrnehmung. Die Eingeschränktheit, die Subjektivität und die Formiertheit des eigenen Wahrnehmungsprozesses werden über ästhetisches Lernen bewusst. Die Illusion, den Wahrnehmungsprozess als wahrhaftige Wahrnehmung zu interpretieren, wird auf spielerische und lustvolle Form zertrümmert, ohne die Identität des Einzelnen zu zerstören. Beim ästhetischen Lernen geht der Verlust an universellen Deutungsmustern einher mit der Erfahrung der Multioptionalität von Seh- und Handlungsoptionen. Das „Multiversum der Wirklichkeiten" (Maturana 2002, S. 19) wird als Zugewinn erlebt.

Ästhetische Bildung als Handlungsraum

Mit Medien (Foto, Video, Datenerfassungsgerät) können Sinneseindrücke festgehalten werden. So kann z.B. die Lebenswelt, die jeweils subjektiv wahrgenommene Wirklichkeit, mit einer über Symbole verknüpften Wahrnehmungswelt konfrontiert werden. Beabsichtigt ist dabei, mit Hilfe der ästhetischen Bildung über die Deskription des Vorhandenen hinauszukommen, die Strukturen der Lebenswelt besser verstehen zu lernen. Die aktuelle Lebenserfahrung kann unter einem neuen Gesichtspunkt, mit einem anderen Standpunkt rekonstruiert, die Stabilität des Selbst gestärkt und die sinnliche Kraft gemeinschaftlichen Lernens und Lebens gespürt werden. Während das subjektive Erleben des Lebensraums meist einem spontanen Agieren im Bewusstseinsstrom entspricht, so dass Vergangenheit, Gegenwart und Zukunft als Amalgam verschmelzen, wird durch das Bewusstwerden der visuellen Deutungsmuster der Schein der allumfassenden Wahrnehmung der Außenwelt durchbrochen. Die mediale Beschäftigung mit der Lebenswelt führt zum Erleben der Differenz zwischen dem Wissen und Wahrnehmen des Ichs und der vorhandenen Außenwelt. Die Wahrnehmung der Eindeutigkeit des vertrauten Umfeldes und seiner Denk- und Handlungsmuster wird irritiert.

Da die Erweiterung des bisherigen Bewusstseins, des bisherigen Standpunkts vornehmlich durch die eigenständige Erkundung erfolgt, führt dies nicht zu einer Blockade, sondern zu einer höheren Bereitschaft, sich bisher nicht Wahrgenommenem zu öffnen. Die oft verfestigte Verselbstständigung der lebensweltlichen Perspektive wird aufgebrochen. Das bisher nicht Wahrgenommene wird wie eine archäologische Entdeckung seines eigenen Selbst erlebt. Leben wird nicht mehr als Fluss gesehen. Leben wird als gestaltbarer Raum erlebt, der Projektionen, Entwürfe erlaubt. Weil ich eine bestimmte Erfahrung gemacht habe, verbinde ich mein Tun mit Plänen und Absichten. Der bewusste Prozess des Wahrnehmens meiner selbst wird geschärft und die Vergangenheit wird zu einer vergangenen Erfahrung. Die Gegenwart wird in einer intensiveren Präsenz erlebt. Die unspezifische Zeit- und Raumerfahrung wandelt sich zu einer spezifischen Zeit- und Raumerfahrung. Die Erfahrungen der Konfrontation der Lebenswelt mit einer ästhetischen Erfahrung führen zu einer Transformation der bisherigen Aneignung von Wirklichkeit. Die Lebenswelt wird aus einer anderen Perspektive kennen gelernt, die aktuell zur Verfügung stehenden Deutungsmuster werden erweitert, und die Motivation, das eigene Leben bewusster wahrzunehmen, wird gefördert.

Durch die Individualisierung der Erfahrungswelten bedarf es einer dynamischen Anpassung dieses Konzeptes auf die jeweiligen Zielgruppen. Die Umsetzung muss daher unter zielgruppenspezifischen Aspekten konkretisiert werden. Doch bevor dieses Konzept beispielhaft dargestellt wird, muss daran erinnert werden, dass, damit es zur „Medienbildung" kommt, erst eine Zielgruppe für die Bildungsmaßnahme gefunden werden muss. Dazu ist Öffentlichkeitsarbeit notwendig. Aus diesem Grunde ist es bedeutsam, die Wahrnehmungsdisposition der avisierten Zielgruppe im Auge zu behalten.

Kultur der Aufmerksamkeit

Aufmerksamkeit lässt sich als Leitbegriff des Medienzeitalters bezeichnen. Unsere Ökonomie des Tausches von Waren, Dienstleistungen und Informationen basiert auf der Fähigkeit, Aufmerksamkeit für das eigene „Produkt" zu erzielen. Je mehr Information es gibt, desto höher ist der Wert, der der Aufmerksamkeit zukommt, da immer weniger und Raum Zeit zur Verfügung steht, die eigenen Botschaften zu vermitteln. Nur die Nachrichten und Botschaften können sich durchsetzen, denen es gelingt zur Kumulation von Aufmerksamkeit beizutragen und damit Aufmerksamkeitsverdichtungen zu evozieren, da vornehmlich die Konzentration auf die Bereiche gerichtet wird, die vom eigenen Wahrnehmungsskript erfasst werden.

In der Aufmerksamkeitsökonomie sieht Assmann (2003) die neue Ökonomie des Informationszeitalters. Da die Produktion von Informationen immer mehr wächst, wird es immer schwieriger die eigene Botschaft an die gewünschte Zielgruppe zu transportieren. Aufmerksamkeit wird immer knapper und wichtiger und erhält somit einen zentralen Wert. Während im typographischen Zeitalter das Gedächtnis die zentrale Bedeutung erhält, kommt der Aufmerksamkeit im elektronischen Zeitalter aufgrund der explosionsartige Vermehrung von Wissen und Information eine entscheidende Bedeutung zu. Assmann geht davon aus, dass die voraussetzungsreiche und aufwendige Infrastruktur der neuen Technologien neue soziale und kulturelle Ungleichheiten schafft. „Ungleichheit in Form von Hierarchien stellt sich im Internet auf eine neue Weise wieder her. Die neuen Riesen entstehen durch Verdichtung medialer Aufmerksamkeit." Die aktuelle Entwicklung (Wikis, Weblogs, social software) lässt vermuten, dass die Ungleichheit nicht durch technische Voraussetzungen geschaffen wird. Gleichwohl sind die Befürchtungen, dass die neuen Technologien neue soziale und kulturelle Ungleichheiten generieren, nicht von der Hand zu weisen. Der viel diskutierte „Digital Gap" drückt diese Befürchtung deutlich aus.

Es gibt jedoch keine Chance, mit den Strategien des typographischen Zeitalters auf diese Entwicklung zu reagieren. Wo elektronische Medien die Kommunikationskultur bestimmen, helfen nur elektronische Medien, um gehört bzw. wahrgenommen zu werden. Notwendig wird daher für alle im öffentlichen Raum agierenden Institutionen, Aufmerksamkeitsstrategien für die jeweils avisierte Zielgruppe zu entwickeln. Institutionen, die Bildung anbieten, sind gezwungen eine *corporate identity* zu entwickeln, die in allen Kommunikationsdiskursen Verwendung findet. Alle Kommunikate (u.a. Webauftritt, Flyer, Briefpapier) sollten eine Wiedererkennbarkeit gewährleisten. Diese *corporate identity* muss von einer ästhetischen Struktur geprägt sein, die den avisierten Zielgruppen die Möglichkeit gibt, die zentralen Botschaften emotional zu verstehen. Die sich wiederholenden Elemente dürfen aber nicht zu spezifisch sein, da dies potentielle Zielgruppen ausschließen könnte. Je mehr eine homogene Zielgruppe vorhanden ist, desto geringer sind die Probleme, *corporate identity* und Zeitgeist-Ästhetik, die speziell den einzelnen Zielgruppen als Orientierungsmarken dienen, miteinander zu verbinden. Je stärker die avisierten Zielgruppen in ihren ästhetischen Vorlieben auseinander gehen, desto schwerer wird es eine gemeinsame *corporate identity* zu entwickeln. Eine sich entwickelnde Dynamik immer komplexerer Bilddiskurse ist zu beobachten.

Je divergenter die Zielgruppen sind, (Kinder, Jugendliche, Erwachsene) desto schwieriger ist es, den Widerspruch zwischen ästhetischem Leitbild und Zeitgeist-Ästhetik miteinander in Beziehung zu setzten. Einzelne Institutionen bieten daher folgerichtig unterschiedliche ästhetische Kommunikationsangebote an. Sie sehen es als sinnvoll an, unterschiedliche Kommunikationsdesigns an die unterschiedlichen Zielgruppen zu richten. Dies soll am Beispiel der BZgA (Bundeszentrale für gesundheitliche Aufklärung) vermittelt werden.

Abb. 1: BZgA

Das Portal der BZgA (www.bzga.de) richtet sich vornehmlich an Multiplikatoren. Die Seite ist professionell gestaltet und durch ästhetische Sachlichkeit geprägt. Sie enthält vier Frames (Raumaufteilungen). Im Top-Frame bietet das in linken Feld oben platzierte Bild eines Leuchtturms die Orientierung. Interessant ist in diesem Zusammenhang, dass in der Ikonographie des Christentums der Platz links oben für Christus vorgesehen war. Im Zentrum oben steht der Name und ganz rechts gibt es eine Suchfunktion. Eine Navigationsleiste rahmt diesen oberen Frame. Im linken vertikalen Frame findet man die Verzweigungen, die zu den anderen Seiten führen. Rechts sind weitere Infos, die vor allem zu Informationen führen, die nicht auf der aktuellen Seite zu finden sind. Die eigentliche Information ist in dem Hauptframe (Mitte) platziert. Die formale Aufteilung der Seite basiert auf einer im Internet aufgrund der im Augenblick verwendeten Content-Management-Systeme oft eingesetzten Gliederungsform. Personen, die die Seite besuchen, müssen sich nicht neu orientieren, sondern können aufgrund ihrer Erfahrung sehr schnell die Verknüpfungslogik der Seiten verstehen.

Drei Farben bilden das Korsett der *corporate identity*. Die Institution erscheint im dezenten Grau. Sie tritt in der Darstellung zurück. Der Bildrahmen ist in Blau gehalten. Blau ist ebenfalls eine Farbe, die nach hinten drängt. Klarheit, Reinheit, Nüchternheit und Zurückhaltung sind typische Assoziationen, die mit dieser Farbempfindung verbunden sind. Die Farbe wird in verschiedenen Schattierungen präsentiert. Dadurch wird das Design aufgelockert. Die Navigation zu den einzelnen Leisten und die Überschriften sind in Orange (mit Tendenz zum Apricot) gehalten. Dies ist eine warme Farbe, die im Kontrast zum Blau nach vorne drängt, aber nicht so aggressiv wie Gelb oder Rot. Die *corporate identity* drückt aus, dass eine Institution präzise und sachbezogen Informationen anbietet. In der Institution begegnet man/frau aber auch Menschen die bereit sind, Wärme, Emotionen, und persönliche Komponenten einzubringen. Der Bruch zwischen Blau und Rot im gesamten Erscheinungsbild ist gewagt, da er Uneinheitlichkeit zum Ausdruck bringt. Zugleich ist aber auch der Aspekt der Mehrdeutigkeit damit verbunden.

Wenn es um konkrete Problemlagen geht, haben Zielgruppen den Bedarf, persönlich angesprochen zu werden. Sie wollen in Bruchteilen von Sekunden wissen, ob die angeklickte Seite möglicherweise ihnen persönlich hilft, ein drängendes Problem zu lösen. Daher müssen diese Seite mehr Emotionen hervorrufen oder zumindest den Raum lassen, dass potentielle Nachfrager Emotionen entwickeln können. An der Seite über „Gib Aids keine Chance" (http://www.gib-aids-keine-chance.de/), die als externer Link in die BZgA-Seite integriert ist, wird dieser Effekt durch die Nutzung von Bildern erzielt. Es dominiert eine Dreigestaltung der Seite mit einer Interaktionsleiste oben. Die Grundfarbe ist blau. Damit wird an die Hauptseite der BZgA angeknüpft. Die Beiträge sind durch Schatten oder Kästchen hervorgehoben. Es dominiert der rechte Winkel. Aber an einer Ecke ist der rechte Winkel ersetzt durch eine abgeflachte Ecke. Der rechte Winkel wird oft mit rationalen, konstruktiven und männlichen Denken in Verbindung gesetzt. Der links oben positionierte Slogan „Gib Aids keine Chance" verstärkt den mutmaßlichen Anspruch dieser Seite, Rationalität mit Emotionalität zu verknüpfen.

Abb. 2: Gib AIDS keine Chance

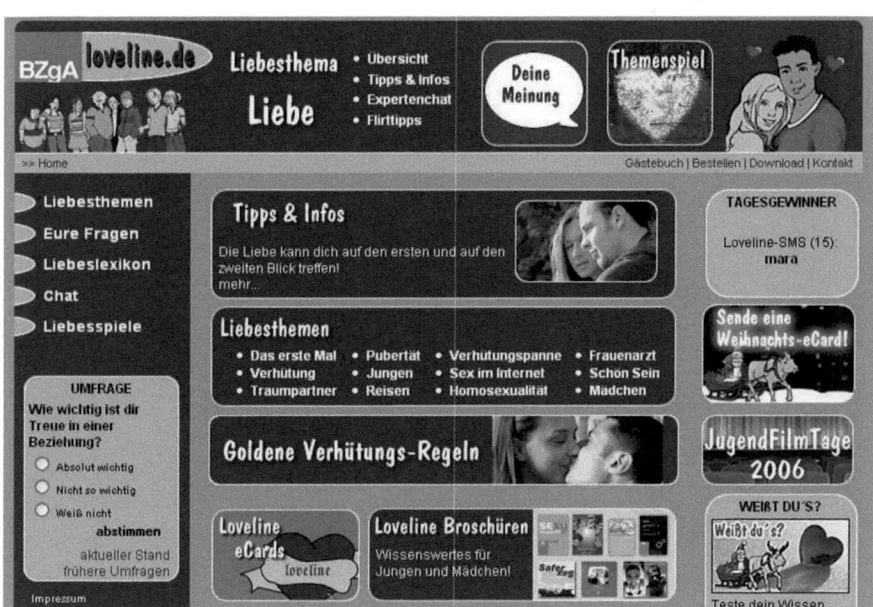

Abb. 3: Loveline

Kinder und Jugendliche sind in der Mehrzahl, insbesondere wenn es um das Thema Liebe geht, nicht durch rationale Diskurse zu gewinnen. Es bedarf eher eines emotionalen Diskurses. Dementsprechend hat die Liebes-Seite der BZgA (http://www.loveline.de/) ein kind- bzw. jugendgemäßes poppiges Aussehen und trifft damit auch das Interesse dieser Zielgruppe. Auf der Seite dominieren warme Farben (rot, orange). Gebrochen wird dies von der Farbe Gelb (nach vorne dringend). Auffallend ist, dass es nahezu keinen rechten Winkel gibt. Das Oval, die Ellipse und der Kreis sind typische strukturelle Formen, die eher mit dem Weiblichen in Verbindung gebracht werden. Die Seite hat damit eine feminine Grundtendenz. Dies wird auch verstärkt durch die violette Farbe, die auf dem Button „Deine Meinung" unterlegt ist. Die Seite ist so gestaltet, dass mit hoher Wahrscheinlichkeit eher Mädchen als Jungen angesprochen werden.

Wie der hessische Jugendring versucht, den Spagat zwischen *corporate identity* und zielgruppenspczifischer Ästhetik zu lösen soll anhand von jeweils einer Ausgabe der Zeitschrift „Hessische Jugend" aus den letzten drei Jahren aufgezeigt werden. Deutlich erkennbar ist das verwendete Grundprinzip: Es wird immer mit fünf gleichen Komponenten gearbeitet: coloriertes Hintergrundbild, ausgeschnittenes Dokumentarfoto aus der Lebenswelt von Jugendlichen, der Titel, die Bezeichnung der Ausgabe des Heftes und ein linker Frame mit vertikaler Schrift, wobei das Hintergrundbild an dieser Stelle abgedunkelt ist.

Abb. 4: Hessische Jugend

Das Hintergrundbild hat die Aufgabe, für die unbewusste Grundstimmung zu sorgen. Sie schafft den „Sound", eine amorphe Stimmung. Durch Aufladung von Symbolen, wie z.B. in Heft 1/04 werden zuweilen zusätzliche Informationen eingebunden. Das zentrale Dokumentarfoto kann als emotionaler Anker angesehen werden. Es ist das Subjekt (die Figur), das sich aus dem Hintergrund hervorhebt. Mit Heft 03/06 verlässt die Redaktion das bisherige Gestaltungsprinzip. Nunmehr ist das Dokumentarfoto mit dem Hintergrund identisch. Der Bezug zur bisherigen Ästhetik wird durch die Colorierung und den linken Frame hergestellt. Das Heft verzichtet somit auf die bisherige avantgardistische Gestaltungsform. Es könnte sein, dass mit der bisherigen Gestaltung vor allem Jungen und darüber hinaus Computer- und Internetfreunde durch das Design angelockt wurden. Die linke Leiste lässt die Assoziation Frame zu. Die Punktlinien, die den linken Teil des Heftes vom rechten Teil trennen sehen wie Tags aus. Die Redaktion war daher gezwungen, sich den unterschiedlichen Seh- und Wahrnehmungsweisen der Nutzerinnen und Nutzer anzupassen.

Deutlich sollte damit geworden sein, dass die ästhetische Ansprache zielgruppenorientiert gestaltet werden muss, um die avisierten Adressaten zu erreichen. Dies gelingt nicht wie früher durch die Inhalte (Texte), sondern vor allem durch das Ansprechen der von der jeweiligen Zielgruppe favorisierten (Zeitgeist-) Ästhetik.

Die Kommunikationsformen und Kommunikationsdesign haben sich in den letzten Jahrzehnten wesentlich geändert. Gleichwohl lassen sich alle Aktivitäten auf eine Strategie aus dem 19. JH, das AIDA-Prinzip (Attention - Interest - Desire - Action), zurückführen. Neu ist, dass dieses Prinzip vermehrt auf der Ebene von Bildkommunikation eingesetzt wird. Dabei ist auffallend, dass das Einzelbild an Bedeutung verloren hat. Zwar lässt sich das Bild weiterhin als Basismedium der technologischen Abbildung und der Visualisierung bezeichnen, allerdings verliert es als unikates Darstellungsmittel an Bedeutung. Dem Internet kommt im Moment die Bedeutung eines Leitmedium zu, da es die Chance optimiert, neben dem Foto weitere Gestaltungsebenen (Text, Grafik, Ton, Film, Tabelle) zu integrieren.

Die Möglichkeit der digitalen Bearbeitung hat nicht nur zu einem Verlust an Glaubwürdigkeit der Bilder geführt, sondern auch zu einem neuen ästhetischen Leitbild. Die „neue" Ästhetik ist gekennzeichnet durch die potentielle Transformation des Ursprungsbildes. Das Bild wird im öffentlichen Diskurs vermehrt als Teil einer multimedialen, multimodalen und multicodalen Ästhetik eingesetzt. Möglich wird diese *intermediale Ästhetik* durch den Computer. Die durch den Computer gegebenen Möglichkeiten, relativ schnell ästhetische Ausdrucksformen zu verändern, tragen erheblich dazu bei, zielgruppenangemessene Angebote zu unterbreiten.

Identifizierung von Wahrnehmungsdispositionen

Folgt man den Prämissen, dass die Seh- und Wahrnehmungsweisen und ästhetische Wahrnehmungen Einfluss auf die Bildungsmaßnahmen haben, bedarf es zu Beginn jeglicher Bildungsmaßnahme der Erkundung der Wahrnehmungsskripte der Lernenden falls diese nicht bekannt sind. Diese sind die Ausgangsbedingung für die intendierten Bildungsprozesse. Jedes Seminar, jeder Workshop, jedes Projekt sollte daher zu Beginn die Möglichkeit öffnen, dass die Lernenden assoziativ, intuitiv, nondirektiv Bilder bewerten, beurteilen oder gestalten. Dabei haben sich folgende Methoden bewährt.

- *Bildbank*. Es werden etwa 200 Fotos aus einer selbst angelegten Bildbank (Aufnahmen mit ganz unterschiedlichen Motiven) ausgebreitet. Jeder Teilnehmer sucht sich je ein Bild aus, das ihm ge- bzw. missfällt. Die Auswahl der Bilder wird begründet.
- *Reiß-Dias*. Tesa-Film in der Breite eines Kleinbild-Dias wird auf ein Bild einer Illustrierten geklebt. Der Tesastreifen wird mit dem Fingernagel fest angedrückt und anschließend abgezogen. Dabei löst sich die obere Farbschicht der Zeitung. Danach wird die Rückseite mit Öl befeuchtet. Durch das Öl ergibt sich eine transparente Struktur. Der Tesastreifen muss dann in ein geglastes Dia gelegt werden, damit es projiziert werden kann. Jedes Thema lässt sich mit dieser Methode bearbeiten.
- *Filmausschnitte*. Es werden Werbefilme, Videofilme und oder Spielfilmauschnitte zur Verfügung gestellt. Die Teilnehmer sollen die interessantesten Szenen aussuchen und dann ihre Entscheidung begründen.
- *Digital-Fotografie*. Die Teilnehmerinnen und Teilnehmer erhalten die Aufgabe ganz schnell 10 Fotoaufnahmen zu machen. Bei der Auswertung wird insbesondere auf den strukturellen Aufbau des Bildes, die Raumnutzung geachtet.
- *Internet-Seiten-Recherche*. Jeder sucht eine Seite im Internet, die ihm gefällt (oder nicht gefällt).
- *Web 2.0-Recherche*. Die Teilnehmer gehen in die Seite Myspace (http://www.myspace.com/) und suchen sich eine Person aus, deren Selbstdarstellung ihnen gefällt (oder nicht gefällt).

Bei der Auswertung können folgende Fragen implizit bearbeitet werden: Was hat beeindruckt, was hat Emotionen ausgelöst, welche persönliche Erinnerung wurde ausgelöst. Beziehen sich die Erinnerungen auf private oder gesellschaftliche Erfahrungen oder mediale Erfahrungen (Intertextualität), sind gestalterische Aspekte aufgefallen, werden Bildkompositionen erkannt, werden ästhetische Gestaltungsmittel registriert, wird über die Intention des Fotografen, Regisseurs nachgedacht, wird der Inhalt oder die Gestaltung reflektiert, werden symbolische Botschaften identifiziert, werden Montagen als intentionale Gestaltungsmerkmale wahrgenommen. Wird bei Filmen die Stimmung identifiziert, die durch die Musik erzeugt wird.

Ausgehend von diesen ästhetischen Annäherungen können bei dem jeweiligen Bildungsprozess dann die bei den visuellen Recherchen gewonnenen Erfahrungen integriert werden. Die Auswertung gibt eine erste Ahnung, dass Bilder bzw. Medienprodukte nicht nur dokumentarische Abbilder von Objekten sind. Es wird sinnlich erfahrbar, dass Medienprodukte bewusst gestaltete oder unbewusste Subtexte, d.h. verschlüsselte Botschaften enthalten.

Diese Seminareinstiege basieren auf der Hypothese, dass bei jeder Entscheidung über visuelle Gestaltung (aktuelle) Gefühlsebenen angesprochen werden. Der Bericht über die ausgewählten Fotos, Filmausschnitte, Webseiten, etc. ist gleichzeitig eine Aussage über die jeweiligen Wahrnehmungswelten. Das Gespräch über die Bildwelten schafft Distanz zur eigenen Person und eröffnet gleichzeitig eine persönliche und ungezwungene Gesprächsatmosphäre. Von Beginn an wird der Lernzusammenhang visualisiert. Die Teilnehmer erfahren darüber hinaus, dass die Seminare hilfreich sein können, mehr oder anderes über das eigene Sehen zu erfahren. Die Auswertungen tragen dazu bei, Prozesse des „inneren Sehen" bewusst zu machen. Mit „innerem Sehen" ist ebenso die Fähigkeit gemeint, den symbolischen Code eines Abbildes (Foto, Dia, Video- oder Filmaufnahme, Computeranimation) zu erkennen und in Bezug zu sich selbst zu setzen. Offenheit ist eine notwendige Voraussetzung. Wichtig ist es daher, eine angstfreie Situation zu schaffen, da die Gespräche über die Bilder substantiell berühren (können).

Im Verlauf der Bildungsmaßnahme wird das innere Bild, die unbewusste Sichtweise, die den Ausgang für die Aneignung von Welt und Wirklichkeit bildet, zunehmend bewusst gemacht und durch eine metakognitive Reflexion bearbeitet. Die Teilnehmenden werden gebeten sich mit einer Sicht-, Wahrnehmungsweise zu beschäftigen, die die in der Regel nicht oder nur peripher in ihrem Wahrnehmungsskript nutzen. Erkenntnis bzw. die Erweiterung der Wahrnehmung soll durch einen eigenständigen, einen selbstgesteuerten Lernprozess angeregt werden. Wesentliches Lernziel ist somit die Erweiterung der jeweiligen Lernskripte. Gelingt dies, erwerben die Lernenden die Fähigkeit ein Thema, ein Fachgebiet, eine Aufgabe aus unterschiedlicher bzw. mehrdimensionaler Sicht zu bearbeiten.

Das Bildungsziel wäre somit die Erweiterung der Möglichkeiten sich mit einem Gegenstand intensiver zu beschäftigen, unabhängig davon ob Ton, Foto, Film oder Computer als Medium eingesetzt wird. Der Medienpädagoge ist verantwortlich für die Lernumgebung. Er setzt die Rahmenbedingungen und stellt Materialien zur Verfügung bzw. gibt Anstöße durch Fragen und durch Kommentare.

Zwei Aspekte sind bei diesem Konzept wesentlich. Die Aufgabenstellung ist offen und kann unterschiedlich bearbeitet werden. Die individuellen Bedürfnisse und Seh- und Wahrnehmungsweisen können sich frei entfalten. Unscharfe Aufgaben umgehen die traditionelle Mixtur aus künstlicher Motivation und aufgezwungener Disziplin. Diese Methode erlaubt, dass die persönlichen Lernpräferenzen Berücksichtigung finden. Die Bewältigung von Aufgaben, ausgehend von der eigenen Selbst-Suche, begünstigt die intrinsische Motivation und fördert das Denken in Zusammenhängen. Denkbar ist es eine Zielorientierung festzulegen, die im Verlauf des Lernprozesses jederzeit verändert werden kann. Jeder Lernende verändert sich, wenn ‚Lernen' eine forschende Fragestellung impliziert und eine aktive Auseinandersetzung im Zentrum des Lernens steht. Dem muss Raum gegeben werden. Ein offenes Curriculum hat den Vorteil, dass keine übergeordnete Instanz Entscheidungen als falsch oder richtig qualifiziert und damit einer Beurteilung unterzieht. Getroffene Entscheidungen legen Schranken fest und verhindern das Erkunden alternativer Erfahrungsräume. Irrtümliche oder ungeeignete Lösungswege zeigen sich oft erst in einem späteren Stadium. Viele Entscheidungen sind in bestimmten Phasen in ihrer Folgewirkung noch nicht einzuschätzen.

Gefordert sind das Zulassen von Suchbewegungen und Gedankenexperimenten. Zufälle und Fehler öffnen den Blick auf andere mögliche Lösungsformen. Manche Fehler machen darauf aufmerksam, dass aus der Sicht des Lernenden möglicherweise die Frage falsch gestellt war. „Diejenige falsche Antwort ist die richtige Antwort, die nach einer Frage sucht. Das Sammeln falscher Antworten ist Teil des Prozesses. Stelle andere Fragen" (Mau 2000, S. 218). Insbesondere bei Innovationsprozessen sind Experimente wichtig und dabei ist nicht jeder Misserfolg (Umweg) „unnötig", da er für den Lernprozess notwendig ist.

Der virtuelle Fachbereich

Wie mit offenen Lernformen (Pädagogik der Unschärfe) unter besonderer Betonung ästhetischen Denkens Projekte umgesetzt werden können soll am Beispiel der Produktion „Der virtuelle Fachbereich" skizziert werden. Vergleichbare Projekte, bei denen jeweils die Aufgabe war, eine Multimedia-CD-ROM, eine Webseite, eine Fotoausstellung, einen Videofilm oder eine Multimediaschau zu erstellen wurden auch mit der Zielgruppe „Kinder und Jugendliche" umgesetzt (Röll 2003).

Bei lernzielorientierten Projekten besteht die Gefahr, dass ein mechanisiertes Denken (Erfüllung einer Erwartungshaltung) erzeugt wird. Die Kreativität wird eingeschränkt und der eigenständige Lernprozess wird behindert. Bei unscharfen Fragen werden kreative Denkprozesse ausgelöst und der Lernende integriert, ausgehend von seinem kognitiven Wahrnehmungsskript, seine bisherige Lebenserfahrung in die zu bewältigende Aufgabe. Diese Methode erlaubt die Entwicklung eigener Lernstile und führt in der Regel zu inhaltlich und ästhetisch anspruchsvollen Ausdrucksformen. Die Bewältigung von Aufgaben ausgehend von der eigenen Selbst-Suche begünstigt die intrinsische Motivation und fördert das Denken in Zusammenhängen. Das führt zu einem erheblichen Kompetenzzuwachs und kreativer Selbstwahrnehmung.

Allen Teilnehmern wird zu Beginn mitgeteilt, dass das herzustellende Medienprodukt öffentlich präsentiert wird und somit die Produktion keinen Selbstzweckcharakter hat, sondern Realtime-Lernen bedeutet. Lernen geschieht durch die Bewältigung einer realen Aufgabe. Es gibt keinen pädagogischen Schonraum. Die Ergebnisse der Bildungsmaßnahmen sollen Kommunikationsprozesse auslösen. Zuerst wird gemeinsam ein Mindmap erstellt, um die unterschiedlichen Aspekte des zu bearbeitenden Themas herauszufinden. Danach entscheidet sich jeder für einen Erfahrungsraum. Die Lernenden können dabei selbst entscheiden, wie das jeweilige Thema gelöst, welche Hilfsmittel verwendet werden und sie sind auch verantwortlich für die konkrete ästhetische Umsetzung.

Die CD-ROM „Der virtuelle Fachbereich" wird von Studierenden des FB Sozialpädagogik an der Hochschule Darmstadt im Rahmen ihrer Ausbildung in Form spiralförmigen Lernens produziert. Die erste Studentengruppe begann im Sommersemester 2000. Jede Studentengruppe setzte an dem vorhandenen Stand der CD-ROM an und entwickelte die CD-ROM weiter. Verblüffend ist, wie die Studierenden, ausgehend von dem jeweils vorhandenen Level, in der Lage sind, die bisher schon erzielten Lernschritte zu adaptieren. Nahezu immer gelingt eine ästhetische und inhaltliche Präzisierung.

Die Aufgabe war, für die HOBIT, eine Messe für Schülerinnen und Schüler zur Studienorientierung, eine CD-ROM zu produzieren, die Studieninteressenten die Möglichkeit gibt, sich über das Studienangebot zu orientieren. Geplant war und ist ein Imageprodukt, das Neugierde und Interesse auslösen soll, mehr an Information zu haben zu wollen. Daher war schon zu Beginn die Absicht deutlich geworden, dass das Produkt vor allem ästhetisch gestaltet werden soll.

Abgesehen von dem Mindmap wird nichts vorgegeben. Jegliche Erweiterungen, Veränderungen, Konkretisierungen waren und sind erlaubt. Jeder Einzelne arbeitet an einem Themenschwerpunkt (Studienordnung, Sekretariat, Praxiserkundung, Moduldarstellung, Fachschaft, Kultur in Darmstadt, etc.). Nach Fertigstellung werden mögliche Verlinkungen erörtert und der Gesamteindruck diskutiert. Mäanderhaft entsteht Stück für Stück die CD-ROM. Da mehrere Studentengenerationen an dem Projekt arbeiten gibt es keinen Autor mehr (Dramaturg). Das Produkt ist die Summe einer Wechselwirkung sich gegenseitig beeinflussender Faktoren. Niemals gibt es ein Endprodukt. Die jeweilige Version bedeutet nur ein punktuelles Festhalten. Jederzeit könnte die CD-ROM wieder erweitert bzw. verändert werden.

Während die Studenten sich damit beschäftigen, anderen zu vermitteln, was Sozialpädagogik ist, lernen sie gleichzeitig die Grundstruktur ihres Studiums kennen und beschäftigten sich wesentlicher intensiver mit der Studienordnung und dem Studienablauf als sie dies ansonsten getan hätten. Darüber hinaus eignen sich die Studentinnen und Studenten den Umgang mit Hypertext an und sind nunmehr in der Lage, eine Multimedia-Produktion selbstständig zu produzieren.

Inzwischen ist ein schon ausgereiftes Produkt mit einer komplexen Seitenstruktur entstanden. Ausgehend von einem topographischen Stadtplan kann mit dem Cursor mit eine virtueller Rundgang unternommen werden. Wenn man mit dem Cursor z.B. auf E 30 geht, erscheint z.B. das Gebäude der Designer. Mit Klicken auf B 10 kommt man zum Lernturm. In einem Rundgang können die Nutzerinnen und Nutzer sich die Architektur der Gebäude anschauen. Von den Gebäuden können sie ganz unterschiedliche visuelle Eindrücke erhalten. Begleitet wird der virtuelle Spaziergang von einer psychoakustische Spannung vermittelnden Musik. Damit wird den Nutzerinnen und Nutzern von Beginn an deutlich gemacht, dass es bei der CD-

ROM vor allem um eine sensitive Annäherung geht. Wer will kann sich noch die Mensa ansehen und beim ASTA vorbeischauen.

Wenn man auf E 10 drückt, kommt man zum Fachbereich Sozialpädagogik. Die Eingangsseite zeigt das Unterrichtsgebäude und heißt alle Besucher willkommen. Von dieser Seite kann man wieder zurück zur FH, kann anschauen wer die CD-ROM produziert hat (Credits), erhält Kontaktadressen und kann sich kundig machen, wo Studierende in Darmstadt wohnen können und welche Abendfreizeitmöglichkeiten Darmstadt außerhalb der Studienzeit bietet (Theater, Kino, Kneipen). Ebenso kommt man von dieser Seite in das Gebäude des FB Sozialpädagogik.

Im Gebäude begegnet man zuerst der Navigationsseite. Es empfiehlt sich zuerst ein Rundgang, produziert als multimediale Diaschau mit Webcam-Integration. Der Rundgang zeigt in kunstvoller Weise das Studienambiente. Dann empfiehlt sich, der Caféte einen Besuch abzustatten. Die Caféte, die von Studenten im Stil des spanischen Künstlers Gaudi ebenfalls im Rahmen eines Selbstlernprozesses gestaltet wurde, wird ebenfalls in Form einer multimedialen Schau präsentiert.

Denkbar wäre es, sich danach im Sekretariat umzuschauen. Im O-Ton berichten die Sekretärinnen von ihren Aufgaben. Ein Bilderbuch zeigt ihre vielfältigen Arbeitsfelder. Wer wissen will, welche Dozenten am Fachbereich lehren und welche Schwerpunkte sie vertreten kann dies tun. Wenn man auf die Rubrik „Dozenten" klickt, erscheint ein Menü , von dem aus alle Dozenten vorgestellt werden. Die Arbeit der Studentinnen und Studenten in der Fachschaft wird ebenfalls gewürdigt. Die Seiten über die Bibliothek geben, unterstützt durch ein ästhetisches Arrangement, Informationen über die Nutzungsmöglichkeiten der Bibliothek.

Das Herzstück der CD-ROM ist die auch visuell sehr gelungene Darstellung des Themas „Was ist Sozialpädagogik?". Der Text wird nicht nur auf dem Bildschirm präsentiert. Durch Animationen, bei denen Bilder zu den jeweiligen Themenaspekten auftauchen, verschwinden oder durch Text ersetzt werden, entsteht ein dichter Eindruck von dem, was Sozialpädagogik ist. Die Hintergründe sind mit ausdrucksstarken Doppelbelichtungen gestaltet, bei denen jeweils das Thema „Mensch und Krise" bzw. Irritation erkennbar ist.

Wegen der Umstellung des Studiengangs von Diplom auf Bachelor musste zwischenzeitlich die Darstellung des Studiengangs vollständig erneuert werden. Die Seiten über den Studienaufbau geben nunmehr Auskunft über die Art und Weise des Studiums, welche Module absolviert und welche Praktika wann und wo gemacht werden müssen.

Beispielhaft zeigt das Ergebnis einer Studentin, die sich im aktuellen Semester mit Modul 2, Theorie und Geschichte der Sozialen Arbeit, auseinandergesetzt hat, die ästhetische anspruchsvolle Gestaltung. Gefordert war, die wesentlichen Inhalte des Moduls gestalterisch zum Ausdruck zu bringen. In dem Lehrangebot dieses Moduls werden die grundlegenden historischen, theoretischen, institutionellen und professionellen Entwicklungen der Sozialen Arbeit vermittelt. Darüber hinaus gibt das Fach einen Überblick über die Arbeitsfelder, die Adressatinnen und Adressaten und die Problemgegenstände der Sozialen Arbeit und führt in deren ethischen Grundlagen ein. Die Umsetzung der Aufgabe zeigt deutlich, dass das Einzelbild zum Segment einer multicodierten Darstellungsebene sich verwandelt. Mit sehr hohem Aufwand wurde Wert auf die Gestaltung gelegt. Die Bilder und die Textbausteine verschmelzen zu einer synästhetischen Einheit. Durch die Integration einer passenden Musik wird dieser Eindruck noch verstärkt. Die ästhetisierte Bearbeitung des Themas soll die späteren Nutzerinnen und Nutzer neugierig machen und zugleich mehrere Sinne ansprechen.

Da die CD-ROM von unterschiedlichen Studentengruppen produziert wurde, haben die einzelnen Teile ganz unterschiedliche Gestaltungsformen. In spannender Weise dokumentieren sie die unterschiedlichen Sichtweisen der Studentinnen und Studenten. Während die jeweilige Gestaltung gänzlich unterschiedlich ist, lässt sich als gemeinsame Nenner der Anspruch identifizieren, Inhalte durch Ästhetisierung mit zusätzlicher Bedeutung aufzuladen. Alle Studentinnen und Studenten ließen sich von der Idee anstecken, künstlerisch-ästhetisch auf den Fachbereich aufmerksam zu machen.

Pädagogik der Navigation

Dieses hier beschriebene Konzept lässt sich als Pädagogik als Navigation bezeichnen (Röll 2003). Dies heißt die Lernenden zum selbst gesteuerten Lernen zu befähigen, sie ebenfalls zu Navigatoren zu machen. In diesem Lernraum übernehmen die Lernenden Funktionen, die im traditionellen Sinne nur den Lehrenden zugestanden wurde. Autonomie erleben wäre ein wesentliches Stichwort. Strukturell gesehen entsteht ein neues Lernverhalten. Die gestellten Aufgaben werden nach den Vorstellungen der Lernenden bearbeitet. Beim Handeln stehen Spielräume zur

Verfügung. Kompetenz erleben wäre ein weiteres Stichwort. Die Lernenden erleben sich und damit ihre eigene Wirksamkeit beim sachverständigen Lösen von Problemen. Da sie dies in einer Gruppe erleben, erfahren sie Anerkennung durch die Peer Group und somit auch das Erleben sozialer Einbindung. „Gleichrangige teilen ihr Wissen, wodurch sich Wissen dauernd neu strukturiert und formiert und von jedem in jedem gewünschten Zusammenhang verwendet werden kann" (Bates 2002, S. 133).

Literatur

Assmann, Aleida (2003): Druckerpresse und Internet. Auf dem Weg von einer Gedächtniskultur zu einer Kultur der Aufmerksamkeit: Oberfläche, Geschwindigkeit und Supermarkt. In: Frankfurter Rundschau v. 18.01.

Bates, Anthony W. (2000): Virtuell Global Zielgruppenorientiert. Der Einfluss der Neuen Medien auf die Universität. In: Christa Maar; Hans Ulrich Obrist; Ernst Pöppel: Weltwissen Wissenswelt. Das globale Netz von Text und Bild. Köln 2000, S. 123-

Beck, Ulrich (1986): Risikogesellschaft. Frankfurt a.M..

Csikszentmihalyi, Mihaly (1985): Das Flow-Erlebnis. Stuttgart.

Dewey, John: Kunst als Erfahrung, 1934. Frankfurt a.M. (Suhrkamp) 1980

Duncker, Ludwig (1999): Begriff und Struktur ästhetischer Erfahrung. In: Neuß, Norbert (Hg.): Ästhetik der Kinder. Frankfurt a.M. 1999, S. 9-19.

Maturana, Humberto R. (2002): Das Multiversum der Wirklichkeiten. Ein Gespräch mit Humberto Maturana über den Terror der Wahrheitsfanatiker und die Sehnsucht nach Gewissheit. In: Frankfurter Rundschau, 05.10.2002, S. 19.

Mau, Bruce (2000): Wachstumsvorgänge – ein unvollständiges Manifest zu den verschiedenen Weisen der Wissenserzeugung. In: Christa Maar; Hans Ulrich Obrist; Ernst Pöppel: Weltwissen Wissenswelt. Das globale Netz von Text und Bild. Köln 2000, S. 217-223.

Röll, Franz Josef: Pädagogik der Navigation. Selbstgesteuertes Lernen mit Neuen Medien. München 2003

Schulze, Gerhard (1993): Die Erlebnisgesellschaft. Kultursoziologie der Gegenwart. 4. Aufl., Frankfurt a. M./New York.

Welsch, Wolfgang (1993): Ästhetisches Denken. Stuttgart.

Zacharias, Wolfgang (2001): Kulturpädagogik – Kulturelle Jugendbildung – Eine Einführung. Opladen 2001.

Autorinnen und Autoren

Angus, Lawrence, Professor and Head of the School of Education, University of Ballarat. Research Issues: Educational politics; Education and society; Social and Educational policy; Equity.

Bonfadelli, Heinz, Prof. Dr., Professor am IPMZ – Institut für Publizistikwissenschaft und Medienforschung der Universität Zürich, Forschungsschwerpunkte: Medienwirkungsforschung, Wissenskluft und Digital Divide, Kinder, Jugendliche und Medienumgang.

Buckingham, David, PhD, Professor of Education at the Institute of Education, London University, director of the Centre for the Study of Children, Youth and Media (www.childrenyouthandmediacentre.co.uk). Research Issues: children and young people's interactions with electronic media, media education.

Haythornthwaite, Caroline, PhD, Associate Professor at the Graduate School of Library and Information Science, University of Illinois at Urbana-Champaign, USA. Her research examines how the Internet and computer media support and affect work, learning, and social interaction, focusing on how information is exchanged, knowledge is shared and co-constructed, collaboration happens, and community forms online.

Hargittai, Eszter, PhD, Assistant Professor at the Northwestern University, USA. Research Issues: Differential uses of information technologies, differences in people's abilities and participation regarding digital media.

Iske, Stefan, Dr. phil., Postdoktorand im Graduiertenkolleg „Qualitätsverbesserung im E-Learning durch rückgekoppelte Prozesse", Forschungsschwerpunkte: Lernen und Bildung in hypertextuellen Umgebungen, Methodologie der Analyse von Navigationsprozessen, Einsatz neuer Technologien in der Hochschule, Digitale Spaltung und Digitale Ungleichheit.

Klein, Alexandra, Dipl-Päd., wissenschaftliche Mitarbeiterin an der Universität Potsdam, Forschungsschwerpunkte: Soziale Unterstützung im Internet, Institutionelle Diskriminierung, Soziale Netzwerke und Soziale Ungleichheit.

Kutscher, Nadia, Prof. Dr., Professorin für Soziale Arbeit an der Katholischen Fachhochschule Nordrhein-Westfalen, Abteilung Aachen, Forschungsschwerpunkte: Bildung im Kindesalter, soziale Ungleichheit und Bildung, Jugend, Bildung und Internet (digitale Ungleichheit).

Marotzki, Winfried, Prof. Dr., Universitätsprofessor für Allgemeine Pädagogik an der Otto-von-Guericke-Universität Magdeburg, Forschungsschwerpunkte: Bildungstheorie und -forschung, Qualitative Sozialforschung, Internet Research.

Mesch, Gustavo S., Dr., Senior Lecturer at the Department of Sociology and Anthropology University of Haifa. Research Issues: adolescents' patterns of use of the Internet, the effect of online and offline ties on the social network structure of adolescents and relationship formation online, effects of membership in electronic bulletin boards on social capital in Israel.

Niesyto, Horst, Prof. Dr., Leiter der Abteilung Medienpädagogik im Institut für Erziehungswissenschaft an der Pädagogischen Hochschule Ludwigsburg; Forschungsschwerpunkte: medienpädagogische Praxisforschung, insbesondere in Hauptschul- und Migrationsmilieus; visuelle Forschungsmethoden in der qualitativen Forschung; Analyse von medialen Eigenproduktionen Jugendlicher.

Otto, Hans-Uwe, Prof. Dr. Dr. h.c., Professor für Erziehungswissenschaft an der Universität Bielefeld, Honorarprofessor an der School of Social Policy and Practice, University of Pennsylvania, Philadelphia (USA). Forschungsschwerpunkte: Soziale Arbeit und Sozialpolitik, Jugendhilfeforschung, Professionalisierung, Bildung und Soziale Arbeit.

Röll, Franz Josef, Dr., Professor im Fachbereich Sozialpädagogik der Hochschule Darmstadt mit dem Schwerpunkt Medienpädagogik und Neue Medien. Forschungsschwerpunkte: Mythen und Symbole in populären Medien, Bürgerfernsehen (Offene Kanäle), Handlungsorientierte Medienpädagogik, Visuelles Lernen, Lernpräferenzen, Web 2.0.

Selwyn, Neil, Dr., Senior Lecturer at the London Knowledge Lab, Institute of Education, University of London, Research issues: sociology of new media, education, technology and society, digital divide, e-policy making.

Neu im Programm
Bildungswissenschaft